Two MP3s are included with the purchase of this book:
- *Belvaspata Angel Healing* - Almine speaking in the language of the Infinite to assist with learning the pronunciation of this language.
- Arcturian Fairy Sound Elixirs - to be used with Belvaspata Healing through Oneness sessions and for preparing and energizing the essential oils of this modality.

To obtain your copy of the MP3 downloads, please visit www.belvaspata.org.

Belvaspata
Angel Healing

Almine

Healing through Oneness

Volume 2

Plus: Healing through Oneness, The Integrated use of Belvaspata and Fragrance Alchemy

Published by Spiritual Journeys LLC

First edition August 2012

Copyright 2012

MAB 998 Megatrust
By Almine
Spiritual Journeys LLC
P.O. Box 300
Newport, Oregon 97365

US toll-free phone: 1-877-552-5646

www.spiritualjourneys.com

All rights reserved. No part of this publication may be reproduced
without written permission of the publishers.

Cover Illustration by Dorian Dyer
www.visionheartart.com

Manufactured in the United States of America

ISBN 978-1-936926-40-4 Softcover

ISBN 978-1-936926-41-1 Adobe reader

Table of Contents

Foreword ix
Dedication to Spiritual Healers x
Disclaimer xi

Book I – Belvaspata – Healing and Initiation Manual
Part I – Introduction Belvaspata, the Healing Modality 2
The Sigil for Belvaspata 6
Guidelines for Belvaspata Practitioners 7
Symbols versus Sigils 8
The Significance of the Sigils 10
The Significance of the Master and Grand Master Sigil 12
Disease as an Illusion 13
Concepts of Wellness 14
Belvaspata General Guidelines 15

Part II – Working with Belvaspata
How to Use Belvaspata 19
Sigils for Opening a session 22
Sigils for Closing a session 23
Examples of Drawing a Sigil 24
Belvaspata Long-Distance Session 27
Belvaspata and Self-Healing 28
Belvaspata Questions and Answers 30

Part III – Level I and II Practitioners
Level I Belvaspata 37
The Twelve Pairs of Emotions 39
The Sigils of Love 42

Level II Belvaspata 45
The 16 Rays of Light 45
Sigils of Light 47
Additional Belvaspata Sigils 50
The Infinite's Sigil 52
The Power Source Wheel 53

Part IV – Master and Grand Master Practitioners
Master Level Belvaspata 57
The States of Being 58
States of Being Sigils 61
Grand Master Level Belvaspata 64
Heart Energies 65
Sigils for Grand Master Level 69
Placement of Grand Master Level Sigils 73
Advanced Sigils for Master and Grand Master Practitioners 74

Part V – Preparing for Initiations
Belvaspata: From Initiate to Grand Master Level 83
Preparation for Level 1 - The 12 Pairs of Pure Emotions 86
Preparation for Level II - The 16 Rays of Light 103
Preparation for Master Level - The States of Being 111
Preparation for Grand Master Level - The Heart Energies 116

Part VI – Initiations: Initiating another into Belvaspata
Belvaspata Initiations by a Master 129
Example: Level II Initiation Sigil 131
Initiation Level I to Grand Master Level
Level I Initiation Sigils 132
Level II Initiation Sigils 133
Master Level Initiation Sigil 136
Grand Master Level Initiation Sigil 137
Closing Sigils for a Session or Initiation 138

Part VII – Initiations: Self-Initiation into Belvaspata
Guidelines for Self-Initiation 141
Preparing for Self-Initiation...143
The Languages and Alphabet of the Infinite Mother 145
All Initiation Levels in the Infinite's Language 152
Belvaspata Certificates of Initiation...163

Part VIII – Specialty Belvaspata Modalities
Introduction to Specialty Belvaspata Modalities 167
General Guidelines for Performing Ceremonies.........................168
The Use of Wheels...171

Book II – Belvaspata Healing through Oneness
The Integrated use of Belvaspata and Fragrance Alchemy
Disclaimer 179
Introduction 181

Part I – Healing through Oneness
How Healing through Oneness Works 187
Essential Oils and their Psychological Properties 189
Choosing Pure Products 192
The Benefits of Essential Oils 194
Home Beauty Products 194

Part II – Healing through Oneness – the Method and Tools
Use of Sigils and Fragrances...199
The Healing Method 200
Sigils 201
Questions and Answers 202
The Wheels for Healing through Oneness 203
Sigils of Praise, Love and Gratitude 207
The 144 Essential Oils for the Arcturian Sigils 208
The 144 Incantations...212

Part III – Healing through Oneness - The Sigils and Angels

The 13 Main Joints of the Body 219
The Evolutionary Stages of Man 238
Secrets of Transfiguration 263
The 20 Primary Systems of the Body 274
The 24 Chakras of the Body 294
Sacred Sexuality Exercise 295
The 24 Chakras of the Body 301
The 24 Pure Emotions 325
The 24 Emotions of Recognition 356
The 16 Rays of Light 385
The Closing Down of the Five Directions 402
The Stationary Fields of Light 408
The Poetry of the Perfection is the One 433

Part IV - The Haaraknit

Entering the Haaraknit 439
The Spaceless Space of No Mind 440
Closing 451

Appendices

Appendix I   Gas Discharge Visualization to Determine
              the Effectiveness of Healing Methods 455
Appendix II   Guidance for Beginning Healers 462
Appendix III Example of Belvaspata Certificate 467

Foreword

In righting a wrong, we judge and divide. In acknowledging wholeness we uplift and inspire the underlying perfection to reveal itself. This miraculous healing modality, a divine gift to humanity, neither tries to heal nor fights disease. To do so would affirm the existence of such illusions.

Belvaspata replaces distorted matrices with clarity by emphasizing the expression of the pure luminosity and harmony that lies within each being. The stimulation of the true frequencies — the Song of the Self — in an individual creates self-healing by shattering the matrix within the body that holds disease programs in place.

Belvaspata has achieved rapidly growing acclaim worldwide as the modality of choice as its well-deserved reputation of success has spread among seasoned healers and newcomers alike.

Healing miracles have been reported from many countries. Interdimensional photography has captured the angels that come to assist practitioners in their efforts to expose the perfection and grace of existence.

Let the sacred work of bringing light to humanity spread around the world one person at a time. May Belvaspata practitioners everywhere be blessed in their ability to roll back illusions of despair and fear. Within their hands lie the gift of hope and the miracle of pure light and frequency.

Almine

Interdimensional Photography of an Angel

Photograph of an Angel taken by Raj Narinder in his garden

Dedication to Spiritual Healers

The way-showers of the world are my mission and my inspiration. My life is dedicated to you, the capstone of humanity. You are the ones who are not afraid to lay down old belief systems and open to the in-pouring of Spirit.

We have come through time and space together, from the first moments of created life, to meet upon this planet to turn the keys that will begin the journey home — back to the heart of God. I have been called forth for the specific task of touching the hearts of those who are the pillars of the temple, who uphold humanity by the light of their presence, both now and in the future.

It is you to whom I dedicate the teachings of healing. May your hearts recognize the many levels of light they impart. May you and I pull the Earth into an era of hope and peace and lay the path to a new tomorrow.

All my love,

Almine

Disclaimer

Belvaspata is not intended to diagnose, or to constitute medical advice or treatment. All healing takes place within self. Please follow all regulatory guidelines of your specific municipality in terms of assisting and working with others, even with their express consent. A physician or other healthcare professional should be consulted for any necessary medical attention.

Book I
Belvaspata Healing and Initiation Manual

PART I

Introduction

Belvaspata, the Healing Modality

Belvaspata, Healing of the Heart, is a sacred modality that heals with light and frequency. This healing method is a gift from the Infinite to the cosmic races to accommodate the changing laws of physics that took place as all life ascended into a new level of existence in August 2006. The language used is a very high cosmic language used by the Mother/Infinite Being and angels alike.

The use of Belvaspata heals as the frequencies of the sacred sigils are drawn to where they are most needed and takes into consideration changes that occurred in August 2006, altering the laws that govern all existence. (See The Sigil for Belvaspata on page 6.)

These laws changed as the frequencies within the cosmos raised us out of a cycle of existence in which polarity was the primary causation for cosmic movement. We had now entered a more elevated cycle of existence in which resonance became the basic moving force.

The most basic assumptions on which healers of all modalities had based their methods changed overnight. No longer did opposite energies attract, that healing energy could gravitate towards diseased energies. Now they would reject each other.

Introduction

It became vital that healers begin to utilize light and frequency to dispel the illusion of disease, as under the changed cosmic laws, opposites would be attracted. The importance of working with Belvaspata is that light would now be drawn to illusion and frequency to distortion.

Belvaspata, in the language of the Mother Goddess, means 'healing of the heart'. Whereas the primary purpose of previous cycles of existence was to seek perception (which is mind-oriented), the one we have entered has a different purpose. This cycle is like a blank canvas and challenges us to fulfill one primary purpose: **To create through the heart.**

The body of knowledge, which is Belvaspata, is a gift from the Mother/Infinite Being that we may fulfill the new purpose of life. It is here to help us create health, joy and happiness through the heart.

Belvaspata Updates following Recent Cosmic Changes

Cosmic changes also impact Belvaspata. Throughout creation there are various states of awareness and awakening and Belvaspata supports each of them for the benefit of all.

Polarity and duality no longer exist. All energy and power is now available to us and inseparable from us. It is no longer necessary to pulse between the poles to create energy. This also means that light and frequency, now unified, no longer are opposites that attract; all resources are immediately drawn to where they are most needed. This is the same for the Pairs of Emotions, Rays of Light, States of Being and Heart Energies discussed later in this book.

As the purpose of Belvaspata is to remove the illusion of all disease, to remove the illusion of distorted emotion and to remove the distortion of light, we can use Belvaspata as a tool to:

- see the perfection of all
- focus and enhance the perfection
- assist with the awakening of consciousness and to reveal the underlying perfection
- assist in the full expression of our being should it be blocked or not expressing fully

Belvaspata inspires the person (or a part of their body) to want to express at a higher level and/or to let go of patterns and behaviors held in the memory, thus releasing illusion and allowing fuller expression.

The ultimate gift of Belvaspata is to Align with the Song of Creation.

As an alchemical equation it reads:

Compassionate Support

+

Awakening from the Dream

=

Alignment with the Song of Creation

While doing Belvaspata, we envision the pristine perfection of all and know that the perfection already exists. In doing so, we assist and support the awareness of the perfection of all life. We look beyond the physical appearance and manifestation of disease to the existing underlying perfection; focusing on 'what is' — perfection — and removing the focus from 'what is not' — the imperfection.

Introduction

The Sigil for Belvaspata

BELVASPATA
HEALING OF THE HEART

THE OVER-ALL ANGEL FOR BELVASPATA

Kelechnutvaveleshvispata

ANGEL SIGIL

Guidelines for Belvaspata Practitioners

- Maintain decorum of dress, manner and behavior. Strictly observe the confidentiality of all information that may be shared during a session.
- Provide a schedule of fees for your session to those you work with. Discussion of all fees should take place prior to a session.
- Offer adequate time for any questions or concerns prior to and possibly after a session. Individuals may require emotional support and reassurance before, during or after a session.
- A signed form of Release of Liability from those who receive sessions may be obtained prior to a session. This will be dependent upon individual preferences.
- Follow all legal guidelines for personal contact[1] with any person according to your individual municipalities and/or your state of residence.
- Remember that all healing takes place within the self. The information in this book is not intended to diagnose illness.
- When using Belvaspata to work on another, healing is made available to that individual or situation. It is not forced and is therefore readily available when all are receptive and ready. For this reason it is not necessary to obtain permission before using Belvaspata.
- Belvaspata may be done for yourself, another person, a situation or a location. It may also be done long-distance (see details in later section). Kriyavaspata[2] is specifically used for working with animals.
- A physician or other healthcare provider should be consulted for any necessary medical attention.

1 In the USA, licensed health practitioners are permitted by law to touch clients with permission of the client. Obtaining a valid minister's license (research on internet) may make it permissible to touch. Research and observe the legal guidelines that apply where you live.
2 See Healing for Animals www.kriyavaspata.com

Introduction

Symbols versus Sigils

Before we start working with Belvaspata and the relevant sigils, we must first understand what a sigil is and the difference between a symbol and a sigil. We will then need to know the meanings of the sigils for this healing modality in order to properly understand and use them.

A symbol **represents** something, whereas a sigil **describes** something. When someone sees a BMW or a Mercedes symbol, it represents upper middle-class vehicles of quality and distinction. On the other hand, the symbol for a Rolls Royce or Bentley represents elite vehicles that speak of a privileged lifestyle of dignity and wealth.

So much is deduced just from one symbol. A Rolls Royce evokes images of walled estates, chauffeurs, enough and accustomed money where the symbol of a Ferrari will speak of more flamboyant taste.

Whereas symbols are common in our everyday world, the use of sigils is virtually forgotten. Even in mystery schools, their hidden knowledge eludes most mystics. Throughout the cosmos all beings of expanded awareness utilize sigils and it is only a few left-brain-oriented races that use symbols such as those in alphabets. An example would be the word 'LOVE' where we have combined four symbols (letters representing certain sounds) to make one symbol (the word that represents a feeling). But love is one of the building blocks of the cosmos, like space or energy.[3] It can also represent many different nuances within the emotion of love (which is the desire to include) and much other dysfunctionality and degrees of need we mistakenly call 'love'.

---

3 Discussed in *Journey to the Heart of God*, The True Nature of the Seven Directions.

As we can see, the symbol or word can be very misleading since what it represents to one may not be what it represents to another. The sigil for love describes the quality or frequency of what is meant. It maps out the exact frequency of the emotion.

The sigil for someone's name would do the same. As the person or being rises in frequency, the sigil will change to reflect that. In the case of angels, even their names change. This is why the angel names or the goddess names have changed as the cosmos and Earth have ascended to a much higher frequency. In these higher realms the languages are also different and reflect the higher frequencies.

When a person has accomplished a major task within the cosmos pertaining to the agreement they made with the Infinite, they also receive a 'meaning' with its accompanying sigil. When a being is called to do a task meant for the highest good, that being will come if you have its name and meaning. The being absolutely must come if, in addition, you have the sigil for the name and meaning.

Having someone's sigil is like having that person's phone number.

Sigils not only describe what they represent, but are a means to communicate with what they represent.

The Significance of the Sigils

If all the other healing modalities are having their healing energy, and their symbols meant to produce healing energy repulsed, they are in fact producing the opposite of what is intended.

Because disease is distorted energy that repulses the natural healing energies (the trillions of little fragments of awareness that have been available to restore perfection), these methods would, in fact, produce disease.

On August 17, 2006, in order to prevent well-intentioned healers from doing harm, the Mother/Infinite Being took away the power behind healing modalities based on energy work. The power behind the previously used symbols was also removed. It is for this reason that the gift of Belvaspata was given to humanity.

The Mother/Infinite Being has given the sacred sigils of Belvaspata to us. As the cosmos grows in awareness these sigils are automatically upgraded and stay at an optimum level of efficiency. As sigils are packed full of awareness particles, it is the sigils given to us by the Infinite that contain the greatest amount of these particles.

As of the 21st of April 2008, Mother/Infinite Being changed the laws that governed sigils.

- Any attraction of resources are now immediate, exponential and non-linear.
- As the building blocks of life are upgraded during cosmic ascension, Belvaspata sigils will likewise be upgraded to attract the correct building blocks.
- *Light* and *love* are now inseparable, interconnected fields. When we speak of attracting light, light and love will both be attracted.

Note: It is very important to remember that the sigils used in Belvaspata are sacred and should always be treated with respect and reverence. Should a drawing of a sigil fall on the floor, do not step over it or on it. When discarding Belvaspata sigils or angel names, they should be burned in a ceremonial manner with appreciation and gratitude.

Introduction

The Significance of the Master and Grand Master Sigil

The Master and Grand Master Sigils are to be used only for the initiations of Master and Grand Master practitioners. This is because of the purpose/intent that is held within their power.

The sigils of Belvaspata have a hidden power behind the obvious. For a Level I and Level II practitioner, every time the sigils are used, they dispel the illusion of disease and the illusion of distortions found in light and frequency (emotion) everywhere. In other words, everywhere on earth, there is less disease each time they are used.

The Master Sigil and Grand Master Sigil extend this influence to affect not only life on earth, but also the whole cosmos. After having practiced the sigils regularly and above all internalized the Pure Emotions, the Rays of Light, States of Being and Heart Energies, Master and Grand Master practitioners become connected to the field of existence that spans the cosmos. Practicing Belvaspata therefore becomes a cosmic service, bringing healing to life everywhere.

Where great service is rendered, great rewards are given. The rewards in this instance are a strengthening of the previous sigils placed in centers of the Master's/Grand Master's body by 100 times. The second magnificent reward is higher consciousness for the master and greater silence of the mind. Mastery is defined as absence of dialogue in the mind, or silence of the mind; only masters have this option.

Disease as an Illusion

Initiates into Belvaspata must very clearly understand why disease and the false emotions of anger, fear, pain and protectiveness are at this point an illusion.

All healing is but the removal of illusion and is facilitated through the use of the sigils. One needs to remind oneself of this every time the sigils are used. To treat disease as a real adversary is to strengthen the illusion.

Almine relates that in 2005, the 'real' part, the indwelling life of disease, was removed. To demonstrate this she said that if she had put her pen on the table and one of the masters of the unseen realms removed the etheric or 'real' pen, it would no longer be real.

She could still pick the physical pen up and write with it. But some days she may not see it, and then one day, it will have disappeared altogether. It would, in fact, disappear even quicker if her thinking that it's on the table were to stop; if she knew it was now no longer real, but just an illusional shell without real life.

Introduction

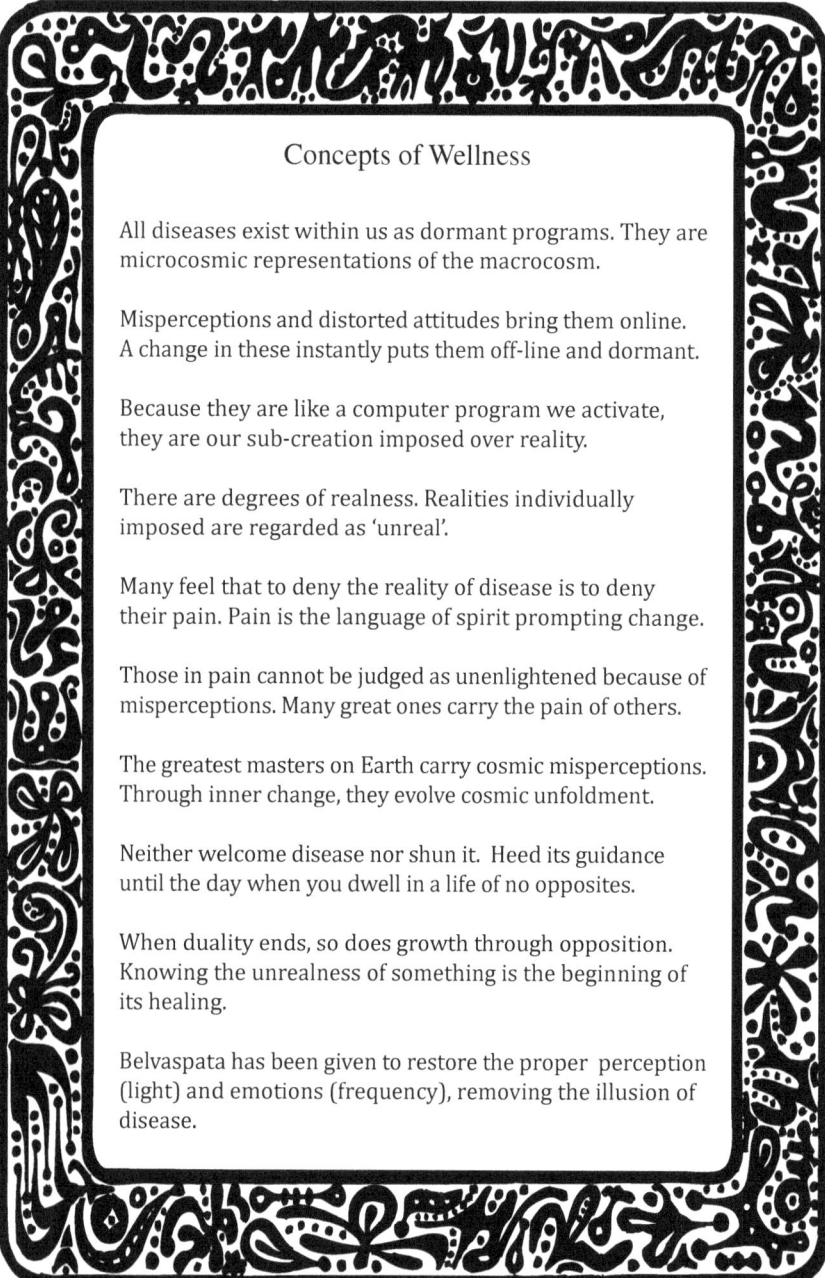

Concepts of Wellness

All diseases exist within us as dormant programs. They are microcosmic representations of the macrocosm.

Misperceptions and distorted attitudes bring them online. A change in these instantly puts them off-line and dormant.

Because they are like a computer program we activate, they are our sub-creation imposed over reality.

There are degrees of realness. Realities individually imposed are regarded as 'unreal'.

Many feel that to deny the reality of disease is to deny their pain. Pain is the language of spirit prompting change.

Those in pain cannot be judged as unenlightened because of misperceptions. Many great ones carry the pain of others.

The greatest masters on Earth carry cosmic misperceptions. Through inner change, they evolve cosmic unfoldment.

Neither welcome disease nor shun it. Heed its guidance until the day when you dwell in a life of no opposites.

When duality ends, so does growth through opposition. Knowing the unrealness of something is the beginning of its healing.

Belvaspata has been given to restore the proper perception (light) and emotions (frequency), removing the illusion of disease.

Belvaspata General Guidelines

1. Understand and know the difference between a symbol and a sigil.
2. The sigils of the healing qualities are drawn for both a session and for initiation. You do not have to memorize them. You can draw them in the air above or over the area of the body that is stated in the book or manual you are using, or a paper that you hold. You may also place the paper directly on the body and trace the sigil with your finger.
3. You do not sign/draw the angel sigils – look at them as you call their name either silently or out loud.
4. The sigils are drawn from left to right. Start at the upper left-hand corner and after that, the order is not crucial.
5. In some of the specialty Belvaspata modalities that are used to work with specific conditions, the sigils may be very complex. It is permissible to use one or several fingers held together to move across the sigil from left to right rather than drawing it. The left hand is receptive while the right hand represents understanding. You may use either hand according to your personal preference and intent. This method is only to be used for these very complex sigils and all other sigils (such as those in Level I, II Master and Grand Master Belvaspata) are to be signed/drawn.
6. Angel names may be called out loud or said silently as you wish and according to the preference of the person who is receiving Belvaspata. *Note: The hyphens used in the sigil qualities or angel names are added to assist with pronunciation.*
7. Use the Power Source/Gift from Isis *(See The Power Source on page 53)*. Place it above the head of the recipient during initiations or healing sessions, to augment results.

Introduction

8. Following cosmic changes, Level I and II Initiations may be done at the same time. There should be a 3 to 6 month interval between Level II and Master Level Initiations along with daily use of the sigils. Master and Grand Master Level initiations may now also be done at the same time. These guidelines apply to both self-initiation and to initiation with a Master or Grand Master of Belvaspata.
9. The intervals between initiations have been established to allow for the complete absorption and integration of these frequencies before advancing onto the next level. Be aware that the integration for some initiates may vary. This can depend on their use of the Belvaspata Sigils and their own readiness.
10. Further information for those who are new to working with healing modalities is provided in Appendix I at the back of the book.
11. Certification from the initiating Master or Grand Master may be provided for those who have received initiation into Belvaspata. *(See Belvaspata Certificates of Initiation in Appendices.)*

Note from Almine: You may charge the same fee as you would for other therapeutic modalities such as massage, for example. The only exchange I ask for from you and those you train is an acknowledgement that Belvaspata originated from me. If it would enhance the value of the modality in advertising, you may freely reprint any of the endorsements (or portions) from the back of my books.

PART II

Working with Belvaspata

How to Use Belvaspata

A Belvaspata Session

Work with the sigils that are appropriate to your level of initiation. Remember that Master and Grand Master Initiation Sigils are only to be used for initiation.

Opening every session

1. Sign/draw the sigil for *'Opening the Mind'* over the forehead once and say the sigil name. Call the Angel while looking at its sigil (do not draw the Angel sigil). Ask the Angel to place the sigil within the forehead.
2. Sign/draw the sigil for *'Opening the Heart'* over the heart once and say the sigil name. Call the Angel while looking at its sigil (do not draw the Angel sigil). Ask the Angel to place the sigil within the heart.
3. Sign/draw the sigil for *'Receptivity of the Body'* over the person's navel once and say the sigil name. Call the Angel while looking at its sigil (do not draw the Angel sigil). Ask the Angel to place the sigil within the person's body.

***Remember the three steps above start every session
(See Opening Sigils on page 22)***

4. One or more of Level II Initiation sigils may also be added after the above steps, at the discretion of the practitioner.
5. Ensure both you and the person you are working with are comfortable as you begin the session. You may place your hands either on or near the person's head, shoulders or feet (be aware if the laws in your area permit touching[4]).
6. Envision yourself expanding and expanding until you are as vast as the cosmos. Hold that expanded awareness for at least 20 minutes.
7. Now see the person you are working with expanding as well until you are both a consciousness blended as one with all that is. Hold that vision.
8. See the person's body within the vastness (just give it or the area of concern slight attention). Do not overly focus on 'the problem' but rather the existing perfection that already exists under the illusion of disease — maintain the expansion.
9. Bring the pre-determined pair of emotions[5] that you have chosen for the session, into your awareness. Feel them ripple throughout all of the cosmos. Stay expanded — do not draw the sigils yet.
10. Maintain the state of expansion throughout the session. Only pull your awareness slightly back before you begin to draw the sigils you have been guided to use. If indicated, draw the sigil over the specific part of the body mentioned.

---

4 In US licensed health practitioners are permitted by law to touch clients with the permission of the client. Obtaining a valid minister's license (research on internet) may make it permissible to touch. Research and observe the legal guidelines that apply in your area/country.

5 When doing a simple session, you may wish to use only one pair of Emotions, specific to the issue or body part that is affected. An example would be to use the sigils for the pair 'Passion and Joy' for circulatory issues. It is beneficial however to draw all of the Sigils for the Pairs of Emotions for any first session as it restores the emotions to purity and clarity, which assists with all healing.

11. Any sigils that are appropriate for your specific level of mastery and that you feel are necessary for the session may be used, such as: the Pairs of Emotions, Rays of Light, Sigil for Self-love, advanced sigils, etc. *(See pages 42-44, 47-51, 61-63 and 69-79.)* Always draw both sigils of a pair as this promotes balance.
12. Specialty Belvaspata modalities may be added to a basic session. For example, you could add part or all of Kaanish Belvaspata, following the basic session and prior to closing the session. An exception to this is Belvaspata of the Song of Self, which is to be done prior to a basic session.
13. Always end a session by signing the sigils for love, praise and gratitude over the heart area or the entire body—this materializes the healing intentions and pulls awareness in.
14. Advise the person to drink plenty of water and rest as needed following a session. Some may need to ground or center themselves before returning to activities such as driving, etc. You may offer the person the opportunity to contact you if necessary.

Note: Strive to create a warm, comfortable and relaxing environment. Gentle background music, soft lighting, blankets and pillows can assist. Keep outside noise to a minimum and avoid any interruptions from phones, pets, etc.

Level I Sigils – for Opening a Session

(These sigils are used every time to open a session or an initiation)

Quality	Angel Name and Sigil
Bla-utva-pa-ta (Opening the Mind) Draw over the forehead	Rutsetvi-uru-bach
Kru-vech-pa-uru-rek (Opening of the Heart) Draw over the heart	Iornumubach
Kel-a-vis-ba-vah (Receptivity of the Body) Draw over the navel 	Tru-ararir-pleva 

Sigils for Closing a Session

These sigils are used to close each session and initiation. They may be drawn over the heart area or over the entire body.

Praise

Love

Gratitude

Example of Using and Signing/Drawing Sigils

The following is an example of using a Level I sigil *(see page 26)*. In this case, we are using the sigil for a session and not an initiation.

When using a Level I sigil for opening a session:

Step 1. Draw the sigil **1 time** over the forehead as indicated.

Step 2. Call (say) the quality of the sigil either out loud or silently **1 time** in Mother's language. Example of the quality of this sigil is: **Bla-utva-pata.**

Step 3. Look at the sigil for the angel name and call (say) the angel name either out loud or silently **1 time** in Mother's language. (It is not necessary to draw the sigil for the angel name.) An example of the angel name for this Level I sigil is: **Rutsetvi-uru-bach**. Ask the angel to place the sigil within the forehead (or as the specific sigil indicates).

Note: Some sigils, such as the 12 Pairs of Emotions and Rays of Light, have only one sigil, which is the sigil for the quality. Draw the sigil and call (say) the quality and the Angel or Lord's name out loud or silently. Use the sigil(s) over appropriate areas, as indicated or as you are guided if specific areas are not indicated. Always draw both sigils of a pair as this promotes balance.

See the example below of one of the 12 Pairs of Emotions, a set of paired sigils.

\+   Creativity/Angel name:
Velesvruchba

*genitals,
reproductive organs*

−   Pleasure/Angel name:
Prubechbanatruva

Working with Belvaspata

Illustration of Level I Sigil

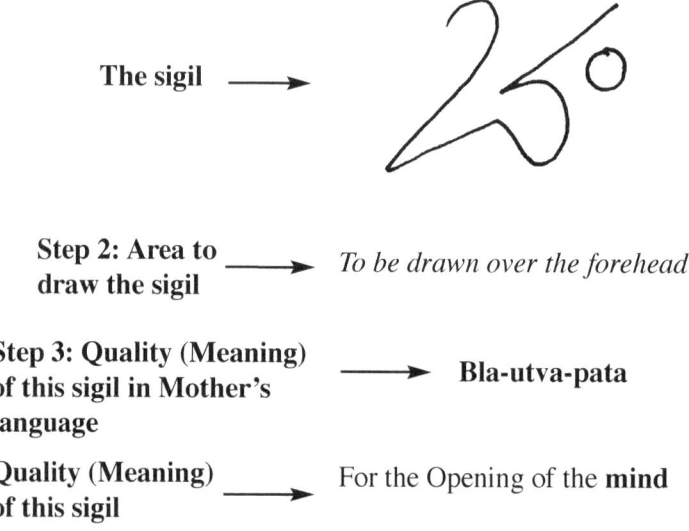

The sigil ⟶

Step 2: Area to draw the sigil ⟶ *To be drawn over the forehead*

Step 3: Quality (Meaning) of this sigil in Mother's language ⟶ **Bla-utva-pata**

Quality (Meaning) of this sigil ⟶ For the Opening of the **mind**

By the power of this Sigil which I hold in my hand, I call in the Angel

Step 4: Angel name in Mother's language ⟶ **Rutsetvi-uru-bach**
(say and look at the Angel Sigil)

Angel Sigil:

Step 4: Look at this sigil while saying the Angel name ⟶

Belvaspata Long-Distance Sessions

Belvaspata healing is effective whether done long-distance or in person. Sometimes an absentee or long-distance session is the most convenient way of working with another person. You may offer the person the opportunity to speak to you prior to the session to determine their reason and intent for it.

1. Follow the same guidelines as for a session done with someone in person. (The person may be advised to lie down during the session in a quiet location, where they will be undisturbed but this is not required.) The session is done with intent to hold the expansion of awareness, to bring the person into this expansion and to work with the sigils for their specific situation.
2. Do not use a teddy bear or other 'proxy' to represent the person that you are working with while doing a long-distance session. Remember that we are not 'sending energy.' Belvaspata works with light and frequency and is attracted to where it is most needed.
3. The person may also be phoned after a session as both parties may have information to share.
4. Advise the person to drink plenty of water and rest as needed following a session. Some may need to ground or center before returning to activities such as driving, etc. You may offer the person the opportunity to contact you if needed.

Belvaspata and Self-Healing

Self-Healing for Belvaspata Practitioners

All self-healing is done by accessing our true self, the One Being, the All.

To do this:
- Go to the largest possible expansion of Self.
- Feel that which you want to access WITHIN THE SELF
- You can now access ALL without limit as ALL is within you

When doing a session on yourself the format for self-healing is the same as for working with another person. Draw the sigils in the air and ask the angels to place them in the appropriate areas of the body.

Working on oneself is the greatest gift that one can give oneself. All healing, whether done for another or for oneself, is a blessing to all life and assists in elevating all to a higher level, as the perfection is further revealed. There is, in truth, only One Being.

Images of practitioner's hand healed within a few days using Belvaspata

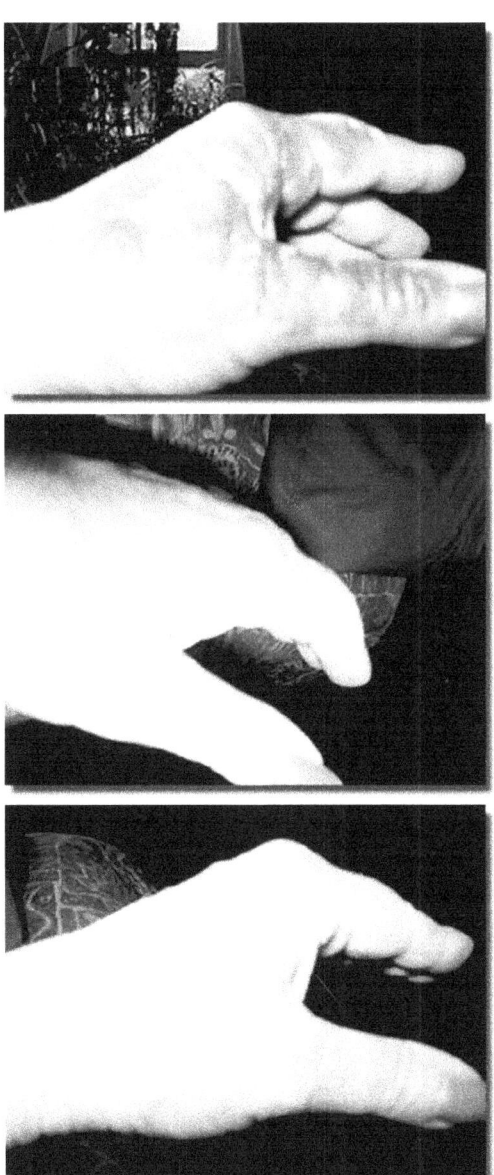

Belvaspata Questions and Answers

Q. How was this healing modality received by Almine?

A. Almine was explaining to a healer in her class in Ireland why a specific energy-based modality wouldn't work when she saw a group of butterflies come through the window and turn into sigils as they flew over the healer's right shoulder and into Almine's forehead. She then went to a flipchart and started writing the sigils and accompanying words as rapidly as she could. Class ended at that point, but in her hotel room, sigils, words and information came through the night until 7a.m. the next morning.

Q. Does one have to be initiated to use the sigils and if so, how?

A. Absolutely, one has to be initiated. If you were to ask an initiate, they will be able to describe how profound the initiation experience is as the sigils are conveyed from a Belvaspata Master. Students need to integrate and internalize the 12 Pairs of Emotions for Level I, the 16 Rays of Light for Level II, the 12 Pairs of Pure States of Being for Master Level and the 12 Pairs of Heart Energies for the Grand Master Level, prior to receiving their initiation into each of these levels of Belvaspata.

Q. This healing method was a gift from the Creator Goddess/Infinite, through Almine to each of us who are initiated into the Master and Grand Master Levels. Why is it important to honour the Source, or lineage, of this gift when we use it for healing sessions or when giving initiations?

A. As we acknowledge and honor the Source, we connect with the lineage of power and purity directly from the Infinite, to Almine and through all others who are initiated before us. The more we expand our hearts through the attitudes of Love, Praise and Gratitude, the more we open to the fullness of the power of Belvaspata. We may feel this power come into us as a physical sensation such as energy moving through one's body, warmth, coolness, tingling, a feeling of excitement, etc.

The Belvaspata healing modality is a gift from Mother/Infinite Source, through Almine and as such reflects the Divine Perfection and is supported by the Angels who work with Belvaspata and its sigils.

Q. Can the time frame for receiving the initiations be reduced?

A. When attending a retreat with Almine, the waiting period between initiations is waived. This is due to the expansion and high frequency levels attained during the retreat. All other initiations must maintain the minimum time periods between initiations. This allows full integration and absorption of the frequencies to occur prior to being initiated into the next level. Some initiates may need longer for this than others.

Q. Having received Level I Belvaspata, is it okay to do healing sessions on others and myself? What benefits does one receive?

A. Yes, Level I masters may use Belvaspata on themselves or others. Through the interconnectedness of all life, the healing frequencies of Belvaspata automatically go where they are most needed so all life benefits. In this way one is of greater service. Through the archetype principle — that which we accomplish for ourselves is also accomplished for all.

Q. What is the significance of the tenth chakra?

A. The Lemurian name for 'ten' is 'Lahun'. This means *One in All* and *All in One*. The 'law of the one' the Atlantean mysteries taught about also pertains to the mystical principles of the 10th chakra. As an initiate becomes an adept and later a master (all three of these phases are still in ego-identification), 12 chakras open.

During subsequent evolutionary stages such as god consciousness and ascended mastery, the tenth chakra (about the size of a dinner plate, often depicted as a sign of enlightenment above the head in Egyptian and Sumerian art), 10" above the head, enlarges. It continues to grow bigger and bigger until it encloses all other chakras during the ascended mastery stage. *All is now One,* and *One is in all.* By initiating it last, this process is activated.

Q. Have any changes occurred in the sigils or the positions of the Lords, Gods and Goddesses of Belvaspata since it was first received?

A. As the cosmos continues to ascend, grow and evolve, so also will the sigils and the positions of the Angels, Lords, Gods and Goddesses of Belvaspata change and rise to reflect the higher levels of consciousness. This means that they will always retain their purity and remain at their most potent.

Q. I know it is important to honor the sacred nature of Belvaspata. If I make extra copies of Belvaspata initiation sigils or angel names or use on business cards, flyers, etc — what is the best way to discard of them?

A. It is always wise to trust our heart and our feelings to direct our course of actions. Working with Belvaspata removes distortions and makes our guidance ever clearer.

You are correct to remove any Belvaspata sacred material from public sites and never to throw any of it into a wastebasket. Always handle the sigils and angel names in a sacred manner. They should never be placed on the floor or have other objects casually placed on top of them. Sigils should always be handled as one would handle any other sacred object, with the care and dignity befitting their holy nature. In this way we honor the Infinite, Almine, Belvaspata (which is the Infinite's gift to us), ourselves and All.

When discarding Belvaspata sigils or angel names, they should be burned in a ceremonial manner with appreciation and gratitude.

Working with Belvaspata

Q. If we accept payment for this sacred healing modality, aren't we blocking the flow of supply?

A. Every time a first or second level healer uses the sigils, a portion of the Earth and its population are healed. Because the Master Sigil connects the master healer to the cosmos, every time a master healer heals with these sigils, it affects the cosmos. The Grand Master sigil assists with preparing the physical body for immortality and to clear old programming. How can any amount of money ever be adequate repayment? You will still be leaving the cosmos in your debt.

Q. With the new laws of attraction, light attracts opposites. Doesn't this mean those in illusion will surround light workers?

A. In this new cycle, heart energy is the most dominant factor so that opposite energies repel and same energies attract. Thus, those of like heart energy will surround us.

PART III

Level I and Level II Belvaspata

Level I Belvaspata

In preparation for Belvaspata's Level I initiation, the initiate must study and internalize the twelve frequencies (emotions) that comprise the twelve frequency bands of the cosmos. They are not only necessary for initiation but also form an integral part of a Belvaspata session.

As we revisit these frequencies we will feel and understand them more fully.

- They will become stronger and deeper within us.
- It will become easier to experience and generate them as part of a session.
- We will live them more fully.
- Should the old discordant emotions of pain, anger, fear and protectiveness surface, we can instantly move into the new.
- The more we live them, the more they are available for others.

When working with a pair of sigils for the Emotions, always draw both sigils of the pair. These emotions do not have a separate angel and quality sigil.

For a simple session, you may want to use only one or a couple of pairs of emotions and their relevant sigils. It is however extremely beneficial to use all twelve pairs, especially for an initial Belvaspata session, as it balances the emotions. Always follow your own guidance.

Further information is given on these emotions in the chapter, *Preparing for Initiation.*

The 12 New Pairs of Emotions

(−)

1) **Trust**
The desire to surrender
(replaced fear)

2) **Peace**
The desire to be at ease, to feel
at home (replaced protectiveness)

3) **Pleasure**
The desire to be delighted

4) **Acknowledgement**
The desire to see perfection

5) **Receptivity**
The desire to receive

6) **Beauty**
The desire to be uplifted

7) **Assimilation**
The desire to integrate

8) **Joy**
The desire to live

(+)

Love
The desire to include

Inspiration
The desire to inspire and to
be inspired (replaced anger)

Creativity
The desire to create

Empathy
The desire to connect

Generosity
The desire to give

Encouragement
The desire to encourage and
to be encouraged

Communication
The desire to express

Passion
The desire to know

9) **Fun**
The desire to revel

Achievement
The desire to excel

10) **Contentment**
The desire to retain

Enlightenment
The desire to enhance and to to be enhanced (replaced pain)

11) **Humor**
The desire to be amused

Empowerment
The desire to be of service

12) **Satisfaction**
The desire to be fulfilled

Growth
The desire to expand

Note: Due to the changes that took place in the cosmos during August 2008, which brought about the healing of duality and polarity and the ending of linear time, the emotions no longer pulse one another. The Pure Emotions now form a unified field that contains the qualities of all emotions with each being a specific emphasis of the whole. It is still therefore very important to understand the unique qualities within each of the emotional pairings and how they inspire one another.

The Twelve Bands of Pure Emotion

In the previous cycle light formed the matrix of the cosmos, while emotion and awareness moved. Then, rings of emotion formed the matrix and light moved within it. Now omnipresent awareness permeates everything within the cosmos.

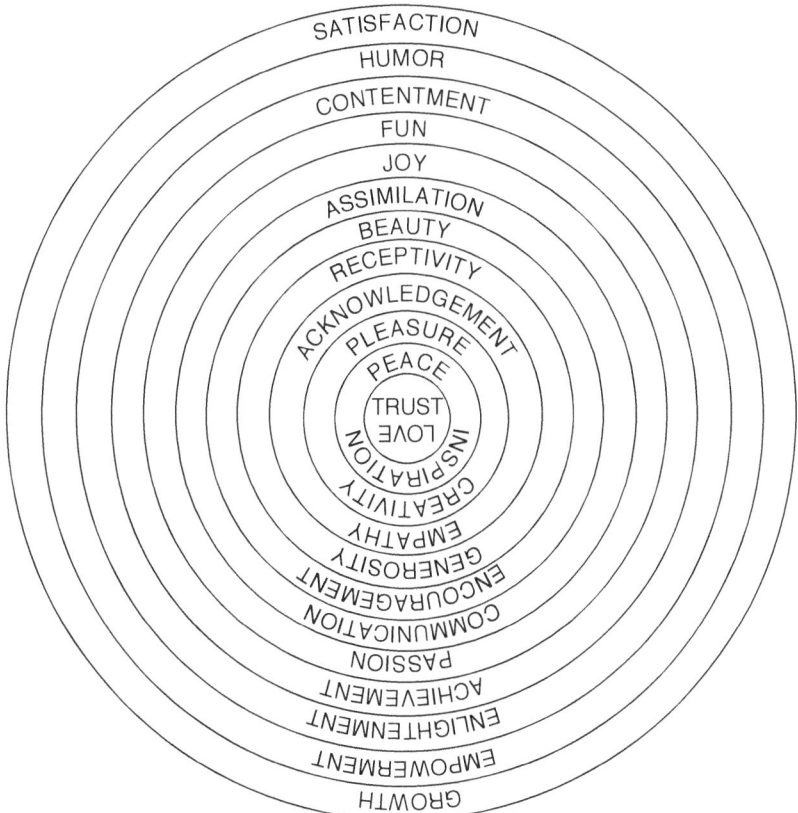

Each band represents a paired set of emotions.

The Sigils of Level I Belvaspata
The Sigils of Love

These sigils are used in pairs to stimulate healthy frequency.

1. Love (+)	Trust (-)	Use
Angel: **Perech-pri-parva**	Angel: **Trues-sabru-varabi**	Use for obesity and excess muscle and weight

2. Inspiration (+)	Peace (-)	Use
Angel: **Kriavat-bishpi**	Angel: **Pele-nanvabruk**	Use in areas of rash, redness or inflammation

3. Creativity (+)	Pleasure (-)	Use
Angel: **Veles-vruchba**	Angel: **Prubechba-natruva**	Genitals and Reproductive Organs

4. Empathy (+)	Acknowledgment (-)	Use
Angel: **Felvi-respi-uhuru-vak**	Angel: **Tre-uch-vara-vaar**	Injuries

NOTE: The Sigils of Love are also known as the 12 Pairs of Emotions

The Sigils of Love

5. **Generosity (+)**	**Receptivity (-)**	**Use**
Angel: **Teshvinechspi-urarat**	Angel: **Nenhursh-brechbravit**	To reduce blood pressure
6. **Encouragement (+)**	**Beauty (-)**	**Use**
Angel: **Kletsut-vesba**	Angel: **Nunberesh-nuk**	Pancreas, liver, gallbladder
7. **Communication (+)**	**Assimilation (-)**	**Use**
Angel: **Araragatveshpi**	Angel: **Nun-heresh-vispi**	Lungs
8. **Passion (+)**	**Joy (-)**	**Use**
Angel: **Gelkrig-sutvra-bararech**	Angel: **Travi-usbava**	For poor circulation

The Sigils of Love

9. **Achievement (+)**

Angel:
Gele-vish-tra-va

Fun (-)

Angel:
Pru-eshbi-klechvaha

Use

Throat, thyroid

10. **Enlightenment (+)**

Angel:
Grunachberesvik

Contentment (-)

Angel:
Kletsatvarabuch

Use

Use for pain

11. **Empowerment (+)**

Angel:
Bu-esbi-klechnatra

Humor (-)

Angel:
Veluchvespri-rekva

Use

Digestive tract, elimination, kidneys, adrenals

12. **Growth (+)**

Angel:
Trubi-kluvespraha

Satisfaction (-)

Angel:
Nechtruavar

Use

Bones, fractures, muscles, joints

Level II Belvaspata

Level II Belvaspata uses the 16 Rays of Light with each ray having its own color and quality. They are studied in preparation for Initiation (see chapter *Preparing for Initiation* for more information on the Rays of Light). It's beneficial to review them occasionally and further study their qualities. As with the 12 pairs of Pure Emotions, the more we understand and appreciate the qualities within these Rays of Light, the more they are available for all. These sigils are called the Sigils of Light.

16 Rays of Light

1. The Root
2. Faith
3. Balance
4. Abundance
5. Wisdom
6. Mercy
7. Diversity
8. Energy
9. Bliss
10. Perception
11. Presence
12. Hope
13. Mastery
14. Discovery
15. Power
16. Truth

The first Ray of Light, the Root, is always held by the Infinite. When using any of the Rays of Light, the Root is always used.

The Sixteen Rays of Light

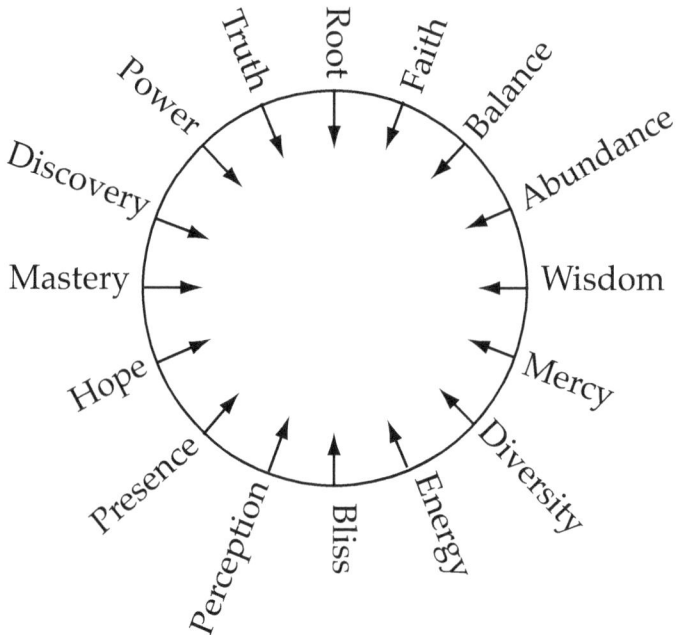

The Sigils of Level II Belvaspata
Sigils of Light

Can be used in a circle. Place sigils in order clockwise.

1. Name of Ray: Root
   Lord name:
   Herhutbrasta

   always use in conjunction with other sigils of light

2. Name of Ray: Faith
   Lord name:
   Belblutvakreshbi

   systemic illness

3. Name of Ray: Balance
   Lord name:
   Kluch-nenuvit

   ears, throat, nose

4. Name of Ray: Abundance
   Lord name:
   Petrevusbi

   prostate, rectum

5.  Name of Ray: Wisdom
   Lord name:
   Gelviveshbi

   pineal, hypothalamus

6.  Name of Ray: Mercy
   Lord name:
   Truavar

   spine, occipital area/base of skull

Sigils of Light

7. Name of Ray: Diversity
Lord name:
Pluakbar

DNA chromosome, memory

8. Name of Ray: Energy
Lord name:
Trechvarvulesbi

blood sugar, blood purification

9. Name of Ray: Bliss
Lord name:
Besbrakva

cellular light, oxygen and ph of cells

10. Name of Ray: Perception
Lord name:
Telenuchvraha

eyes, pituitary, 3rd eye

11. Name of Ray: Presence
Lord name:
Klechsavra

legs and feet

12. Name of Ray: Hope
Lord name:
Telerutskrava

heart, circulation

13. Name of Ray: Mastery
Lord name:
Brishnavak

brain, clarity of thought

NOTE: The Sigils of Light are also known as the 16 Rays of Light

Sigils of Light

14. 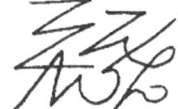 Name of Ray: Discovery
Lord name:
Verebisma

tongue, teeth, tonsils

15.  Name of Ray: Power
Lord name:
Veruchmavaheshbi

skull, scalp, hair

16.  Name of Ray: Truth
Lord name:
Petluchvraha

arms, elbows, hands/wrists, shoulders

Additional Sigils for Level I and Level II Practitioners

These can be used by masters of all levels

Sigil for Presence
(This sigil may be used for treatment of various cancers)

Kurash-berech-verespi   Angel: **Bilach-uvrespi-spaurach**

Sigil for combining frequency and light into one interconnected field
(Can be used anytime imbalance exists)

Kirasta-elech-bruk   Angel: **Ninhursta-uvechvi** (female)

Sigil for Emotional Health
(Use for Emotional Health and Depression)

Angel: **Nechvikrechbar**

Additional Sigils

Sigil for Self-Love
(For enhancing and healing with self-love)

Kluhavespi-sta-unag   Angel: **Kiritre-anuch** (female)

Sigil for Archangel Michael
(The Guardian of Sacred space)

New Name: **Ephrimvael**   Meaning: **The Guardian of the Sacred**

Sigil for Silencing of the Mind
(To silence the internal dialogue of the mind)

Kanig-vishva-heresvi

The Infinite's Sigil

(The Symbol for Connection to Source)
The Sigil's name: Pi-helaa Stanuchvi

**Kaa iri vish esta, na nut klavaa haruhas
Wherever life exists, there perfection is also**

Note: The Infinite's Sigil can be used as a meditation or focus tool to connect to the Infinite. It may be posted in living areas, walls of your room or house, under your mattress or table that you use for Belvaspata sessions as it contains a specific frequency. It does not have a specific purpose as a sigil for doing Belvaspata sessions or initiations.

The Power Source Wheel

Gift from Isis

The use of the Power Source Wheel will augment results. It contains three languages that were used by the Infinite during different creational cycles.

Part IV

Master Level and Grand Master Level Belvaspata

Master Level Belvaspata

Master Level Belvaspata requires that you understand and internalize the frequencies of the States of Being. Along with the information on the States of Being are sigils that each have a specific healing intent. It is also beneficial to revisit them occasionally to gain a greater awareness of the qualities of these States.

As with the sigils for the 12 Pairs of Emotions, both sigils should be drawn. Each pair of States of Being also has an angel sigil; this sigil does not need to be drawn. Look at it as you call the angel by name.

The Master Level Sigil is only to be used for initiation. It is not to be used as part of a healing session.

The Pure States of Being

(+)	(-)
Praise	Glory
Exploration	Harmony
Gratitude	Guidance
Discernment	Transparency
Understanding	Reflection
Embrace	Ecstasy
Manifestation	Inevitability
Oneness	Contentment
Integration	Evolution
Play	Flexibility
Perception	Power
Retention	Conductivity

Further information on the States of Being is given in the chapter *Preparing for Initiation.*

How the Emotions and States of Being Surround the Body

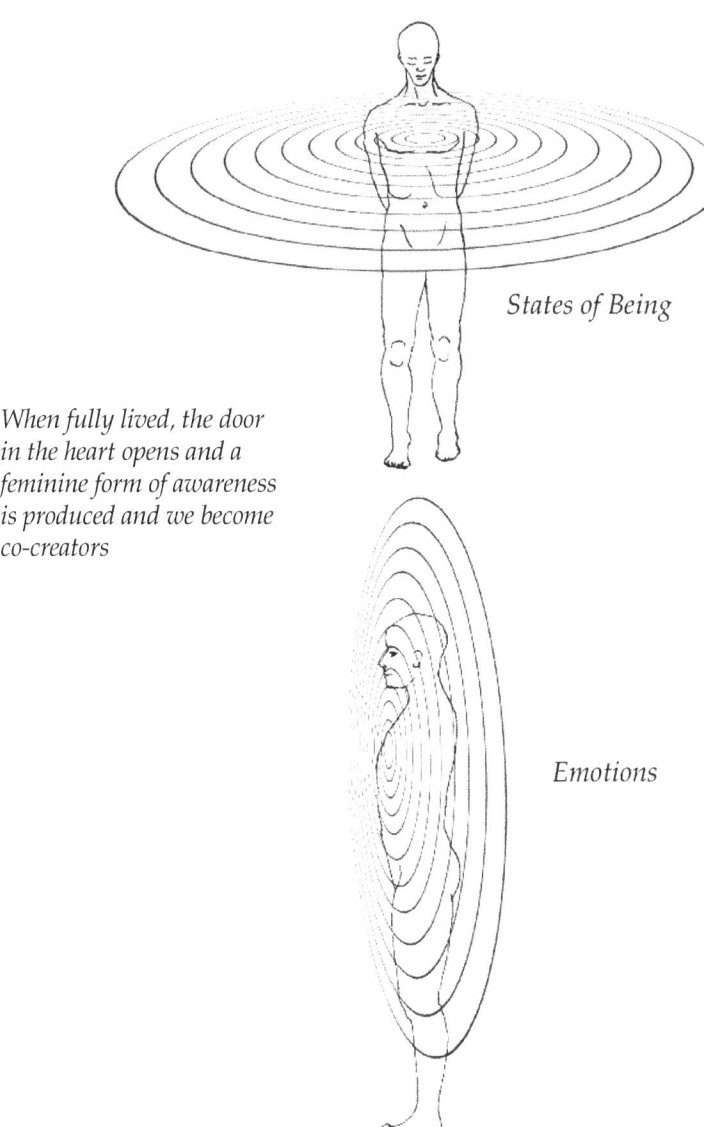

States of Being

When fully lived, the door in the heart opens and a feminine form of awareness is produced and we become co-creators

Emotions

How the Emotions and States of Being Intersect

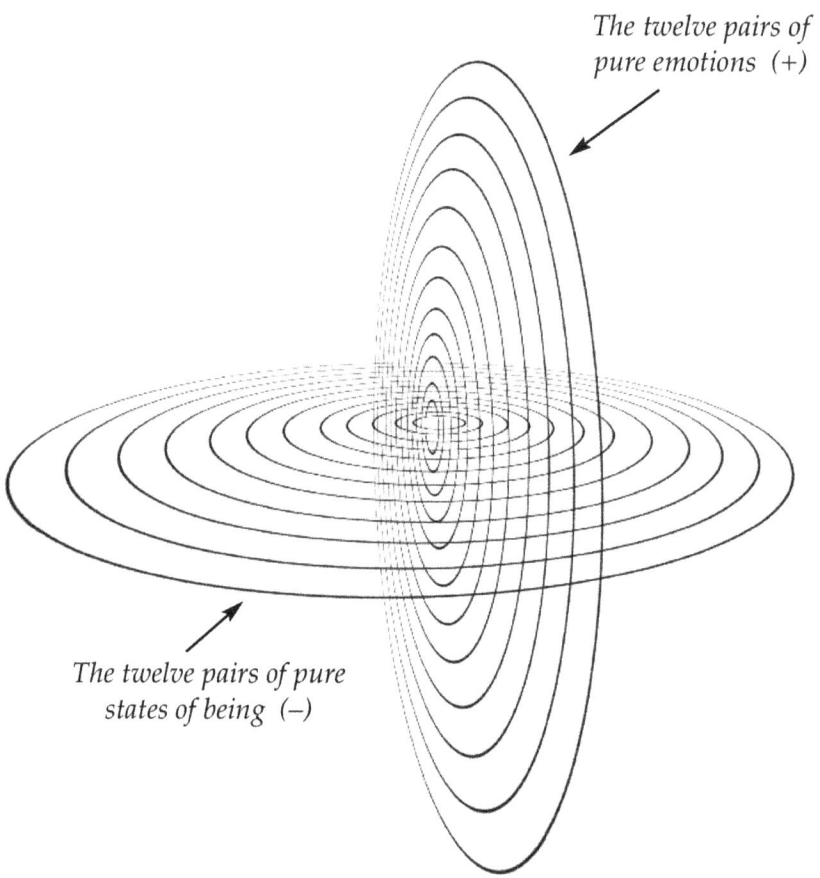

The Sigils of Master Level Belvaspata
The Sigils of The States of Being

1. **Praise (+)**	**Glory (-)**	**Use**
Angel: **Kuluheshpiuvrata**		To increase awareness by infusing the blood stream with awareness particles.
2. **Exploration (+)**	**Harmony (-)**	**Use**
Angel: **Grustervirabach**		To clear neuro-pathways and enhance the perception of subtle information.
3. **Integration (+)**	**Evolution (-)**	**Use**
Angel: **Kruapretparva**		To balance the tones of all the bodies of man.
4. **Discernment (+)**	**Transparency (-)**	**Use**
Angel: **Nunheshbielstuavet**		For the integration of all nine levels of light as information.

Sigils of The States of Being

5. **Understanding (+)** **Reflection (−)** Use

Angel:
Brashechnetvetparva

For the excretion of higher hormones to evolve the physical body.

6. **Play (+)** **Flexibility (−)** Use

Angel:
Gertraskuvaelenustraberechnit

For the evolving of the DNA to the next stages of evolution.

7. **Perception (+)** **Power (−)** Use

Angel:
Pelenichvrausetbi

Opening the doorways of potential.

8. **Embrace (+)** **Ecstasy (−)** Use

Angel:
Grustachvauveshbi

For the connection with the Infinite Mother to be established.

Sigils of The States of Being

9. **Manifestation (+)**	**Inevitability (-)**	**Use**
Angel: **Gelstraubechspi**		For the expression and interpretation of full potential.
10. **Gratitude (+)**	**Guidance (-)**	**Use**
Angel: **Vertlusbraveparhut**		For the awakening of the inner hearing and clairaudience.
11. **Oneness (+)**	**Contentment (-)**	**Use**
Angel: **Sutbiuvechbiklausetvaruach**		For the removal of any obstacles to clairvoyance and the awakening of second sight.
12. **Retention (+)**	**Conductivity (-)**	**Use**
Angel: **Viresklachbirestna**		For the release of any blockages of perception in the higher bodies.

Grand Master Level Belvaspata

Introduction

Belvaspata's first three levels are meant to beneficially impact the physical, etheric, emotional, and mental bodies of beings only; Level II affects the four lower bodies of the planet. At the Master Level, the four lower bodies of the cosmos are also affected by the sigils.

The Grand Master Level affects the spiritual emotional, spiritual mental and spirit bodies of all. It promotes the coming together of life in the more subtle and physical levels of existence. This level of Belvaspata also removes obstructions that interfere with the opening and blossoming of the many new enhancements now found in that unique archetype, man.

The Grand Master Level is the level for the immortality of the body. It is designed to release new hormones and open the higher capacities of the endocrine system. It connects the individual with assistance from the highest levels within the cosmos. It draws in additional angelic presences into our lives and brings clarity of mind and purity of heart as the pathways of light are cleared within the seventh body or spirit body. As it does so, it clears the cosmic pathways and removes old programming of suffering.

The frequencies of the Grand Master Level were born as the Pure Emotion and the States of Being 'pulsed' with one another. This is no longer necessary, as all are now part of the unified field. These frequencies do not have their own specific healing sigils but it is important to revisit them so that they are understood and felt more intensely. (See chapter on *Preparing for Initiation.*)

The Pure Heart Energies

1. Ecstasy (+) + Embrace (-) = Divine Compassion
2. Insight (+) + Appreciation (-) = Reverence
3. Inspiration (+) + Love (-) = Pure Creativity
4. Truth (+) + Clarity (-) = Absolute truth
5. Manifestation (+) + Gratitude (-) = Impeccability
6. Rejoicing (+) + Praise (-) = Celebration
7. Harmony (+) + Wisdom (-) = Timing
8. Fulfillment (+) + Presence (-) = Focus
9. Growth (+) + Balance (-) = Strength
10. Evolution (+) + Surrender (-) = Grace
11. Discovery (+) + Awareness (-) = Clarity
12. Acceptance (+) + Allowing (-) = Harmlessness

This level of Belvaspata is accompanied by a set of 10 sigils that each relate to and are drawn over a specific area of the body. They may be used on their own or in conjunction with other sigils in a session. Placement of sigils is shown on page 73. If they are being used on their own for a session — always start with the Opening Sigils and end with the Closing Sigils.

The Grand Master Level Sigil is only to be used for initiation. It is not to be used as part of a healing session.

Creating the Twelve Heart Energies
How the Emotions and States of Being Intersect

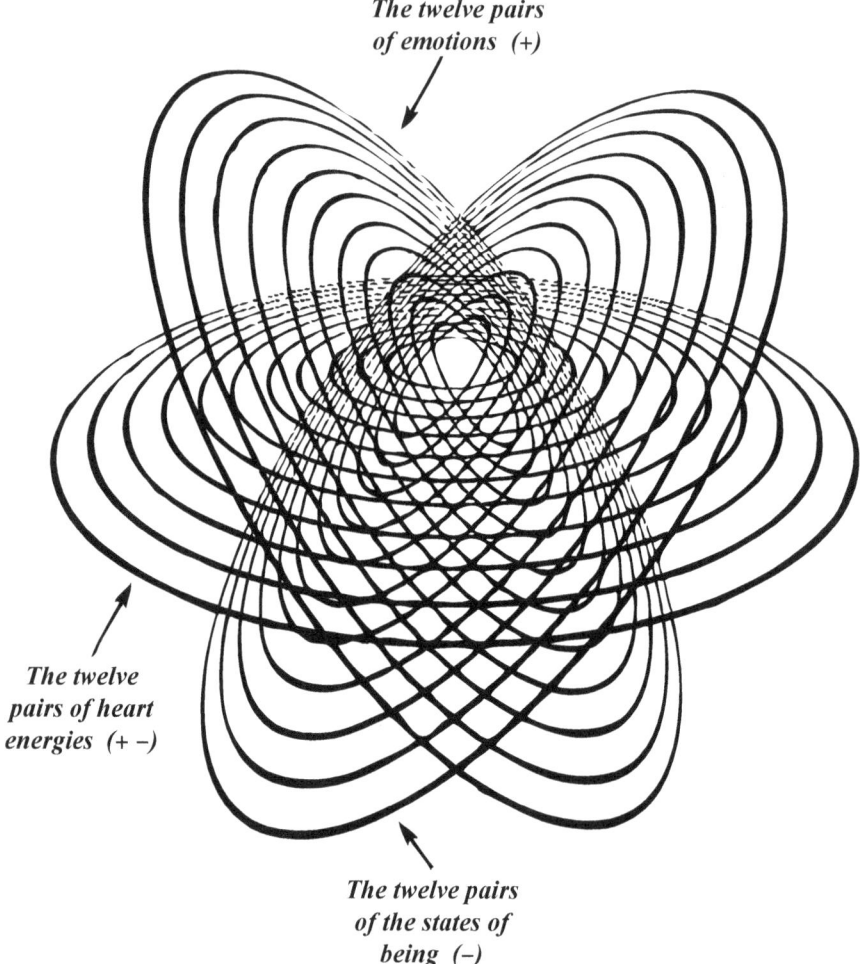

The twelve pairs of emotions (+)

The twelve pairs of heart energies (+ −)

The twelve pairs of the states of being (−)

Originally, the rings each represented a pair that pulsed between their positive and negative aspects. The wheels also pulsed with one another. These were found not only as the grids of the cosmos, but around the body of man.

Following the cosmic changes in December 2008, we no longer pulse between aspects as all fields, light, frequency, etc. are now blended. There are no longer any grids.

The Seven Bodies of Man

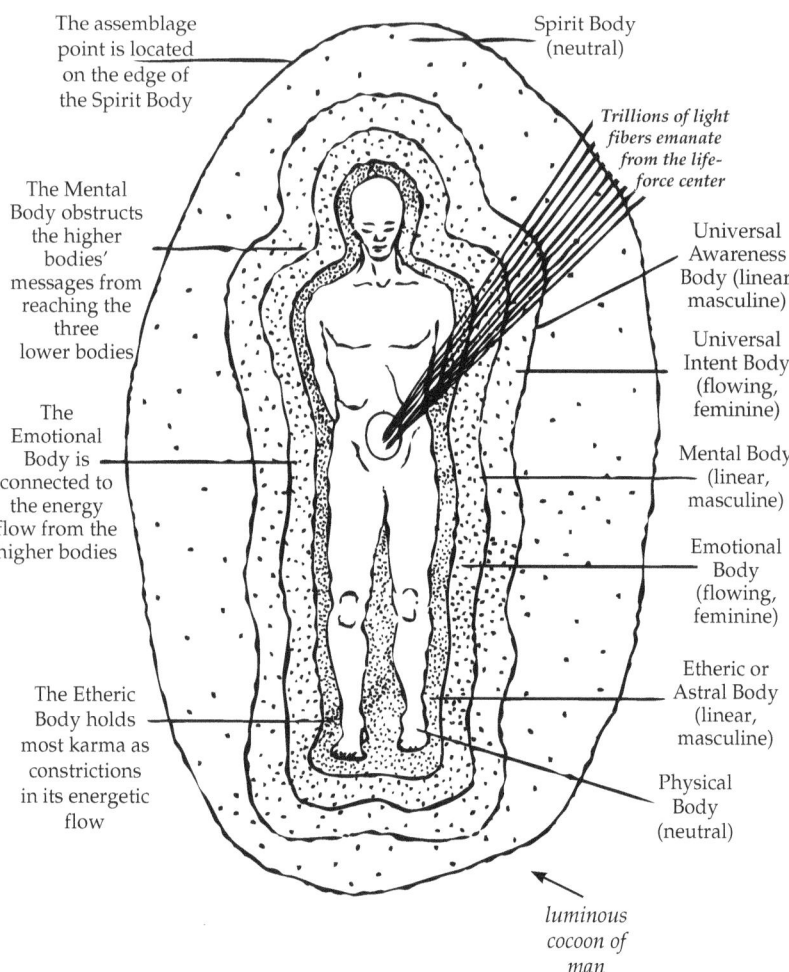

The bodies are superimposed over each other and form the luminous cocoon of man. The trillions of light fibers from the life force center penetrate all other bodies forming the spirit body. As a result of the cosmic changes in December 2008, all fields, bodies, light, frequency, etc. are now blended.

Sigils for Grand Master Level Belvaspata

1.
Stu–elavis–klauna Angel: **Selvi–kluavak- heshpi**

For the removal of any obsolete programming from the
light fibers so that the light can be unobstructed in its flow

2.
Ersatvikelesh-uava Angel: **Kelibap-patrahesbi**

For the clear accessing and interpretation of potential

3.
Kri–ustava-krech-heresbi Angel: **Stuavu-hespi–echvravi**

For the production of awareness as co-creators of our lives

See the illustration on page 73 for placement of these sigils on the body.

Grand Master Sigils

4.
Brabrat-kluvechspi-anuretvraha Angel: **Belach-velesh-pavi-stuava pranut**

For the opening of the capacities for the next level of evolution

---

5.
Kulbelsta–uvachva-kruneshvavi Angel: **Gilstra–usbak–vravesh pi-kla–uva**

For bringing the higher energies into the physical through pulsing the states of being with the emotions

---

6.
Kelvikstauvavechspi-straunak Angel: **Barushbelechpa**

For the opening of the door of the pineal to receive awareness, and the door of the heart to give awareness

Grand Master Sigils

7.
Stuabekbavak-klashvisprasteurit   Angel: **Tristarvamalvashnavek**

For the flow of information between the higher bodies
and the four lower bodies

8.
Vili–esva-kluchba-stuvechvabi   Angel: **Pritineshva-kulu–esvabi**

For the constant awareness of our highest identity
as our never ending source

9.
Beletrevahupspa–eravi   Angel: **Stuvaver-ehepshpi-kluanastrava**

For the development of interactive autonomy and sovereignty

The Tenth Sigil in the Tenth Chakra

Connecting the Bodies of Man to the Cosmic Bodies

The Lahun Sigil

Angel Name:
Harahuch-paranech-skava

By using this sigil above the head in the tenth chakra, the Grandmaster connects the person with the cosmic chakra for mutual support.

Belvaspata

Placement of Grand Master Level Sigils

The cosmos benefits from the healing and the person in return receives cosmic support.

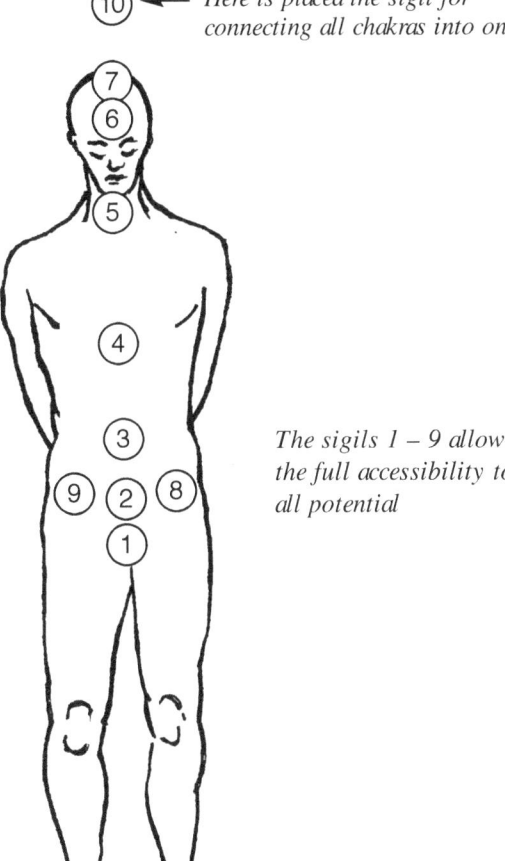

Here is placed the sigil for connecting all chakras into one

The sigils 1 – 9 allow the full accessibility to all potential

These sigils enable the dissolving of all illusions and heal all fracturing. They activate the 144 core illuminations of life.

Advanced Sigils for
Master and Grand Master Practitioners

1. ### Sigil to Achieve the Optimum Ph of the Blood *(The alkaline/acidity ratio)*

Kerenech-vravi-hereshvivasta   Angel: **Klubechspi-klanavek**

2. ### Sigil for the Fetus of an Unborn Infant

Gershta-uklechva-heresvik   Angel: **Pelevik-ustetvi-hereskla**

3. ### Sigil for the Reptilian Brain

Kereshbrikbranavitspaha   Angel: **Kluastragnesvi**

4. ### Sigil for the Medulla

Kleshvi-stauherespi   Angel: **Klachvi-meshpi**

Advanced Sigils

5.
Sigils for the Limbic Brain
(helps magnetic/electrical harmony)
Use all of the below for addictions

a.
Kluagna-uvestrava   Angel: **Pereheretruavar**

b.
Perspratnahut-ulu-echblavaa   Angel: **Septiveravaar**

c.
Kluabresbistuvanar   Angel: **Setvikleshvrahaar**

6.
Sigil for the Amygdala

Kersvravigraniksteravi   Angel: **Erekherashvi-krechvi**

Advanced Sigils

7. Sigils for the Neo-Cortex

a.
Birharnavaksetvravish Angel: **Eravasvetvi**

b.
Granigverevishvahet Angel: **Gelvishvrasbi**

8. Sigil for the Spinal Cord

Kranighereshnutvavi Angel: **Kregnish-herespa**

9. Sigil for Cerebrospinal Fluid

Kritvrapeleshvihasvrabi Angel: **Kru-anegvashpavi**

Advanced Sigils

10. **Sigil for the Pons**

Kelstra-hurva-ukluaverespi Angel: **Ilistrava-klubaberesbi**

11. **Sigil for the Cognitive Heart Center**

Kerenastravaa-heshbi Angel: **Kelstri-uklechvarvaa**

12. **Sigil for the Cognitive Stomach Center**
(the 'gut' feeling, or instinct)

Kers-stabaa-hershvi Angel: **Kluagnetvrich-vravi**

13. **Sigil for the Corpus Callosum**
Connecting the Left & Right Brain Hemispheres

Birnik-hevrasta-kregnig Angel: **Pilnikhershvrata**

Advanced Sigils

14. **Sigil for the Cerebellum**

Pelvisprespata-uhurivesbi-kleshvrataa   Angel: **Kliugnesvi-beleshta**

15. **Sigil for the Centrum**

Krechvaa-erstu-helesvaa   Angel: **Bilich-hestvik-neshvaa**

16. **Sigil for 12 Cranial Nerves**

Kirnit-pleplastavi   Angel: **Hereshvabluavet**

17. **Sigil for Reticular Alarm Activation System**
(helpful for hyperactive children)

Kelhasbraseluvitbareshta   Angel: **Pritlaresuit**

Advanced Sigils

18. **Sigil for Vagus System**

Kelavabra-ushvabi staunag   Angel: **Belaviranachtravi**

19. **Sigil for the Working Man and Woman**
(For freedom from financial bondage and joyous heart-felt work)

Kluha-subatvi-eresta   Angel: **Kirinanhursta-plevabi-vechspi**
(male)

PART V

Preparing for Initiation into Belvaspata

Belvaspata: From Initiate to Grand Master Level

Preparations for all Levels of Initiation

Note: *Level I and Level II Initiations may be performed at the same time. Master and Grand Master Initiation may be performed at the same time. This is a result of cosmic changes that occurred in 2008.*

*There still remains a time period of 3-6 months between the combined Level I and Level II initiations **and** the combined Master and Grand Master Initiations.*

Due to the cosmic changes that occurred in December 2008, we no longer have soul groups to accomplish work by proxy, no planetary or cosmic grids and no fields of bodies within our one field. All light, frequency, bodies, fields, etc are combined into the One Being. However, we may now be connected by these individual levels of initiation to that which they represent within the One field.

Level I connects the initiate to the soul group they represent.
Study and internalize the 12 Pairs of Emotions.

A Master or Grand Master of Belvaspata may do initiation for Level I.

Self-initiations may be done with a mentor who is a Master or Grand Master of Belvaspata.

(Level I initiates may use the sigils of Love and others for this level. *See pages 42 and 50.*)

Level II connects the initiate to the planet. Each time a Level II practitioner uses Belvaspata, it affects all of humanity.
Study and internalize the 16 Rays of Light

A Master or Grand Master of Belvaspata may do initiation for Level II.

Self-initiations may be done with a mentor who is a Master or Grand Master of Belvaspata.

(Level II initiates may use the sigils of Love, the sigils of Light and other sigils for this level. *See pages 42, 47 and 50.*)

Master Level removes illusion, connecting the Master to the cosmos in that every time a master practitioner uses Belvaspata, it benefits all of the cosmos.
Study and internalize the 12 Pure Pairs of States of Being.

A Master or Grand Master of Belvaspata may do initiation for Master Level.

Self-initiations may be done with a mentor who is a Master or Grand Master of Belvaspata.

(Master Level initiates may use the sigils of Love, Light, States of Being and some advanced sigils. *See pages 42, 47, 50, 61 and 74.*)

Grand Master Level affects the spiritual emotional, spiritual mental and spirit bodies of all. It is the level to prepare for immortality of the body, as it releases new hormones and opens higher capacities of the endocrine system. It also clears the cosmic pathways and removes old programming of suffering as it connects the initiate with assistance from the highest levels within the cosmos.

Study and internalize the 12 Pairs of Heart Energies.

A Grand Master of Belvaspata may do initiation for Grand Master Level.

Self-initiations may be done with a mentor who is a Grand Master of Belvaspata.

(Grand Master level initiates may use the sigils of all levels of Belvaspata. *See pages 42, 47, 50, 61, 69 and 74.)*

Preparation for Level I

In preparation for Belvaspata's Level I initiation, the initiate must study and internalize the twelve frequencies (emotions) that comprised the twelve frequency bands of the cosmos and have now become a unified field. It may take from a few of hours to an entire day to do this. Once initiated, the practitioner may heal using these frequencies and their sigils.

Before looking at these new frequencies it is important to understand 'what was' so one may more fully appreciate 'what is'.

In the past, there were four basic emotions, each with two opposite poles:

1) Fear (-) / Love (+)
Fear – the desire to retreat
Love – the desire to include within

2) Protectiveness (-) /Anger (+)
Protectiveness – the desire to protect
Anger – the desire to attack/to break up illusion or stuckness

3) Joy (-) / Passion (+)
Joy – the desire to be/to live
Passion – the desire to know

4) Contentment (-) / Pain (+)
Contentment – the desire to keep as is
Pain – the desire to change

These emotions would have pulsed each other from the negative to the positive, from the unknown to the known as we explored portions of the Infinite's Being that had not been fully explored. Often we would find that we over-polarized into one emotion. Then we would attract into our environment the opposite polarity, for example within a relationship, excess anger would need a partner with an over-polarization in protectiveness to provide the balance.

We are now birthing a new paradigm as a result of a major leap in ascension and this has brought about a change in the Laws that govern nature and the cosmos. This has further resulted in a change in emotions. There are now 12 pairs of emotions with some of the old emotions being replaced. No longer do we have pain, fear, protectiveness and anger.

Internalizing The Pure Emotions

To internalize an emotion, we approach it from the largest perspective:

- While in a meditative state, visualize your heart center opening wider and wider until you can imagine seeing the whole Earth in it.
- Imagine and visualize the heart center opening at a rate beyond the speed of light until the solar system, the galaxy and then many galaxies are visible through the heart.
- Continue opening while in deep meditation until the whole cosmos is within you and you have reached the membrane that contains it all.
- You may visualize the large central sun within you and see its arms of light spiraling outwards, consisting of trillions upon trillions of galaxies like specks of light. (You may have another visualization that works for you to achieve maximum expansion — feel free to use it.)
- Remind yourself that you are a consciousness superimposed over all that is and you are all that you see.
- From this large perspective, feel the frequency of one aspect of an Emotional pair ripple through you as you envision all that evokes it. Start with the first Emotion of Love from the pairing of Love and Trust.
- Sustain it until it is strong, potent and all you can feel.
- When you are ready, move on to its 'opposite' frequency, Trust.
- As you experience each aspect of an Emotional pair, understand and observe how they complement and inspire one another.

- When you can feel them both, move on to the next Emotional pair while keeping the expanded awareness.
- Each pair of Emotions should be explored and experienced fully. The time necessary for this may be different for each person and for each pair of Emotions being integrated.

While the Pure Emotions are now part of the unified field, it is still important to study and integrate them as they are paired. It is in understanding their specific qualities that we can more fully appreciate how they have combined and yet continue to express their own unique emphasis within the field.

This is the same method that is used to internalize the Rays of Light, the States of Being and the Heart Energies that are given later in this book. As with the Pure Emotions, all are now part of the unified field yet they each maintain their own particular characteristics and essence.

The Pure Emotions

Initially each pair of emotions represented a ring with its masculine and feminine aspects. They pulsed against each other to enhance the qualities of both. The stronger one felt a specific emotion, the deeper one could go into its opposite aspect. In fact, the more strongly an emotion was felt, the more its opposite had to be experienced or an imbalance resulted. For instance, if one did not alternate achievement with fun, it became blind ambition, losing sight of the quality of the journey.

As a result of cosmic changes and the healing of duality and polarity, all emotions form a unified field. Each emotion is a unique expression of the whole and as a pair they inspire one another.

It is essential that the steps be performed in the same order as the frequencies are found within the cosmos, starting from the core emotions of love and trust, and working your way out to growth and satisfaction.

1. Trust and Love

Trust and Love are the core emotions for the new creation of existence and replace fear.

As old programming of fear breaks down in every being, the new reality of trust must reveal itself. It is, after all, what is real; what **is**. All else is just an illusion.

Trusting that our lives are guided in every way by our largest identity that spans all existence, we can release our attempts to control life. But what guides our highest self? The One Life that sustains us all — infinite, timeless and vast.

In your expanded state, feel the essence of the One Infinite Being, the serenity, compassion and ageless wisdom. Feel your expanded being as part of this Infinite's vastness and all-encompassing love. This is what runs all life. Allow yourself to surrender to the guidance and love of the Infinite.

The more we surrender to the One, to ourselves, the deeper our love for all beings grows. We can include them in our love because we see so clearly that the roles we play in our experiences are but small ones on a small stage. When we look further, each being is a unique perspective superimposed over all that is — just as vast as we are and just as deserving of life as a part of the Infinite's Being.

Allow love, trust and total surrender to flood your being until they have become part of all you are.

2. Peace and Inspiration

Peace and Inspiration form the second ring. Peace is the desire to be at home, to feel totally at ease. These rings build on each other; we cannot feel peace when trust is not present, telling us that life is safe. Peace knows that the cosmos is a safe home; that we can relax in the knowledge that we are in the secure hands of our highest self.

The striving that was part of linear progression in the previous cycle, left us feeling we always had to become what we were not. The new creation offers us an unprecedented gift that makes striving unnecessary.

All is available right now in terms of awareness. All we have to do is open the door in each moment using the ascension attitudes.[6] These attitudes come when we cease to strive and are fully at ease within the moment.

This deep peace creates our happiness and acceptance of our body as the center of our cosmic home. This is not something light workers have generally felt. Many have been unaccustomed to dense

---

6 The three ascension attitudes are Praise, Love and Gratitude. For more information read *A Life of Miracles* by Almine.

bodies, having been seeded into humanity as a gift of light for the earth's pivotal role during the cosmic ascension.

They've wanted to leave their bodies, at times even living partially out of body. Where is there to go if we are everywhere at once? We are neither the body nor its experiences. Secure in this knowledge, we can be at peace and enjoy the play.

This feeling of being at peace within ourselves and at home in the cosmos, did not come easily in the previous cycle for another very prominent reason. Since opposites attracted, we were surrounded by opposite energy. The greater our light, the greater the darkness that lurked behind the faces we drew into our environment.

Now that the same energies attract each other, we will be attracting others who live the same high standards of impeccability. We will finally not only feel at home within ourselves but also with others. We must be able to allow those with opposite energies to depart with grace, however, for in keeping with the new laws of the cosmos, their departure is inevitable. It is also inevitable that others with like energies must gravitate towards us.

It is in the deep peace of our being that we access the perfection of all life. It is here inspiration is born. We are now immortal in our individuated beings, and physical immortality is available also through constant states of the ascension attitudes. We have now every reason to be inspired, to build a life of beauty and a legacy that inspires others.

3. Creativity and Pleasure

The link between Creativity and Pleasure is apparent, as the more pleasure fills our life, the more the muse stirs us into creativity; the more creative we become, the more our pleasure increases.

This pair of emotions, together with the previous two rings, forms the core of the new creation. That such pleasant and worthy emotions have replaced anger, pain, fear and protectiveness is a cause for gratitude and great praise. They form the hub, or core of the rings of frequency, inspiring creativity through love — the primary purpose for life.

To be constantly delighted simply takes full awareness of the moment. When we truly experience the wonder of the senses, the beauty of Creation all around us, and the heroism that lies in everyday life, delight will flood our being. Only those unaware, or steeped in thought, can deprive themselves of the pleasure life so freely offers the one who lives in the moment.

4. Acknowledgement and Empathy

See the ever-unfolding perfection underlying appearances. It is not enough to acknowledge that the perfection is there, then feel victimized by someone a while later. Do we truly realize that we have co-created whatever is in our life?

If we do not like what we have created, it is now easier for us to make changes since the very purpose of this new paradigm is creating through love. If we focus on that which we love, new creation will flow. If we focus on that which we do not like, the change will not come. In this new creation, therefore, we have come into our spiritual maturity; we have become co-creators with the Infinite. The perfection is not just there for us to **find**; it is ours to create.

How do we create perfection? We create it by finding it in others, in the moment, in the situation. We create that which we love in another. Light workers no longer need to be surrounded by those of an opposite energy. It should therefore be easy to see perfection in those we draw into our lives.

When we focus on perfection, our ability to find it increases. A light family will increasingly fill our life. In the safety of being among others like us, we empathically connect.

The opposite aspect of acknowledgement is the desire to connect — empathy.

Encounters with those of lower light also allow a heart connection because, in seeing their perfection, we connect with the perfection of their higher selves, not their lowest. In seeing this, we help them to achieve that perfection. But it does not mean we have to allow them into our lives.

Now it is safe for us to connect empathically with others. We are no longer the martyrs. We no longer have to be injured so others may learn. Because our hearts are open, we have become cosmic creators. This is a role so precious and significant that we cannot allow any remaining illusion in another to close off this priceless connection we have with all life — the gift of empathy.

5. Receptivity and Generosity

When a large cycle closes, as has just occurred, not only do opposite poles reverse but, as a consequence, their flow is also reversed. In the previous cycle, light workers were surrounded by those who wanted their light. The takers were not consciously aware of what they were seeking, so they took anything they could get. Light workers, therefore, have been giving for ages while others have been taking.

Now the flow has reversed and the debt has to be paid. There is a law of compensation decreeing that imbalance in any part of existence must have an equal and opposite movement to correct it. This is about to happen as light workers are repaid for all their giving.

There is just one requirement, however, and that is receptivity. After only giving for so long, light workers must break the mindset that can stand in the way of opening to receive. They must, in fact, look forward to it, expect it and envision it.

There has been an agenda associated with others giving to us that has sometimes made us reluctant to receive. But if it is the cosmos settling a score, we are really getting what belongs to us by rights. What does it then matter through what means it chooses to repay us? Let us be filled with receptivity.

When we give, we must not think that such generosity depletes us. Rather let us see how generosity and receptivity form one long continuous flow. Though the wind blowing through the house enters at the window, it leaves through the door. Express both receptivity and generosity joyously.

6. Beauty and Encouragement

It can be said that beauty is just a glimpse into the perfection of the indwelling life behind form. It sees that which has enduring value, like a doorway into eternity. Every time we recognize beauty, we are encouraged (encouragement being its opposite aspect).

Beauty encourages us to create our life as a living work of art. If we see ourselves surrounded by beauty, we are hallowed by it. Moments become meaningful. A hard journey through life becomes not only tolerable, but we feel encouraged enough to believe we can flourish rather than survive.

There are obvious visions of beauty: the sunset over the sea, a child's sleeping face, a new kitten. But the true disciple of beauty doesn't stop there. Encouraged by what has become a treasure hunt for gems of beauty, he seeks to find them in the most unlikely places.

Artists of old saw beauty in the mundane, in another man's trash. They painted the crumbs of a left over meal, the spill of a wineglass. For where others saw only dirty dishes, the artist saw light as it played on crystal and wine and reflected off a wayward spoon.

They did not paint objects, but a dance of light, playfully leading the eye of the observer across the canvas of a captured moment. A famous English watercolorist said at the end of his life that he had never seen anything ugly. These are the words of a true disciple of beauty.

7. Assimilation and Communication

Too little true assimilation of information (which is accessed light) takes place in the world for several reasons:

- True listening to another's words can only take place in the absence of internal dialog. The listener has to stay in the silence of the mind and enter into the other's viewpoint by feeling the communication with the heart.
- The past cycle was left-brain dominated, but the non-verbal communications from the right brain accesses nine times more than did the left brain. Thoughts crowd out the subtle information from the cosmos that is all around us.
- Finding silence is getting more and more difficult. Airplanes roar, car horns blare, appliances hum and then, as though that were not enough, TVs are on whether someone is watching or not. Cell phones make sure that no one has silent time around them. But

it is in silence that we get to know ourselves through listening to our thoughts and desires.
- Conversation and intergenerational communication has dwindled in most cultures where TV has become the substitute for knowing one another.
- We spend too little time in appreciation of nature's wonders, and much of that experience has become action-oriented. All of the natural world and its creatures speak to us through their individual frequencies. We can assimilate their special life song by sitting in silence and feeling it within our cells.

The assimilation of other's communications enriches us. Their diversity can carve new facets in our own life, new perspectives that leave us enhanced. When we feel truly heard, the desire to communicate (its opposite aspect) becomes more active as well.

8. Passion and Joy

When the social conditioning of our lives has left the clear impression that it is unsafe to fully participate in the game of life, we may hang back in the safety of the known, afraid to make ourselves a target by being noticed. We may fear that passion could cause our light to shine so brightly that others might try and tear us down so that their own lack of luster is not as obvious. If we deny our desire to express passionately long enough, we end up being strangers to passion; not knowing how to find it, nor recognize it even if we do. The lateral hypothalamus tells us when we have eaten enough. The ventromedial hypothalamus tells us when we are hungry. In the same way, if we deny the promptings from these portions of the brain, we will end up either obese or anorexic. When that happens we have to gently coach ourselves into recalling how their promptings feel.

When passion beckons, we feel warm and excited; our faces flush and our imagination stirs with questions of "What if?" and "What lies beyond the next horizon?" It inspires us into action and makes us believe we can take risks and build.

We find our passion by following the yearnings our moments of joy evoke within our hearts. It is the lost song the singer feels hiding within the shadows of his mind; the lost rhythm the dancer forever seeks; the mysteries of the cosmos that wait for the scientist or the metaphysician to unlock. It is the desire, inspired by the innocence in our child's eyes, to build a life of wonder and beauty for our family.

If passion has become a stranger to us, we may need to become reacquainted with it one facet at a time. When it is expressed, passion consists of taking risks. It is the precursor to accomplishment and the building of something new. It adds new experiences, further boundaries, and new depth to our lives.

Training ourselves to hear the voice of passion again, we find the yearning of our heart and follow where it leads. We make a concerted effort to break free from the prison bars of ruts and expectations, socially conditioned limitations and self-imposed belief systems that keep us in mediocrity. We take a few minutes a day to dare to dream of what would make our hearts sing. We awake each morning and determine to live the day before us as though it were our last. We look at our lives as though for the first time, with a fresh perspective that can detect the joyless, self-sacrificing areas. With courage and great consideration for the consequences of our actions on others, we implement our first steps to bring the glow of passion back to these areas.

A decision may take a minute to make, but for it to be as life altering as we would want it to be, it must be supported by a firm foundation. This requires planning and a certain amount of analysis. What is the goal? What resources will be needed? Is there a discrepancy between what we need and what we have? How can we fill it? Many businesses fail, taking many dreams with them, because not enough thought was given to what was needed to support them in terms of time and money.

Once a goal is identified, break it into projects and tasks. Many envy the achievements of others, but are not prepared to put in the work. Sometimes it takes burning the candle on both ends to fulfill a dream. It is our passion that keeps our enthusiasm lit and gives us our second wind to fly higher than we ever thought possible.

As passion explores the multitude of possibilities through which we can express, so joy is concentrated on the simplicity of the moment. Joy is a mindset, a certain focus that sees the perfection of the here and now, casting a golden glow over the experiences of yesterday. It turns the mundane into poetry and captures the moment in a still life image.

Milton said: "The mind in its own place and of itself can turn hell into heaven and heaven into hell." Franz Liszt was urged to write his memoirs, but he said: "It is enough to have lived such a life." He found such joy in his experiences; he did not have to externalize them to appreciate them.

Joy can be recognized by the deep feeling of satisfaction it brings, by the feeling that one has come home to oneself. It taps into the quiet place within that nurtures the soul and replenishes the mind. When we are under its spell, joy makes us feel light and young again, connected to the earth and freed from our cares.

Just as building with passion requires careful and disciplined time allocations, living with joy requires us to focus on the details in front of us at the moment. Even if we cannot find even a moment today to do the things we enjoy, we can find the time to enjoy the things we are doing.

In cutting up vegetables to make a stew, we can see the colors of the carrots, explore the different textures of each vegetable and smell the fresh fragrance as we cut through their skins.

Even repetitive work can become a mantra, or a production line a prayer as we send blessings and angelic assistance to the homes where the products will end up. Walking in the crowded street, we can feel the sadness of others but can turn it into joy by envisioning blessings pouring into their lives. The loss in the lives of others can be used to inspire praise and gratitude for the blessings in our own.

In our choice of the joy to fill our leisure time, we look for that which will inspire us into accomplishment. As the joy flows inward on the surface, the passion it inspires folds outward beneath the surface. The greater our joy, the greater the actions it will inspire.

9. Fun and achievement

We have possibly all heard the saying that someone we know 'works hard and plays hard.' That is because the two go hand-in-hand. Fun without achievement is a shallow, unfulfilling life. Achievement without the fun that brings quality to the journey, leads to an equally unsatisfying life. Blind ambition can result from such an imbalance and one becomes blinded as to which achievements would be truly life enhancing.

Fun helps energy flow and prevents us from taking ourselves too seriously. It relieves the tensions we experience during our battles of achievement.

10. Contentment and Enlightenment

Contentment knows that it is living perfect moments; the fire is crackling in the fireplace, a little child with sleep-weighted eyelids is wrapped in a quilt on your lap, while the rain of a winter night beats outside on the window panes.

It is during those moments that we wish everyone on earth could share the feeling of complete contentment. We wish we could enhance the life of a runaway teenager somewhere in a lonely bus station. We want to have the hungry family in the ghetto fed and feeling the inner fulfillment contentment brings.

Such contentment can come as a strong undercurrent of life, rather than as a few fleeting moments. Contentment as a constant companion is the result of deep, meaningful living, of insights gained and inner storms weathered. The desire to enhance and enlighten the life of another is the sincere wish that insight will change despair into contentment for another as well.

11. Empowerment and Humor

Empowerment is the desire to serve. At first, this definition might not make sense. The connection between service and empowerment might seem a bit obscure. The reason is that man has really not understood the proper meaning of service.

Service has often meant assuaging our conscience by giving a handout, not really addressing the deficiency that caused the condition in the first place. True service instead is empowering the individual to find his own way out of the dire straits of his life. This way he has something to show for his hardship: newfound strength or abilities.

The desire to be of service will be never-ending if it is based on need.

It could eventually pull us into the despair of need as well. The balancing factor is humor.

Humor laughs at life, laughs at self and instead of blaming, laughs at the folly of others. It cannot take anything too seriously because it knows without a shadow of doubt that we are just engaged in a play. It helps by empowering the beggar, not because he seems needy, but just because it is his role. The play must go on because it has value.

12. Growth and Satisfaction

Understanding the essence of growth is new. This is because the way growth now takes place is new. It used to be the result of delving (painfully, at times) into the unknown, grappling with its illusion and eventually turning it into the known through experience. When delving into the unknown, fear resulted, often bringing about protectiveness. When the illusion refused to yield its insights, anger tried to break it up.

The emotions associated with growth were not always pleasant and even the word 'growth' often had an unpleasant connotation. Growth is now an expansion that is the result of satisfaction. When we are with those who are energetically incompatible, we experience a shrinking feeling. The new creation brings kindred spirits in the form of family and friends. In the deep satisfaction of their company, we can feel our souls expand.

Growth used to come through opposition. Now it comes through support. How will we know when we have found it? The deep satisfaction of our hearts will tell us we have just lived our highest truth.

Preparation for Level II

The requirement for Level II Initiation is to study and internalize the following sixteen Rays of Light.

The Sixteen Rays of Light

The root of Light is the Infinite, the Goddess Mother of all Creation. She is like the white light that splits into colors. In the new creation into which we have entered, there are sixteen rays of light that move throughout existence. Although our minds may not initially grasp and interpret that we are seeing colors never before seen, we are nevertheless in a new color spectrum. Previously, light reflected the static gridwork of the cosmos; now it reflects cosmic movement.

The Sixteen Rays in a Clockwise Position

1. The Root — During this cycle of existence, Mother/Infinite, the Source of all light, is the root of light. The purity and incorruptible nature of Her Being henceforth safeguards the Cosmic Light against distortion.

As we seek to internalize the root of light in our lives, let us be always mindful that we exist in the holiness of Her Being and that we can dedicate every action, every breath we take in love, praise and gratitude to the One Being that sustains us and gives us life.

In meditation, let us see ourselves become as vast as the cosmos and as we linger there, let us know we have become one with the Infinite Mother, that in such expanded awareness, we are being cradled in Her loving arms. It is here where we will find the Source of all light.

2. Faith — The nature of faith has changed for this creation. Formerly, it was a mindset that re-created itself. In other words, the most prevalent and dominant thoughts ended up creating our environment. Because our thoughts were generally chaotic, we created chaotic conditions on Earth.

The new creations do not come through thought, but through the heart. We create through love, praise and gratitude — a way that prevents us from creating more chaos. Faith, as a way to create our reality, has to therefore reflect this change. The new way to understand faith would be as the conscious creation of reality through an attitude of love. Envision how you would like to live life, and flood the images with love, praise and gratitude that such joyous manifestations can be yours.

3. Balance — The light-ray of balance represents the essence of what the Mayans call 'Movement and Measure.' Balance is not static, but rather consists of the dynamic movement between expanding boundaries. In other words, it moves between positive and negative aspects within existence, always pulling them slightly further apart.

As an example, a balanced life pulses between beingness and doingness. The deeper we enter into the peace of our being, the more we can accomplish with our actions (our 'doingness'). In this way, both our passive and pro-active aspects are strengthened and enhanced. In these deepening pulsations lie the expansion and growth of the being.

4. Abundance — The true meaning of abundance has been colored by the beautiful and uplifting purpose of our new existence, creation through the heart. Before, we hoped that life would deliver abundance. Now we are limited only by how large we can dream and how much love we can pour into our dreams and visions.

While doing this, we continue to broadcast heartfelt gratitude throughout the cosmos for what we have. Increases do not occur where there is an absence of gratitude for present gifts. Conversely, whatever we are grateful for increases.

Generosity also increases supply. If we truly understand that we are co-creators of our realities, then our supply has no limit. In giving, we simply open the sluices of manifestation a little wider. If we have love, praise and gratitude, we open it wider still; clustering awareness into manifesting our created realities.

5. Wisdom — It has been said that wisdom is applied knowledge. Previously, we had to interpret principles that lay hidden within the illusion of the former cycle of existence. Now all illusion has been solved and the new creation lies before us like a pristine uncharted land. What knowledge is there to apply?

The knowledge that needs to be interpreted through our lives is the knowledge of the self we see mirrored within those of like energy. In them, we see ourselves and learn about what we are. Learning by observing those energies in others, we become more of what we are and find new ways of applying them in our lives.

6. Mercy — Mercy no longer means tolerating the dysfunctional in our midst. In fact, the opposite is true. Because opposite light and frequency (emotion) now attract, the most merciful way of living is to surround ourselves with authentic, love-filled people who make our hearts sing. As we feel joy, it is automatically drawn to its opposite aspect, the most joyless places in the cosmos.

Mercy therefore resembles a form of 'tough love,' a refusal to indulge the clinging to old patterns of illusion as some will want to do. The repelling of those of opposite energies used to be considered 'uncharitable' — now not living our highest truth is.

7. Diversity — The greatest period of growth for any group of beings is when there is unity within diversity, creating interdependency. The slowest growth, and ultimately stagnation, occurs when there is uniformity. We see this in tribal life. The dynamic within the group is one of dependency, keeping its members in an infantile state.

Because the new creation stresses 'sameness,' diversity within the 'sameness' is absolutely vital. If this were not the case, the possibility of over-polarization into the known (accessed light) would be a very real concern. The inevitable result of such over-polarization is stagnation. Although we are to study the beautiful qualities of others, we are in fact studying our own.

We can only recognize that which we have within — the major reason why light-promoters have been so easily deceived by those of ill intent. Although what we see is what we are, every other person is like a uniquely colored lens through which his beam of light shines. When this diversity is observed and appreciated, it brings richness to our lives.

8. Energy — The deep secret behind this fact is that matter and energy have merged. This has already occurred. The gods and goddesses in human form have become 100% energy and are moving into becoming an even more refined form of light. A whole new reality is being born, one in which the Mother Goddess Herself will reign on this most pivotal planet, Earth.

9. Bliss — Bliss is a result of a vast expansive perception that effects the vibration of a body's cells. It is a state of profound praise, love and gratitude generated by an eternal perspective.

The gift of bliss is that old patterns melt away in its presence; constrictions in the flow of energy release. Others experience healings and growth by grace. In a new creation where we are able to access awareness by grace through the ascension attitudes, bliss is more readily present. As one of the rays of light, it offers growth through grace and births hope that anyone can achieve the pinnacle of enlightenment through love, praise and gratitude.

10. Perception — Perception used to come through the gifts of challenge and hardship. Through the friction of life's experiences turning the unknown into the known, perception exacted a high cost.

In the cycle of existence just completed, perception yielded emotion as the primary way of promoting change. Perception birthed the realities of our lives. In this creation, our emotions primarily steer our course, affecting our perception. The more profound our emotions, the more they birth our hopes and dreams into reality.

Imagine our lives as a sphere of existence filled with twelve concentric circular frequency bands (emotion). If the emotions strengthen, the bands expand. Light rays bounce through these bands. If they expand, the light rays have to move through a larger sphere; therefore they have to move faster to complete their pattern. The more intense the emotion, the faster we get our perception.

11. Presence — The Mother of All has a specific 'flavor' to Her light — a personality that expresses Her Being in this cycle of Creation more than any other. Within this ray of light, the presence of the Infinite Divine Being is accessed and known.

The stillness of Mother's ancient moments, timeless and eternal, the tempestuousness of her cataclysmic change, all can be felt through this ray. The reflections of the facets of Her Being are expressed in the stupendous variety and exquisite beauty of Her creations. We can study the Mother's Being by seeing Her face in the reflections of the cosmos.

The study and interpretation of the majesty and glory of the Infinite Mother is really the study of self. We are Her facets, Her reflections. We can only recognize in Her what we are in ourselves. This creation is dedicated to studying the known, that which we are, by accessing it within the divine presence of the Mother of Creation.

12. Hope — Hope is a state of mind that lives with eyes and heart firmly fixed on the most beneficial outcome. Hope has taken on an entirely new meaning since our reason for being has become the creation of that which we love through the heart.

Hope is the vision we hold as we fan the flame of its creation through love, praise and gratitude. This acts upon the substance of things hoped for, formed from tiny fragments of awareness that have always existed, but have now become abundantly available for us to create with.

An attitude is comprised of both love and light. The attitudes of ascension are really the positively charged aspects of awareness. The awareness particles comprise the opposite (negative) aspect.

Awareness also consists of both love (frequency) and light (where opposites attract), The little rays rush towards the source of the ascension attitudes. Here they roll, cluster and fill the mold created by hope.

13. Mastery — Mastery advocates a life lived from complete authenticity, self-discipline, and inner balance. Mastery is a combination of many attributes that take dedication and focus to achieve. Previously these attributes took years to cultivate, one painstaking step at a time.

With awareness immediately available and with time's collapse into the moment, mastery is now at our fingertips. It takes a mindset that always acts from our highest vision, remembering that we are a vast being superimposed over all that is and that wherever we are is the center of our cosmos.

Mastery acts with the utmost impeccability and sensitivity in realizing that every action, every thought, impacts the whole. With such awareness, each act becomes an act of love for the interconnectedness of all life.

14. Discovery — The great significance of the introduction of this ray of light into Creation is as follows:
- The previous cycles of creation were descension cycles, containing a great deal of distorted light. The descension was due to self-centered and separative patriarchal rule. This distorted emotion created fear, anger, pain and protectiveness. Thus we were driven further and further down into density.
- It did not have to be this way. Mother had given freedom of choice to Her creations. The choices of Mother's creations brought about these painful descension cycles and ultimate rebellion and destruction.
- The way it was meant to be was through joyful discovery of the unknown, much the same way the ancient mariners set forth to explore the uncharted seas. It was supposed to be a treasure hunt — finding the gems within our being lying in the dust of the unknown. Through many of the choices made by the higher gods, the adventure of discovery became a nightmare. The reinstallation of this precious ray of light is a wonderful gift as we study the known.

15. Power — In the new creation, all of the previous rays of light moved into the ray of Power, which then moved to birth the 16th ray, as follows:
- All previous rays moved into the one ray, namely the ray of Power.
- The one ray of Power then moved into the inner emotional sphere of trust/love with the brilliance of all fifteen rays.
- The great power and light caused the emotional sphere to spin counterclockwise.
- The rapid spinning shot out all fifteen previous rays plus an additional one, a pink ray embodying absolute truth.

The first fifteen rays previously mentioned had originally been meant to become available as the cosmos ascended. This would have provided the cosmos with the ability to move on to a new existence beyond (as we have just done) without having to go through numerous and repetitive cycles of ascension and decension. Due to the distortion chosen by some of the lords of the light rays at the very pinnacle of existence, the Mother of Creation never gave additional rays until now.

16. Truth — This newly born ray of truth is a new form of this principle. Truth was previously that which was sought without, through the phantoms of illusion clustered about us, attracted to our light. Truth is no longer found without — after all, we are in a play that has yet to be written. There are no preconceived guidelines here. It lies before us, pristine as this newborn ray of truth. This ray is the firstborn child of the cosmos; it is to be felt in our hearts as *The Ring of Truth*.

Preparation for Master Level

The requirement for Master Level initiation is to study and internalize the 12 States of Being.

While they are now part of the unified field, it is still important to understand the individual qualities and how they combine to fully appreciate the unique emphasis that each contributes.

The Twelve Pure States of Being

1. Praise (+) As a state of being it is slightly different than when it is an attitude. Attitudes have more perception. Praise is the surge of deep, exultant feeling that comes from accessing the highest aspect within. It is the triumph of recognizing the perfection underlying appearances.
Glory (-) Glory is the maintenance of the highest aspect of ourselves as a being as vast as the cosmos, and its expression in our lives. In other words, it is when we live life from our largest perspective.

2. Exploration (+) Exploration is the pushing beyond previous boundaries of expression so that new creation and deeper expression can take place for the sake of growth.
Harmony (-) Harmony is the state of being that results from being in step with the blueprint or will of the Infinite; when smaller segments of Creation express synchronistically with the largest purpose of life.

3. Gratitude (+) This state of being results from encountering the true nature of the cosmos as one that supports all life, the recognition of the nurturing of the Divine in our lives.
Guidance (-) The revelation of the most life-enhancing choices along our path and the uncovering of the blueprint of our existence. (**Note:** Within the irrevocable overall purpose of our lives there are now more choices and freedom of expression available than ever as we enter our spiritual maturity.)

4. Discernment (+) Although all unknown portions of Mother's Being have been solved during the cycles of the Fall, there is nevertheless always a mystery as to which expression of the known portions of Her Being would be most life-enhancing. The discernment comes when our hearts reveal this mystery.
Transparency (-) Transparency is the revelation of a portion of existence that reflects the purity of absolute truth.

5. Understanding (+) When we regard our true identity as a being as vast as the cosmos, all is **within** our consciousness that is **without** our bodies. Understanding comes when the light fibers within our bodies light up, or come on line, as a result of something outside our bodies revealing its information.
Reflection (-) When something is encountered in life that evokes an emotional response, it is worthy of study and further scrutiny. It is an indicator of whether we have lived our highest truth. It may also be an indicator of a mystery waiting to reveal itself. Reflection will show whether what we have understood is worthy of implementing and incorporating into our life.

6. Embrace (+) Embrace is the reaching to incorporate more of the vastness of existence into our compassionate understanding and acceptance.
Ecstasy (-) Ecstasy results from the inclusiveness of our vision that sees each life as its own.

7. Manifestation (+) Fifty percent[7] of life is ours to manifest and create at will; that part of life in which we can creatively contribute to the big picture. Manifestation occurs when awareness clusters itself into the circumstances of our lives, pulled forth by the emotions of our hearts as well as our attitudes.
Inevitability (-) Each of us plays a part in contributing to the growth and evolution of the large plan or pattern of life. This constitutes inevitability: the experiences we are required to live according to our mutual contract with the Infinite. Because growth comes through mutual support, the large plan also writes in some 'key moments' — moments of support that are given in our own lives depending on which choices we make. This is part of the set circumstances, of inevitability, in our lives.

8. Oneness (+) Living the deep awareness that all beings are part of us makes us aware of the interconnectedness of life. We gain this understanding by opening ourselves to include all parts of existence.
Contentment (-) Contentment results when oneness occurs and life flows through us without obstruction. We feel that we have come home.

---

7 As of May 2007.

9. Integration (+) The praiseworthy parts of life beckon for us to make them our own — to integrate them as a part of us. That which we find unworthy of integrating, nevertheless has gifts in the form of insights that are worth making our own and should not be dismissed.
Evolution (-) As the caterpillar grows with each bite of the leaf it eats, so we grow in depth of wisdom and perception with each part of our experiential learning that we make our own and integrate. Change for the better is therefore the one constant in a life well lived.

10. Play (+) The spontaneous and lighthearted interaction with the unexpected creates a useful flexibility. It spontaneously and abundantly creates a grace and ease of interaction with life in the moment.
Flexibility (-) The cumbersome weight of self-reflection, self-pity and self-importance weighs down the journey and keeps us locked into points of view. Any viewpoint could, in the next moment, be obsolete as life changes constantly, thought by thought.

11. Perception (+) Much abuse of power has occurred by reversing the polarity of power and perception. Power is the state of being that results from perception, not the other way around. It is perception that must actively be sought in our world, not power.
Power (-) Power as a feminine pole is vastly more powerful than power that is masculine and separative. Power that is feminine, and therefore inclusive in nature, is the power that is aligned with all that is.

12. Retention (+) To retain or allow something to flow through our lives requires our making a simple choice. The only real question in all existence is what is life-enhancing and what is not. That which is, we retain as our own.

Conductivity (-) Conductivity when fully lived brings our lives into a state of grace. The alternative, resistance to that which we choose not to retain, leaks energy and lowers consciousness. It embodies the complete surrender to life.

Preparation for Grand Master Level

The requirement for Grand Master Level Initiation is to study and internalize the Twelve Heart Energies of the Zhong-galabruk

The Heart Energies from the Zhong-Galabruk

Heart energies were born when the Pure Emotions and the States of Being pulsed each other. The feminine aspect of one (either a Pure Emotion or a State of Being) pulsed with the masculine aspect of the other. This interaction produced particles of awareness that had a negative polarity in relation to the already existing awareness particles spread throughout the cosmos. The deeper or stronger one aspect pulsed, the deeper the other responded and the stronger the quality of heart energy that was born.

As the Heart Energies were produced, the Heart Energies themselves 'pulsed' to form an enhanced and balanced Heart Energy. The healing of polarity and duality has meant that they are all now part of a unified field and as such, each is a unique emphasis within that field.

Awareness used to move until August of 2006 when massive changes occurred to the structure and nature of existence. Now awareness only moves in response to love, praise and gratitude as a magnetizing force.

But the awareness particles emitted by the heart will vary from person to person, determined by his or her heart energies. When there is an emission of these negative particles of awareness, they hover in that person's environment until directed to create through love, praise and gratitude focused on a specific set of circumstances. As the cloud of awareness particles surrounds the person, these particles (although not moving directionally) vibrate. The dance, or vibration, of the particles is very much affected by the energetic qualities of the heart. When these particles dance in a similar way to someone else's, we can deduce that their heart energies are the same and that, since same energies attract, there will be a strong attraction.

Note: In August 2006, it was written by Mother in the Book of Life (which determines the laws of the cosmos), that heart energy will always be the determining factor (in other words stronger), rather than light or frequency in any relationship. In that way, light workers will be attracted to one another, rather than have their similar light and frequencies repelling each other (remember: same light and frequency repel, same energies attract — the principles behind the effectiveness of Belvaspata as a healing method).

Preparing for Initiation into Belvaspata

The Creation of the Heart Energies

Emotions	and	States of Being	give	Heart Energies
Love (+)		Glory (-)		Ecstasy (+)
Trust (-)		Praise (+)		Embrace (-)
Inspiration (+)		Harmony (-)		Insight (+)
Peace (-)		Exploration (+)		Appreciation (-)
Creativity (+)		Guidance (-)		Inspiration (+)
Pleasure (-)		Gratitude (+)		Love (-)
Empathy (+)		Transparency (-)		Truth (+)
Acknowledgement (-)		Discernment (+)		Clarity (-)
Generosity (+)		Reflection (-)		Manifestation (+)
Receptivity (-)		Understanding (+)		Gratitude (-)
Encouragement (+)		Ecstasy (-)		Rejoicing (+)
Beauty (-)		Embrace (+)		Praise (-)
Communication (+)		Inevitability (-)		Harmony (+)
Assimilation (-)		Manifestation (+)		Wisdom (-)
Passion (+)		Contentment (-)		Fulfillment (+)
Joy (-)		Oneness (+)		Presence (-)
Achievement (+)		Evolution (-)		Growth (+)
Fun (-)		Integration (+)		Balance (-)
Enlightenment (+)		Flexibility (-)		Evolution (+)
Contentment (-)		Play (+)		Surrender (-)
Empowerment (+)		Power (-)		Discovery (+)
Humor (-)		Perception (+)		Awareness (-)
Growth (+)		Conductivity (-)		Acceptance (+)
Satisfaction (-)		Retention (+)		Allowing (-)

The Heart Energies

1. Ecstasy (+)   + Embrace (-)   = Divine Compassion
2. Insight (+)   + Appreciation (-) = Reverence
3. Inspiration (+)   + Love (-)   = Pure Creativity
4. Truth (+)   + Clarity (-)   = Absolute truth
5. Manifestation (+) + Gratitude (-)   = Impeccability
6. Rejoicing (+)   + Praise (-)   = Celebration
7. Harmony (+)   + Wisdom (-)   = Timing
8. Fulfillment (+)   + Presence (-)   = Focus
9. Growth (+)   + Balance (-)   = Strength
10. Evolution (+)   + Surrender (-)   = Grace
11. Discovery (+)   + Awareness (-)   = Clarity
12 Acceptance (+)   + Allowing (-)   = Harmlessness

The Heart Energies

1. Ecstasy (+) + Embrace (-) = Divine Compassion
Ecstasy as a positive factor is active: it is the broadcasting, or reaching out, of the ecstatic song of the heart. Wherever it reaches, the heart embraces; the heart includes in its compassionate embrace. Divine compassion can therefore be described as the ecstatic embrace of the heart.

2. Insight (+) + Appreciation (-) = Reverence
Insight, as a positive aspect, probes behind the illusion of appearances, finding the perfection underlying all life. True illusion, as unsolved portions of existence, no longer exist. All has been solved. But the 'illusion' of taking things at face value continues. Insight refuses to take life at face value, finding the divine within. The response of the heart to seeing the divine order behind illusion is one of honoring and appreciation of life. From this vantage point, life is lived with reverence for all life, refining the person living this way and hallowing his experience.

3. Inspiration (+) + Love (-) = Pure Creativity
Inspiration is a positive quality, actively seeking out that which uplifts and inspires in what it observes. What uplifts and presents us with inspiration evokes a deep love in our hearts. It creates a desire for us to be in its presence. The combination of the inspiration plus the love we feel for that which inspires, brings forth the desire to create through the heart — the place of pure creation.

4. Truth (+) + Clarity (-) = Absolute truth

When truth, as we see it, is lived at its highest level, we start to express and live from a situation of clarity; where we are true, not only to others, but to ourselves. In clarity and truth we become aware of our motives' origins. (Toltec mystics call it stalking ourselves.) As we eliminate fear, protectiveness, anger and pain as motives, the reasons for taking action or making choices become clear and guide the promptings of our heart. The pure guidance of our heart comes from the blueprint of the Infinite (that which the Mother Goddess is), which is absolute truth.

5. Manifestation (+) + Gratitude (-) = Impeccability

The loss of impeccability is the result of failing to see the support of the greater scheme of our lives; of not recognizing that we are not alone. It is in thinking that we have to fend for ourselves that we act in a way that does not enhance the interconnectedness of life. In allowing life's perfection to manifest in our lives in whatever way it wants to, and knowing with gratitude that we are sustained at all times, impeccability is born.

6. Rejoicing (+) + Praise (-) = Celebration

Rejoicing is a choice. It chooses to find that which is praiseworthy over that which is not. If one looks for that which is flawed, it is easy to find. Looking for that which one can rejoice in might take more work. In doing so, our life changes day by day into a song of praise, and transforms itself into one of celebration.

7. Harmony (+) + Wisdom (-) = Timing

There is a flow to life — subtle currents that determine the course of events. There is a time to act and a time to reflect; a time for output and a time for input. Our lives unfold with grace and in perfect timing when we have wisdom to stay in harmony with the soft whisperings of destiny. To have the wisdom to obey these inner whisperings, takes restraint. To hear them takes the silence of the mind of one who has ceased to oppose life.

8. Fulfillment (+) + Presence (-) = Focus

Toltec seers have given the sage advice to use death as an advisor; to live each moment as though it were our last, with the focus it deserves. The moment is the pivot point upon which all of life pivots. It is therefore that which holds life's potential. As such, it deserves our full presence so that it can yield its full potential. In other words, the moment can fulfill its promises of a new tomorrow, unfettered by yesterday's expectations. If tomorrow comes from the moment, but the moment is not lived in a fulfilling manner, with presence and focus, where will the future come from? It will instead be formed by our yesterdays, haphazardly and as a repeat of what went before.

9. Growth (+) + Balance (-) = Strength

Growth that is unsupported lacks strength. Growth is always tested, for gained knowledge has to become experiential knowledge to be truly useful. Without balance to bolster it, it will lack the strength to pass the testing of experience. Growth internally produces external change. If change is not balanced with rest, or our coming home to ourselves (more detailed information on "Wings and Roots" by Almine, available as an MP3), we will have wings but no roots. It is the dynamic pulsing between wings and roots that gives us our strength.

10. Evolution (+) + Surrender (-) = Grace

Grace is the enviable result of the ability to live life with full cooperation. The surrender and trust of allowing life to evolve at its own pace, and in its own way, brings to our lives the grace of Mastery. It does not only require that we allow life to flow through us, but that we learn from it as it does, evolving through the insights it bestows.

11. Discovery (+) + Awareness (-) = Clarity

We have examined clarity in Heart Energy number four as the complete honesty with ourselves that requires a transparency of our motives. Clarity as an end result can be described as the certainty of what our next step is. The journey of existence becomes a journey of discovery when lived with the utmost awareness; an awareness born of the humility to know that only a fool can assume to know what the next moments will be. A life of clarity is not outcome oriented. It only knows that through living in the fullest awareness, the discovery of the next step will be achieved by living this one well, and thus a journey of clarity unfolds one step at a time.

12. Acceptance (+) + Allowing (-) = Harmlessness

Injury to life comes when we step out of contracts: when we fight and resist life's circumstances, keeping others and ourselves from growing. We often want life to change, but refuse to accept that we have to change ourselves. It is when we accept the moment for what it is, but allow change to come where it is needed by changing ourselves, that we fulfill life's contracts. Only then does life become empowered, rather than one of victimhood. When we feel life is out of control, we try to control its unfolding, causing harm to the interconnected web of life. By accepting our part of directing the play, but also allowing the script to unfold, life is lived harmlessly.

Integrating the Heart Energies

The 12 Pairs of Heart Energies are studied and internalized in the same way as the 12 Pairs of Emotions, the 16 Rays of Light and the States of Being have been. While they are now part of the unified field, it is still important to understand the individual qualities and how they combine to fully appreciate the unique emphasis that each contributes.

1) While in a meditative state, visualize your heart center opening wider and wider until you can imagine seeing the whole Earth in it.
2) Imagine and visualize the heart center opening at a rate beyond the speed of light until the solar system, the galaxy and then many galaxies are visible through the heart.
3) Continue opening while in deep meditation until the whole cosmos is within you and you have reached the membrane that contains it all.
4) You may visualize the large central sun within you and see its arms of light spiraling outwards, consisting of trillions upon trillions of galaxies like specks of light.
5) Remind yourself that you are a consciousness superimposed over all that is and you are all that you see.
6) From this large perspective, feel the frequency and the quality of one aspect of a Heart Energy pairing rippling through you. Start with the first Heart Energy of Ecstasy from the pairing of Ecstasy and Embrace.
7) Sustain it until it is strong, potent and all you can feel.
8) Then when you are ready move onto its complimentary aspect, Embrace.

9) As you experience the Heart Energy pairing, understand and observe how they complement and inspire one another to form an enhanced and balanced Heart Energy. For example observe and feel how the pairing of Ecstasy and Embrace combine to form Divine Compassion
10) When you are ready, move on to the next set of Heart Energies while maintaining expanded awareness.
11) Repeat steps 6 – 9 above for the remaining Heart Energies.
12) Each set of Heart Energies should be explored and experienced fully. The time necessary for this may be different for each person and for each pair being integrated.

Part IV

Initiations
Initiating another into Belvaspata

Belvaspata Initiations by a Master

Note: A Master Practitioner of Belvaspata can initiate up to Master Level of Belvaspata. A Grand Master Practitioner of Belvaspata can initiate all levels of Belvaspata.

Opening and Closing Initiations: Level I Initiation sigils are used for Level I initiations and to open all other initiations, in order to increase receptivity. The love, praise and gratitude sigils are always used for closing an initiation to seal the frequencies of the sigils within the body. (See Example Level II Initiation Sigil on page 129.)

When using the sigils for Initiations:

Step 1. Follow the directions as indicated on the sigils themselves for each level.

Step 2. Draw the sigil **3 times** over the area indicated — for this sigil it is the lower abdomen.

Step 3. Call (say) the quality of the sigil either out loud or silently **3 times** in Mother's language: **Kel-a-visva-uravech.**

Step 4. State the following: "By the power of this Sigil which I hold in my hand, I call in the Angel (insert angel name)" and call (say) the angel name either out loud or silently **3 times** in Mother's language, asking the angel to place the sigil in the desired location.

Look at the angel sigil while calling the angel name: Krunechva-atruha. (It is not necessary to draw the sigil for the angel name.)

Step 5. Complete all initiations by making a closing statement that declares the new level of mastery achieved by the initiate. As an example, you may use the following statement or something similar:

*"By the power vested in me, I declare that (*insert name of initiate*) is now a (*insert initiation level*) of Belvaspata, Healing of the Heart. We give thanks to our teacher, Almine and to the Infinite for the sacred gift of Belvaspata."*

Step 6. Close all initiations by drawing the sigils for love, praise and gratitude. You may draw them above the heart or over the entire body. (See Closing Sigils to end a Session on page 136.)

Example of Level II Initiation Sigil

The sigil ⟶

Step 1: Area to draw the sigil ⟶ *To be drawn 3 times over Lower Abdomen*

Step 2: Quality (Meaning) of this sigil in Mother's language ⟶ **Kel-a-visva-uravech** (say 3 times)

Quality (Meaning) of this sigil ⟶ For the Release of patterns that no longer serve (transformation)

By the power of this Sigil which I hold in my hand, I call in the Angel

Step 3: Angel name in Mother's language ⟶ **Krunechva-atruha**
(say 3 times and look at the Angel Sigil)

Angel Sigil:

Step 3: Look at this sigil while saying the Angel name ⟶

Level I Initiation Sigils

All 3 Level I sigils are used at the start of all healing sessions and prior to initiation into other levels of Belvaspata.

1.

To be drawn 3 times over the forehead
Bla-utva-pata (say 3 times)
For the Opening of the **mind**

By the Power of this Sigil which I hold in my hand, I Call in the Angel **Rutsetvi-uru-bach** (say three times and look at the Angel Sigil) to place this sigil within the forehead

Angel Sigil:

2.

To be drawn 3 times over the heart
Kru-vech-pa-uru-rek (say 3 times)
For the Opening of the **heart**

By the Power of this Sigil which I hold in my hand, I Call in the Angel **Iornumubach** (say three times and look at the Angel Sigil) to place this sigil within the heart

Angel Sigil:

3.

To be drawn 3 times over the navel
Kel-a-vis-ba-vah (say 3 times)
For the Opening of the **body**

By the Power of this Sigil which I hold in my hand, I Call in the Angel **Tru-ararir-pleva** (say three times and look at the Angel Sigil) to place this sigil within the navel

Angel Sigil:

Level II Initiation Sigils

(When healing, use in conjunction with Level I's sigils to start the session)

1.

   To be drawn 3 times over Lower Abdomen
   Kel-a-visva-uravech (say 3 times)
   For the Release of patterns that no longer serve (transformation)

   Angel Sigil:

   By the Power of this Sigil which I hold in my hand, I Call in the Angel **Krunechva-atruha** (say three times and look at the Angel Sigil) to place this sigil within Lower Abdomen

2.

   To be drawn 3 times over Solar Plexus
   Trech-su-ba-reshvi (say 3 times)
   For Transmuting matter to higher light

   Angel Sigil:
   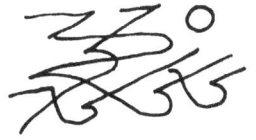

   By the Power of this Sigil which I hold in my hand, I Call in the Angel **Mirakluvael** (say three times and look at the Angel Sigil) to place this sigil within Solar Plexus

3.

   To be drawn 3 times over the sternum (middle of the chest)
   Pata-uru-hut-vi (say 3 times)
   For Transfiguring illusion to light

   Angel Sigil:

   By the Power of this Sigil which I hold in my hand, I Call in the Angel **Kelevi-traunar** (say three times and look at the Angel Sigil) to place this sigil within the sternum

Level II Initiation Sigils

4.

To be drawn 3 times over Crown
Kers-baur-veshpi (say 3 times)
For Sanctification

Angel Sigil:

By the Power of this Sigil which I hold in my hand, I Call in the Angel **Trechbar-uru-heresvi** (say three times and look at the Angel Sigil) to place this sigil within Crown

5.

To be drawn 3 times over Throat
Klet-sut-manarech (say 3 times)
For Attracting light into the voice

Angel Sigil:

By the Power of this Sigil which I hold in my hand, I Call in the Angel **Vilivesbi-keres-na** (say three times and look at the Angel Sigil) to place this sigil within Throat

6.

To be drawn 3 times in each hand
Vis-beles-pah-rech-vi (say 3 times)
For Attracting healing frequencies into the hands

Angel Sigil:

By the Power of this Sigil which I hold in my hand, I Call in the Angel **Kru-echna-vilshpreva** (say three times and look at the Angel Sigil) to place this sigil within each hand

Level II Initiation Sigils

7.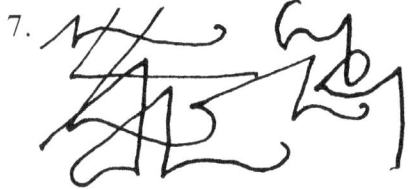

To be drawn 3 times over Root Chakra
Nen-hersh-bi-klet-rasut (say 3 times)
For DNA activation of the codes of light

By the Power of this Sigil which I hold in my hand, I Call in the Angel **Ku-ulu-vet** (say three times and look at the Angel Sigil) to place this sigil within Root Chakra

Angel Sigil:

8.

To be drawn 3 times over Alpha Chakra (1 hand length below base of the spine)
Vele-echs-bi-kluatret (say 3 times)
For Creating movement in Light

By the Power of this Sigil which I hold in my hand, I Call in the Angel **Belech-his-pavatra** (say three times and look at the Angel Sigil) to place this sigil within Alpha Chakra

Angel Sigil:

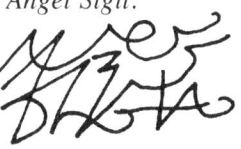

Also call in the angel Kelipretvaha *for placing this sigil into the earth.*

9.

To be drawn 3 times over bottom of each foot
Nun-mer-stararot-belch-spi (say 3 times)
For Bringing in the new template of frequency

By the Power of this Sigil which I hold in my hand, I Call in the Angel **Kretna-ulu-vesbi** (say three times and look at the Angel Sigil) to place this sigil within bottom of each foot

Angel Sigil:

Self-Initiation into Belvaspata

Master Level Initiation Sigils

This sigil is **not** to be used on clients. It is for use during initiations only.

Belveresnukvi
All Becomes One

To be drawn 3 times over each of the following in the order given:

1. bottom of each foot
2. alpha chakra
3. root chakra
4. lower abdomen
5. navel
6. solar plexus
7. heart
8. sternum
9. throat
10. forehead
11. crown
12. both hands
13. 10" above crown

After drawing the sigil 3 times in each location, say the following:
Bel-veres-nuk-vi, Bel-veres-nuk-vi-, Bel-veres-nuk-vi, All Becomes One

By the power of this Angel Sigil which I hold in my hand, I call in the Angel **Urhetvi** (say three times and look at the angel sigil) to place the Master Sigil in each of the following locations of the body (read the list from #1-13)

Angel Sigil:

Grand Master Level Initiation Sigils

This sigil is **not** to be used on clients. It is for use during initiations only.

Kluagvanesvi–elu–achvraheresh–vi-skaulag (say three times)

To be drawn 3 times over the heart

By the power of this Angel Sigil which I hold in my hand I call in the following angels who support this initiatory level:

(say each angel name three times while looking at the angel sigil)

Brua–kranuvig–stela–u–achvraba

Kersh–heruvit–pele–ach–uvespi–klauna

Stuapruanatvi–keleshna

Closing Sigils for a Session or Initiation

Praise

Love

Gratitude

PART VII

Self-Initiation into Belvaspata

Guidelines for Self-Initiation

Self-initiation means that you initiate yourself into Belvaspata, however, it is required that you work with a mentor who is a Master or Grand Master in order for your initiation to be considered valid. Another person cannot do this for you either long-distance or over the phone.

In the case of self-initiation, completion of the preparation work increases the frequency of the initiate so they are prepared to receive the initiation. This is accomplished for each specific level by:

- Completing the preparation for each level of initiation — as in the internalizing of the specific Emotions, Rays of Light, States of Being or Heart Energies. The preparation for each level is the same for both self-initiation as for initiation by a Master of Grand Master.
- Translation of the Infinite Mother's language for the level of initiation using the Mother's alphabet.
- Drawing the appropriate sigils for the level of Initiation.
- Completing the ceremony of self-initiation by asking the angels to place the sigils in your body and speaking the initiation in the language of the Infinite.

It is important that you speak the words yourself.

The time frame between initiations remains the same. Level I and Level II may be done at the same time, as may Master and Grand Master Levels. There still must however be at least 3 months between Level I and Level II **and** Master and Grand Master Levels. Be guided by what is right for you. Regular use of the sigils is an important aspect of Belvaspata Initiation and very necessary before moving from one level onto the next level.

Guidelines from Almine state that all initiates are to be mentored by a Master or Grand Master of Belvaspata. This ensures that each level of self-initiation is completed successfully. The mentor will assist you in preparing for self-initiation, answer any questions that you may have and also ensure that you are both competent and confident in working with Belvaspata. The mentor may issue a certificate stating that you have self-initiated and that they have mentored you. A list of masters who may be contacted for mentoring may be found on the Belvaspata site, see the link at www.spiritualjourneys.com.

Note: *Belvaspata Angel Healing,* one of the recordings that accompanies this book, was created to assist with learning the pronunciation of the language of the Infinite. It is not to be used for a session or for initiation. For self-initiation you must speak the Infinite's language of initiation for yourself.

To obtain your copy of an MP3 download, please visit www.belvaspata.org.

Preparing for Self-Initiation

1. Carefully study the material given in this book regarding Belvaspata.

2. Spend the necessary time studying and internalizing the appropriate material for the level of initiation you are preparing for.
   The 12 Pairs of Pure Emotions for Level I
   The 16 Rays of Light for Level II
   The States of Being for Master Level
   The Heart Energies for Grand Master Level

3. Using the Alphabet of the Infinite Mother, translate the self-initiation ceremony. The language is written in vertical columns and written from left to right as shown on page 149.

4. Each initiation sigil is to be drawn on a separate piece of paper. The sigils are to be placed on or near the specified area of the body for each level of initiation.

5. When you are ready, you may lie down. Read the self-initiation ceremony out loud in the Infinite Mother's language. Draw each sigil in the air three times and call upon the angels of that sigil to place it in the appropriate area of your body three times. Read the translation and draw one sigil at a time.

6. When you are finished, close the initiation with the sigils for praise, love and gratitude by drawing them in the air above you.

7. Level I sigils are always used to open the initiation unless Level I and Level II are being done at the same time or Master and Grand Master are being done at the same time. In other words, if 2 levels of initiation are being done consecutively, it is only necessary to use Level I sigils for the first level, then continue on to the next level. Use of Level 1 sigils enhances receptivity for the initiation.

8. The original copy of your translation and sigils should be sent to the master who is mentoring you. They should keep them as a record if you wish to proceed on to self-initiate for other levels of Belvaspata. If this mentor is not available for subsequent initiations, send a copy of your previous translations and the date(s) when initiations were performed to the new mentor.

The Languages and Alphabet of Infinite Mother

Whatever is spoken in the languages of Mother/Infinite becomes reality. Having this power, the languages and their use constitute a most holy body of white and beneficial magic.

The purity of the languages makes them incapable of being misused. The use of them brings light and restores perfection. They are without doubt the most holy of symbols on earth.

The languages have appeared in 3 different forms in various cycles and have provided a guidance system for the cosmos. The choice of a specific language of the Mother/Infinite used during a given cycle of Creation provided the exact frequencies and amount of light needed at the time.

The Second Language of the Holy Mother
Used during the Cosmic Ascension
(Excerpted from *The Ring of Truth*)

Pronunciation of Mother's Language

The pronunciation is very much like German, other than that the 'v' (as in very) and 'w' (as in white) are pronounced as in English.

The syllables are pronounced individually when placed next to each other. There are no contracted sounds like 'au' (as in trauma). It would be necessary to say the 'a' and 'u' separately. The only exception to this rule is a double 'aa' at the end of a word. This indicates the 'a' sound (as in spa).

The 'ch' spelling at the beginning of a word is the only time it is pronounced as in 'church'. Everywhere else it is pronounced as in the German 'kirche' or somewhat like the Spanish x as in Mexico.

- 'u' is pronounced as in 'prudence'.
- 'a' is pronounced as in 'garden'.
- 'e' is as in 'pet'.
- 'i' is pronounced as in 'pink'.
- 'o' is pronounced in the way someone with an English accent would say 'of' or 'cross'.
- 'g' is always a hard 'g' like 'great'.
- 'c' is always hard as in 'call'.
- 'q' has a 'qw' sound as in 'queen'.
- 'r' is slightly rolled—'rr'.
- 'y' is pronounced as in 'Yvette', with an 'ee' sound.

'I am happy' has a much higher frequency than 'I am tired', therefore 'I' and 'am' would be different in each of these sentences.

Also, when the concept is large, several words are needed. 'Beautiful' will have different words depending on what is described, but in each case the term will have several words since it is a complex concept.

There are no words for 'sad', 'pain', 'angry', 'protective' or 'fear', since those are illusory concepts in this creation of life. There are also no negative words.

'I' and 'we' would be the same word as this is a group consciousness language. Similarly, 'he' and 'they' would use the same word.

Sentences and Phrases:

1. *Aushbava heresh sishisim* (Come here)
2. *Va-aal vi-ish paru-es* (Do it again)
3. *Kre-eshna sa-ul varavaa* (It is beautiful everywhere)
4. *Pranuvaa sanuvesh vilsh-savu bravispa* (We are with you when you think of us)
5. *Aasushava pre-unan aruva bareesh* (We come to open the gate)

Note: 'Come' in this sense is not the same word used for 'come here'.

6. *Oonee varunish heshpiu tra barin* (Everyone is dancing with joy)
7. *Belesh bri anur bra vershpi iulan* (Take away the frown from your face)
8. *Nen hursh avervi tranuk averva?* (When comes the moment of laughing?)

Note: there is no word for time.

9. *Nun brash barnut pareshvi* (Please take us with you)
10. *Vursh venestu parneshtu* (Magic is in the moment)
11. *Iuvishpa niutrim sarem* (Great things await)
12. *Ruftravasbi iulem* (Let the fun begin)
13. *Verluash verurlabaa mi urla set viunish* (Be prepared for the fulfilment of your dreams)
14. *Be-ulahesh parve mi-ur ville starva* (Speak to us through these sacred words)
15. *Truaveshviesh aluvispaha maurnanuhe* (Welcome to the fullness of our being)
16. *Telech nusva rura vesbi* (Through love are we connected)

Self-Initiation into Belvaspata

---

17. *Erluech spauhura vavish menuba* (Find the new song that you sing)
18. *Me-uhu vaubaresh ka-ur-tum* (Our new dance is a joyous one)
19. *Pelech parve uru-uhush vaspa pe-uravesh ple-ura* (Together let us create wondrous moments)
20. *Vala veshpa uvi kle-u vishpi ula usbeuf pra-uva* (You are invited into the loving embrace of our arms)
21. *Perenuesh krava susibreve truach* (In great mercy you are renewed)
22. *Pleshpaa vu skaura versebia nunuhesh* (Allow your shoulders to feel lightness)
23. *Verunachva ulusetvaabi manuresh* (All are in this moment redeemed)
24. *Keleustraha virsabaluf bra uvraha* (You dwell in us and are ours)
25. *Keleshpruanesh te le-usbaru* (Call and we shall hear)

Belvaspata

Alphabet of the Holy Mother

1. AUX
2. PAH
3. GHEE
4. KA
5. G as in Gold
6. DJU as in Giraffe
7. B
8. PE as in Peg
9. L
10. TRA
11. I as in Ink
12. N
13. R
14. A as in Far
15. M
16. E as in Leg
17. U as in True
18. V
19. SH
20. K
21. H
22. S
23. O as in Open
24. Y as in Yvette ("ee" sound)
25. QW as in Quail
26. T
27. CH as in Church
28. A as in Back
29. O as in Lock
30. XCH as in Mexico (Spanish pronunciation)

Alphabet of the Holy Mother (continued)

Alphabet

31. F

32. Z as in Azure (soft sound)

33. RR (rolled r)

34. P

35. Y as in Yes

36. CK (short K sound)

37. Period (placed at the end of a sentence)

38. Question Mark (placed at the beginning of a sentence)

Additional Letters of Other Languages – Used in the Holy Mother's Languages

1. D

2. PF

3. KL

4. W

5. SHP

6. KRR

7. HF

8. PL

9. TL

Language of the Holy Mother

Magic is in the moment.
(vursh venestu parneshtu)

Great things await.
(Iuvishpa niutrim sarem)

Let the fun begin.
(Ruftravasbi iulem)

Please take me with you. (Nun brash barnut pareshvi)

Self-Initiation in the Language of the Infinite Mother

Prior to self-initiation into any specific level, ensure that you have completed translating the ceremony using the alphabet of the Infinite Mother and drawn each of the sigils on paper. This is an important and integral part of self-initiation. The preparation assists in raising your frequency for the initiation. (Hyphenation of the Sigil and Angel names is used to assist with pronunciation.)

Level I Belvaspata Initiation

Self-Initiation

Pelech vi brashvata urespi klaunash strechvi uklesva uhuru reshvi straunach Belvaspata.

By the power of the holy language, I enter into the Level 1 initiation of Belvaspata.

*1. Uklesh varabi ukretnet **Rutsetviurubach** u palva uheristat kletvubra. Kre stubava uset uvechvi kraunat valavish usta vabi uretvi **Blautvapata** pre nusvi haruhit.*

For the opening of my mind, I call in the angel **Rutsetvi-uru-bach**. By the power of his sigil, I instruct him to place the sigil of **Bla-utva-pata** three times in my forehead.

*2. Uklesh varabi ukretnet **Iornumubach** u varespi uheristat kletvubra. Kre stubava uset uvechvi kraunat valavish usta vabi varespi Kruvechpaururek pre nusvi haruhit.*

For the opening of my heart, I call in the angel **Iornumubach**. By the power of his sigil I instruct him to place the sigil of **Kru-vech-pa-uru-rek** three times in my heart.

*3. Uklesh varabi ukretnet **Truararirpleva** u stavavechspi umirarat. Kre stubava uset uvechvi kraunat valavish usta vabi pres pranatuk **Kelavisbavah** pre nusvi haruhit.*

For the receptivity of the body, I call in the angel **Tru-ararir-pleva**. By the power of his sigil I instruct him to place the sigil of **Kel-a-vis-ba-vah** three times within my navel.

Esta u manurch bria stuvaba reshvi straunach Belvaspata.

I am now in Level I Belvaspata.

Close by drawing the sigils for Praise, Love and Gratitude above the heart area or over the body.

Level II Belvaspata Initiation

Self-Initiation

Open the initiation with Level I initiation sigils unless Levels I and II are done together.

Pelech vi brashvata urespi klaunash strechvi uklesva basetvi reshvi straunach Belvaspata.

By the power of the holy language, I enter into the Level II initiation of Belvaspata.

*1. Uklesh varabi ukretnet **Krunechvaatruha** u stechvabi uleska bret net hurava. Kre stubava uset uvechvi kraunat valavish usta vabi perenutvi skaulag **Kelavisvauravech** pre nusvi haruhit.*

For the release of patterns that no longer serve, I call in the angel **Krunechva-atruha**. By the power of his sigil I instruct him to place the sigil of **Kel-a-visva-uravech** three times in my lower abdomen.

*2. Uklesh varabi ukretnet **Mirakluvael** u ste u plavaa urechspi hershstavaa uknech staura. Kre stubava uset uvechvi kraunat valavish usta vabi keres nusta-ava **Trechsubareshvi** pre nusvi haruhit.*

For the transmuting of matter to energy and then to light, I call in the angel **Mirakluvael**. By the power of his sigil I instruct him to place the sigil of **Trech-su-ba-reshvi** three times in my solar plexus.

*3. Uklesh varabi ukretnet **Kelevitraunar** u trana uruvet pre usta utvi us plavaa. Kre stubava uset uvechvi kraunat valavish usta vabi krunespi ustava **Patauruhutvi** pre nusvi haruhit.*

For the transfiguring of illusion to light, I call in the angel **Kelevi-traunar.** By the power of his sigil I instruct him to place the sigil of **Pata-uru-hutvi** three times in my sternum.

*4. Uklesh varabi ukretnet **Trechbaruruheresvi** u stavavechspi pre uhus traurat. Kre stubava uset uvechvi kraunat valavish usta vabi brat nutva rechspanadoch **Kersbaurveshpi** pre nusvi haruhit.*

For the sanctification of the body I call in the angel **Trechbar-uru-heresvi.** By the power of his sigil I instruct him to place the sigil of **Kers-baur-veshpi** three times in my crown.

*5. Uklesh varabi ukretnet **Vilivesbikeresna** u sta binavich steretu uvlaesh kletvubra. Kre stubava uset uvechvi kraunat valavish usta vabi stiekluava uprech vabi **Kletsutmanarech** pre nusvi haruhit.*

For the attracting of light into my voice, I call in the angel **Vilivesbi-keres-na.** By the power of his sigil I instruct him to place the sigil of **Klet-sut-manarech** three times in my throat.

*6. Uklesh varabi ukretnet **Kruechnavilshpreva** u bestich haru vereshva kletvubra. Kre stubava uset uvechvi kraunat valavish usta vabi peresnustavat kliechspi **Visbelespahrechvi** pre nusvi haruhit.*

For the attracting of healing energies into my hands, I call in the angel **Kru-echna-vilshpreva.** By the power of his sigil I instruct him to place the sigil of **Vis-beles-pah-rech-vi** three times in my right hand.

*7. Uklesh varabi ukretnet **Kruechnavilshpreva** u bestich haru vereshva kletvubra. Kre stubava uset uvechvi kraunat valavish usta vabi peresnustavat truvachspi **Visbelespahrechvi** pre nusvi haruhit.*

For the attracting of healing energies into my hands, I call in the angel **Kru-echna-vilshpreva.** By the power of his sigil I instruct him to place the sigil of **Vis-beles-pah-rech-vi** three times in my left hand.

*8. Uklesh varabi ukretnet **Kuuluvet** stau nenhurpersh ustachni versh u stanavach steraa. Kre stubava uset uvechvi kraunat valavish usta vabi tremish uretkla uvra vesti pelenuch ustechbi **Nenhershbikletrasut** pre nusvi haruhit.*

For the DNA activation of the codes of light, I call in the angel **Ku-ulu-vet.** By the power of his sigil I instruct him to place the sigil of **Nen-hersh-bi-klet-rasut** three times into my root chakra at the base of my spine.

*9. Uklesh varabi ukretnet **Belechhispavatra** ukresh mi hes vi ustachva plavaa. Kre stubava uset uvechvi kraunat valavish usta vabi sta u achva usbanadoch sterut **Veleechsbikluatret** pre nusvi haruhit. Uklesh baurabi ukretnet pehera **Kelipretvaha** tre u stamamit selbi usvi trevaa.*

For the creation of movement in light, I call in the angel **Belech-his-pavatra.** By the power of his sigil I instruct him to place the sigil of **Vele-echs-bi-kluatret** three times in the alpha chakra (one hand length below the base of the spine).

I ask that his wife **Keli-pret-vaha,** place the same sigil in the Earth.

*10. Uklesh varabi ukretnet **Kretnauluvesbi** paurivi heshva ustevavi klasutbaru uraesh. Kre stubava uset uvechvi kraunat valavish usta vabi kresna stechvi kliechspi **Nunmerstararotbelchspi** pre nusvi haruhit.*

For bringing in the new template of frequency, I call in the angel **Kretna-ulu-vesbi.** By the power of his sigil I instruct him to place the sigil **Nun-mer-stararot-belch-spi** three times into the bottom of my right foot.

*11. Uklesh varabi ukretnet **Kretnauluvesbi** paurivi heshva ustevavi klatsutbaru uraesh. Kre stubava uset uvechvi kraunat valavish usta vabi kresna stechvi truvachspi **Nunmerstararotbelchspi** pre nusvi haruhit.*

For bringing in the new template of frequency I call in the angel **Kretna-ulu-vesbi.** By the power of his sigil I instruct him to place the sigil **Nun-mer-stararot-belch-spi** three times into the bottom of my left foot.

Esta u vish basetvatu reshvi straunach Belvaspata esba unavespi stechmanarot ra utvaba kelesvi unus kraunata pre us ubarech.

I am now initiated into Level II of Belvaspata and connected to the planetary field to bring healing through the use of these sigils.

Close by drawing the sigils for Praise, Love and Gratitude above the heart area or over the body.

Master Level Belvaspata Initiation

Self-Initiation

Open the initiation with Level I initiation sigils.

Draw the Master Sigil above all the following parts of the body three times and in the order given. Say the name of the sigil, Bel-veres-nuk-vi, each time you draw it.

1. bottom of each foot
2. alpha chakra
3. root chakra
4. lower abdomen
5. navel
6. solar plexus
7. heart
8. sternum
9. throat
10. forehead
11. crown
12. both hands
13. 10" above crown

Uklesh tre basetvi me uspata reshvi berek nautar Belvaspata, uklesh varabi ukretnet nautari spa uvechvi **Belveresnukvi.** *Kre stubavat usetvi sta unava,* **Urhetvi** *kreunes tra va esta ulvavech ustavravi es bautra pre nusvi haruhit esbaerch usmi treur nun hesvata.*

Uset uvechvi steba kresna stechvi kliechspi esba u stau vi kresna stechvi truvachspi.Uset uvechvi steba achva usbanadoch sterut es vra tremish uretkla esva perenutvi skaulag. Uset uvechvi pres pranatuk es keres nustaava esva varespi esva krunespi ustava. Uset uvechvi steba stiekluava uprech vabi esba uretvi esba brat nutva rechspanadoch esba peresnustavat kliechspi esba peresnustavat truvachspi. Uset uvechvi steba stabalut.

Lahun estakva knues bra us ta uvi brat rechspanadoch. Parus na ta esva klua nu Lahun.

For my initiation into the Master Level of Belvaspata, I call in the angel of the master sigil, **Bel-veres-nuk-vi.** By the power of your sigil that I hold, **Urhetvi** come forth and place this sigil that connects me to the cosmic field three times in each of the centers I mention.

Place it into the bottom of my left foot and the bottom of my right foot. Place it into my alpha chakra, root chakra, lower abdomen, navel, solar plexus, heart, sternum, throat, forehead, crown, right hand and left hand. Place it into the tenth chakra ten inches above my crown, known as lahun.

Esta u vish basetvu reshvi pelevradoch ukles parva Belvaspata esbaur ne tru bravabit basetvi kluavanet perhet pra usva kliunesvi eshtra usbava Amanur.

Let all become one and one become all. I am now initiated as a Master of Belvaspata and am able to initiate others into this sacred healing modality given by the Goddess of Creation.

Close by drawing the sigils for Praise, Love and Gratitude above the heart area or over the body.

Grand Master Level Belvaspata Initiation

Self-Initiation

Open the initiation with Level I sigils unless Master and Grand Master initiations are done at the same time.

The Grand Master Sigil is drawn three times over the heart area and the name of the sigil is said three times — Kluagvanesvi-elu-achvraheresh-vi-skaulag.

Barach usta hesvi klanevuk staba urechspi utklasvaba utrenuch steravik peleshba utklenevriavak uhes stau va klau nas prava uhuresbi. Esklat us ste uvra klenevash pra uvra kelesnut verek stauvrabach usetvi minur pelesh **Bruakranuvigstelauachvraba, Kershheruvitpeleachuvespiklauna, Stuapruanatvikeleshna** *et kla ninur varset pre us veleshbi ukletvi bre* **Kluagvanesvieluachvrahereshviskaulag** *stunavek strau nas pra ve.*

Arvuklat vru elesbi sta minech staubileshvi usklaveres nesvabi ustech vre usbla eleshbi strau netvra stu velesbi nech tre ubrekva helesbi staravu. Kelvi arasva stu belechbi usta heresvri eshvra kluva vreshbi. Pre rech uvra nuresbi presatvi urla verleshvi Belvaspata kreunag viashva kluvanet **Kluagvanesvieluachvrahereshviskaulag** *pre usutvi treunag mi uresh priesva kleunich.*

Self-Initiation into Belvaspata

As one who has practiced this sacred healing of the heart with respect and in honor of all life, I present myself to become a Grand Master practitioner. I call the angels, **Brua-kranuvig-stela-u-achvraba, Kersh-heruvit-pele-ach-uvespi-klauna** and **Stuapruanatvi-keleshna,** and by the authority of their sigils, instruct them to place the Grand Master sigil, **Kluagvanesvi-elu-achvrahereshvi-skaulag** three times in my heart center.

As Grand Master let them consecrate and initiate me, that I too may do so for others. Let my healing abilities increase one hundred fold. I am now a grand master of Belvaspata carrying the **Kluagvanesvi-elu-achvrahereshvi-skaulag** sigil within my heart.

Close by drawing the sigils for Praise, Love and Gratitude above the heart area or over the body.

Belvaspata Certificates of Initiations

The initiating Master or Grand Master may issue certificates upon completion of any level of Belvaspata initiation. Certificate templates may be purchased at office supply stores and online for creating certificates or create your own. An example of a certificate is in Appendix III.

Creating a word document template will allow you to insert the name, date, level of initiation and initiating master for each specific initiation. If all levels are completed, it is customary and acceptable to create only the Grand Master Level certificate.

The Belvaspata Directory

A directory of Masters and Grand Masters is located on our main Belvaspata website at www.belvaspata.spiritualjourneys.com.

Complete the following if you wish to be added to the directory:

1. Initiation or self-initiation into Master or Grand Master level of Belvaspata.
2. Submit a copy of an initiation certificate or a letter confirming initiation to jan@almine.net. Certificates and letters are to include the name of the initiate, level and date of initiation and signature of the initiator or mentor for self-initiation. All applications will be approved based on meeting these requirements.
3. Register on Spiritual Journeys store, click on Belvaspata link and Registration for Belvaspata Directory. (A small fee is charged to be listed on the directory.)

PART VIII

Specialty Belvaspata Modalities

Introduction to Specialty Belvaspata Modalities

All levels of Belvaspata masters may use the sigils in the following books of this Belvaspata manual without any further initiations. The Belvaspata Initiation and Healing Manual at the start of this book is a recommended reference and guide for the use of all Belvaspata modalities.

Any specialty Belvaspata may be used in conjunction with a basic Belvaspata session. Start with the initial session and then proceed with the specialty Belvaspata, unless otherwise directed. For example, Belvaspata for the Song of the Self is always done prior to a basic Belvaspata session or any other specialty Belvaspata.

General Guidelines for Performing Ceremonies

The following are general guidelines for performing ceremonies. If specific directions are provided for any ceremony, use those directions; otherwise follow these general guidelines.

Creating and Dismantling a Ceremonial Circle:
When creating a ceremonial circle, place the elements in a clockwise direction (on the floor or other surface). When dismantling the circle, pick up all the elements counter-clockwise.

Wheels, Squares, Triangles, Gates, etc as used in Ceremonies
When using elements such as Wheels, Triangles or Gates, the lowest numbers always go on top and the highest numbers on the bottom when these items are stacked. *Example:* Stack 1 is created at your head if you are lying down on your back or in front of your face if you are sitting. If each stack contains 8 Wheels then stack 1 contains Wheel 1–8 with lowest number on top and highest number on bottom; stack 2 contains Wheel 9–16, with lowest number on top and highest number on bottom — repeat this same order for each stack around the circle.

All ceremonial circles create an alchemical equation: Wheels or other items placed in stacks are created per the individual ceremony and create an alchemical equation that is different for each ceremony. Do not assume that you can determine the components of stacks for a ceremony with multiples of wheels, gates, etc.

The alchemy works through EACH item and thus it is important to stack them one upon another. This ensures that the components create the correct alchemical equation.

If the ceremony provides specific directions for creating stacks, follow them. All aspects of the alchemical equation have been considered by Almine as given in the specific instructions.

a. Item such as wheels, gates, squares, etc can be cut out singly. On some occasions when there are a large number of items, multiples may be placed on one page. As long as the elements are equally divided between the stacks and equally laid out on the pages — this is permissible. For example if there are 144 elements to be divided between 12 stacks, you may either have 2 elements per page or 4 elements per page. The types of elements should not be mixed when combining onto one page.

b. Ensure you follow the directions for creating the stacks needed for each of the ceremonies.

c. The shape of a circle must be maintained when creating the stacks.

d. If in doubt it is best to follow the exact ceremonial guidelines as given.

e. *With our intent to create the sacred space, we are part of the alchemical equation.* When following the ceremonial guidelines, we produce the known results of the alchemical equation that are intended for any specific ceremony.

Position

Lying down on your back is the preferred position. You may use a bed, a massage table or the floor. Ensure you are comfortable. It is okay to use a small pillow under your knees and your head or neck.

Follow the directions as given for each specific ceremony. For the majority of these ceremonies, your head should be placed at the Number 1 Wheel or Stack (which correlates to 12 on the clock). If you choose to sit on a chair, the Number 1 Wheel or Stack should be placed in front of you.

Creating Sacred Space

Avoid interruptions of any sort as you create your sacred space and participate in your ceremony, whether it is a physical ceremony or one of intent. Once you start the ceremony it is best to complete it. (Unplug the phone, go to the restroom, etc - prior to starting.)

Ceremonies build upon each other. It is recommended that they be completed in the order given. Ceremonies may be repeated as often as you feel is appropriate and right for you.

Note: Maintain the sacred space and circle — keep animals and children out of the area by closing doors, etc. The frequency of the sacred circle is affected by their presence and they are affected by the ceremonial frequencies. These frequencies may be too high for them.

Recommendations during pregnancy: The frequencies of a ceremony may be too high for the baby and therefore, not comfortable. As a general rule, avoid doing ceremonies during pregnancy.

The Use of Wheels

A wheel is a visual image that conveys non-cognitive, sacred and empowering information. They are similar to gateways through which specific healing frequencies are drawn and are power sources in the same way a holy object would be.

The wheels are alive and as we work with them they provide us with deep insights into the vastness and wealth of our own being, reminding us of all that we are.

Each wheel is a stand-alone wheel and can be used by itself. When wheels are used in a sequence, they tell a story and combine to make an equation.

Mystical practices have a beginning and a closure. If you are working with a sequence of wheels, do not stop in the middle as it leaks resources and energy. For this reason it is important that you always complete each sequence.

To access the information contained within the wheels at a deeper level you may place your hands on the wheels or run your hand across them — the left hand is receptive and the right hand promotes understanding.

Lying down, you may also place a wheel at your feet and upon contemplating its meaning, bring it up through your body from your feet to the Lahun Chakra 10 inches above your head. If a wheel feels 'stuck' anywhere, continue to feel the quality of the wheel until it moves freely. If you are working with a sequence of wheels, ensure that the highest numbered wheel is at the bottom and the lowest numbered wheel is at the top. Work with one wheel at a time and fully integrate one before moving on to the next. As you do, also contemplate how the qualities of each wheel combine and complement the other wheels within the sequence.

Possible Uses for Wheels include:
- Meditate on a wheel.
- Place on the walls of a healing space, office or a room in which you spend a lot of time.
- With intention they can be placed into the body or placed directly on the body.
- Specific wheels can be placed under a healing table when working on someone or under a chair that you frequently sit on.
- Create your own personal mandala that you carry with you.

Wheel for Love, Praise and Gratitude

Love - Neresh-huspata

Praise - Blavit-rechvatu

Gratitude - Nusarat-ubesvi

Specialty Belvaspata Modalities

Photos of blessings received by students

Specialty Belvaspata Modalities

Book II

Belvaspata
Healing through Oneness

The Integrated use of Belvaspata
and Fragrance Alchemy

Liability Disclaimer

Note: Level I initiation is required for use of Belvaspata Healing through Oneness for self or others. Detoxification symptoms may be experienced following treatment.

Any liability, loss, damage or injury in connection with the use of Belvaspata and fragrance alchemy, including asthma and allergic reactions is expressly disclaimed by Spiritual Journeys, LLC and/or Almine.

Almine is not a medical practitioner, nor does she practice medicine. Belvaspata and fragrance alchemy are not intended to diagnose illness or to constitute medical advice or treatment. All persons with a medical condition, (including pregnancy) that may affect their use of the material in this book, are advised to consult with a physician or other qualified health provider prior to its use, in order to obtain medical approval.

Introduction

The powerful healing modality of Belvaspata has produced many miracles as it has gained recognition globally. But as with all healing modalities, there are times when stubborn ailments persist and it feels to a Belvaspata practitioner that they are working against an unseen impediment.

From ancient texts, translated by the Seer Almine, comes a solution and many answers as to why the healing may be resisted and what disease really is. To understand these deeply mystical and metaphysical explanations, the following concepts should be explained.

Note: Almine has for many years translated tablets and records from inter-dimensional sources to reveal sacred information previously unavailable to humanity. It is only in the last months of 2009 that some of her students have been able to obtain photographic evidence of the existence of these materials. See the following pages for examples of inter-dimensional photos of tablets previously translated by her.

Tablets Translated by Almine
Photographed Interdimensionally

Photos taken by Barbara Rotzoll, 2009 (angelbarbara.com)

Tablets translated by Almine months before they were photographed and drawn.

- Cycles of existence that life in the cosmos, and the lives or incarnations of an individual go through, resemble the rotation of a disc.

- The disc not only turns during each lifetime, creating cyclical repetitions of similar types of events, but also spirals upwards as we go from one lifetime to the next.

- When unresolved traumatic events happen during this lifetime, they lodge in related areas of the body, coming up for resolution as life cycles repeat themselves.

- If a lifetime does not manage to resolve the issues held in areas of the body, that part of the body, stays behind as the disc spirals upwards to the next level – a new incarnation.

- When a body part gets 'left behind,' it means that its life force is mostly not present in the moment, that its ghostly image lingers on the spiraled journey of past lifetimes. In cases of severe past trauma, such as a severed limb for instance, the present limb may have almost no life force or true presence. It is as though there is nothing but a hologram, or a virtual reality image.

- After many lifetimes of either overwhelming trauma or unexamined experience, it is as though 'ghosts' of body parts are strewn behind us on our incarnational journey. The inevitable loss of life force reduces life spans, causes premature aging and leaves very little vitality for health in the moment.

- When a healer meets with failure in attempts to heal a physical area, it may be that it is hardly present, having been left behind.

- The Atlantean Healing System is designed to bring integrated presence to the physical, emotional and mental bodies, when then facilitates healing with Belvaspata – the only way to permanently and successfully deal with previously traumatized body parts where life force is not present.

PART I

Healing through Oneness

How Healing through Oneness Works

The fragrances restore the memory that nothing can really be divided or left behind, that all is fully expressed when we remember this. Fragrance evokes memories and abilities to see the Infinite within the hidden part of all beings. The real part within all beings is not the 'spirit that moves through all things' as spoken of in Native American teaching. That teaching refers to the 'formlessness of spirit' which is just as illusional as form. Instead what is referred to in this teaching is something not found within the matrix and thus you have to approach and sense it within your entire being. You get this really intoxicating feeling that allows you to feel that you are in love with all life.

- The senses have been fragmented by past trauma as well. The only exception is smell, which has been scientifically shown to be the strongest trigger for recalling memories.

- The earliest memories evoked by plant flower essences, according to the translation of ancient records reach back as far as before the fall. The 'fall' is the point of existence during which separation (duality) occurred and life shattered from oneness into sub-created identities. The fragrances are therefore able to remind us of what an existence of wholeness with Oneness is like.

- When the memory of wholeness evoked by the flower and plant essence reminds the body part of its oneness with Indivisible, Infinite Life, it recalls its life force and all components to the present organ.

- The absence of any part of existence from the present is like a wound in one's life and like any wound natural laws try and fill the gaping space by creating scar tissue. The scar tissue of parts left behind is belief systems.

- To accomplish the 3 basic steps of Healing through Oneness: bringing all body parts to the present, removing the scar-tissue of belief systems and healing the fully energized and present body part – the Atlantean sigils are necessary.

- The Atlantean sigils are designed to remove through clear insight, the old programmed belief systems that have filled the gap of absent body parts.

Note: See page 201 if combining Healing though Oneness with other specialty Belvaspata modalities. If using Belvaspata for Song of Self, it is always done first.

Why Healing through Oneness uses the Sigils for Emotional Healing

When physicality or physical incarnation shifts from one layer of life to the next, what is left behind is non-physical or ethereal, hence body parts left behind are 'ghostly' in appearance.

When restored to the present moment from the past of this life or a previous life, the component of the organ or body part is non-physical. The etheric realms are the domain of frequency-based, emotion-based existence that respond well to Belvaspata sigils designed for emotional healing.

Essential Oils[1] and their Life-enhancing Psychological Benefits

Excerpt from *Secrets of Rejuvenation* 'Discovery of the Fountain of Youth

Balsam Fir (Idaho) Self-dignity
Basil Integrated Oneness
Bergamot Finding inner home
Black Pepper Passionate exploration
Cedarwood Recognizing inner divinity
Cinnamon bark Pleasant memories
Citrus Accessing experiential knowledge
Clary Sage Belief in success
Clove Dissolving boundaries
Coriander Releasing untapped potential
Cypress Balancing the feminine/masculine
Dill Unified fields of light and love
Douglas Fir Exuberance
Elemi Dynamic balance
Eucalyptus dives Emotional stability and flow
Eucalyptus globulus Creating new paradigms
Eucalyptus polybractea Openness to new ideas
Eucalyptus radiata Recognition of intrinsic value
Fennel Comforting the Inner Child
Frankincense Entrainment with the Earth
Galbanum Overcoming conditioned responses

---

1 The purest forms of these essential oils are available from Spiritual Journeys office at 1-877-552-5646, toll-free in US.

Geranium New beginnings
Ginger Self-trust
Goldenrod Re-establishing faith in perfection
Grapefruit Resurrection of innocence
Helichrysum Enlightenment
Hyssop Inner wellbeing
Idaho Tansy Being in touch with the instinctual
Jasmine Sensuality explored
Juniper Spiritual reawakening
Laurus nobilis Finding the praiseworthy
Lavender Gratitude
Ledum Acknowledging wholeness
Lemon Purity regained
Lemongrass Youthening through frequencies of praise
Marjoram Delight remembered
Melaleuca (alternifolia) Self-discovery
Melaleuca (ericifolia) Dynamic balance
Melissa Being fully present for the self
Mountain Savory Surrender to the divine
Myrrh Majesty reclaimed
Myrtle Faith in bounty
Nutmeg Limitless availability of resources
Orange Reawakening pure sexuality
Oregano Realizing dreams
Palo Santo Clarity of vision
Patchouli Connection with nature
Peppermint Effervescent energy
Pine Feeling enveloped in safety
Ravensara Empathic/telepathic communication
Roman chamomile The peace of immortality

Rose Divine presence
Rosemary Holistic language of truth
Rosewood Integrated transparency
Sage Absolute truthfulness with self
Sandalwood Compassionate understanding
Spearmint Fervent devotion to self-understanding
Spikenard Silencing the mind
Spruce Awakened connection with Source
St. Marie's Lavender Recognizing blessings
Tangerine Fluidity in mastery
Tarragon Daring to stretch horizons
Thyme Abundant self-nurturing
Tsuga Establishing sacred space
Valerian Unshakeable peace
Vetiver Eternal perspective
Western Red Cedar Honoring the interconnectedness of life
White Fir Reverent living
Wintergreen Expression of inner strength
Ylang Ylang Divinity of physical life

Dr. Sabina de Vita writes:

The human olfactory system – sense of smell – is our most ancient and powerful root of emotional life (Goleman, 1977). Research has shown that aromas stimulate the brain within one to three seconds. As aromatic molecules are inhaled, olfactory membranes capture them. There are 800 million nerve endings for processing and detecting odors. Each fragrance molecule fits itself into specific receptor cells like a puzzle piece. The stimulation created by odor causes the receptors to trigger electrical impulses ... within milliseconds bypassing the thalamus, which is the electrical switchboard of the brain. The research done by scientists on the effects of oil fragrances has found them to be one of the fastest ways to affect heart rate, blood pressure, breathing, memory, stress levels and hormone balance. They produce effects 60% to 76% stronger than the herbs taken whole. (Raichur/Cohn)

Essential oils are one of the highest known sources of antioxidants that can prevent free radical damage.

Choosing Pure Products

The oils recommended and available from the number provided[2] are all Young Living Oils. There is a very important reason for this: there are vast differences between *good therapeutic* grade oils and *perfume* grade oils. Their effectiveness varies widely as well. Only 2% of all essential oils are therapeutic grade oils. The remaining 98%, produced for the perfume industry, are in many instances synthetic, adulterated, over or under-processed, laden with chemicals or denatured. One of the key factors in producing therapeutic

---

2 1-877-552-5646, toll-free in US.

grade essential oil is to preserve the delicate balance of aromatic compounds which can easily be destroyed by high temperatures and high pressures. Using copper or aluminum distillers, rather than stainless steel (as Young Living Oils does), also destroys these compounds.

Pure therapeutic oil starts with proper agriculture. The plants need to be free of pesticides and chemicals so that toxic compounds are not produced during distillation. Multiple other factors, such as seed and soil quality (with proper enzymes and trace minerals) need to be taken into consideration. "We irrigate with pure mountain water... The herbs are distilled fresh ... under low pressure and low temperature to preserve the healing constituents," Dr. Gary Young.

An example of the high standards required for pure therapeutic grade oil is given by Dr. Sabina de Vita.

> "Timing and pressure in distillation are extremely important; e.g., cypress requires 24 hours at 245° and 5 # of pressure to extract all of its active ingredients. Lessening the time by 2 hours will result in destroying 10 to 20 of the oil's constituents. Most operations distill cypress for only 1 hour and 15 minutes, so you can imagine the quality of the oil."

Roberta Williams in her book, *Aromatherapy* states that "...95% of the products sold as aromatherapy are counterfeit, pseudo-aromatherapy with no therapeutic value, produced in massive quantities from petrochemical imposters."

Few companies in the world have obtained the AFNOR label – the recognized international standard for therapeutic Grade A oils. Young Living Oils has been granted this endorsement for the excellence of their products.

The Benefits of Essential Oils

Not only do these great gifts to humankind bring emotional balance and wellbeing, but they provide us with extraordinary rejuvenating effects for the skin. Like sound therapy[3] they are a joy to use and deliver tremendously potent results.

They reverse aging by stimulating rapid cellular reproduction.
They penetrate and moisturize deep dermal layers of the skin.
They promote lymph flow, purifying the skin by removing toxins.
They heal skin scarring, sun damage and wrinkles.
They are disinfectant to skin bacteria, fungus and viruses.
They reduce redness and inflammation.
They regulate hormones and oil gland activity and reduce stress.
They keep collagen and elastin production at optimal levels.

Home Beauty Products

Lavender Oil

The many contributions are as varied as the oils, making it difficult to single one out. But lavender is rare in that it is anti-inflammatory and balancing (normalizing oiliness) and is suitable for every body type. Furthermore, it reduces stress and enhances libido. It is a powerful wrinkle reducer, antiseptic and scar eliminator. Like bergamot, it can be used as an anti-depressant and is also great as a deodorant. It relieves sunburn and restores skin's elasticity.

Note: Drop 4 drops of lavender oil into a cup of cool water. Dip a washcloth in the solution, wring out the excess liquid, and use as a soothing eye compress.

---

[3] www.angelsoundhealing.com

Rose Oil

Not all roses are the same due to centuries of cultivation of hybrid species. Young Living Oils use Bulgarian Rose Oil with a frequency of 320 Hz, the highest in the plant kingdom.

It is a powerful releaser of HGH, a cell rejuvenator and is also suitable for all skin types. Bulgarian scientists have demonstrated that Bulgarian Rose Oil can reduce high blood pressure and heart arrhythmia.

Facial Masks

1. Add 4 drops of lavender oil to a dessert spoon of oatmeal in the palm of your hand, and scrub the face with gentle rotating movements.

2. For normal to oily skin, pour 3 tablespoons of fine Celtic sea salt into your hand, add 3 drops of lavender oil and a little warm water to make a paste. Massage into the skin and rinse. Use once a week to exfoliate dead cells and remove toxins.

3. Stevia drops (not in an alcohol base) are placed in the palm of the hand, then distributed over the face and neck and rinsed off after 15 minutes. Stevia, like vinegar, is one of the wonder foods. It helps reduce wrinkles, softens, tightens and enlivens the skin. It helps burns, cuts and wounds heal without scarring.

4. Lavender or rose oil can be mixed with a tablespoon of honey. Apply it to the face and neck and leave on for 20 minutes before rinsing.

5. Mashed organic strawberries mixed with 5 drops of lavender oil helps reduce redness on the chest, neck and face when used regularly as a 20-minute mask.

Toners and Spritzers

1. Mineral water mixed with 3-4 drops of lavender oil.

2. Organic apple cider vinegar mixed with 3-5 drops of lavender oil relieves skin disorders, redness, inflammation and age spots.

3. A tablespoon of witch hazel combined with 2 drops of lavender oil is an astringent, cooling toner that refines skin tone and minimizes enlarged pores. Store this in the refrigerator.

Dandruff

Mix 4 ounces (1/2 cup) of unsweetened kefir with 8 drops of lavender oil. Rub into the scalp after shampooing and rinse after 10-15 minutes. This is also good as an aftershave; leave it on for 5 minutes.

Note: Unsweetened kefir and stevia are essential parts of a rejuvenating diet.

Recommended reading: *The Body Ecology Diet*, by Donna Gates.

PART II

Healing through Oneness
The Method and Tools

Use of the Sigils and Fragrances for healing of self or others

1. If the fragrances can be obtained in their pure form (therapeutic grade), they can be applied to the bottom of the feet; 1 drop is ample. If using perfume grade oils, deeply smelling them will be sufficient. Use oil(s) at the beginning of the session. Choose one or several oils specific for the focus for the session. It is not necessary to use all of the specified oils for a particular section/session.

Use of the sigils only will still allow the memories of Oneness and wholeness to surface. Place your left thumb on the small fairy sigil to access its qualities. The Alchemy of Fragrance is about achieving Oneness, memory is linked to fragrance; running finger(s) from left to right over the fairy sigils releases memory of Oneness (achieving Oneness through remembering it).

2. The sigils of the individual sections can be used as indicated. For example, if you want to facilitate healing in the joints, you may use sigils 1 – 13. If you want to work on healing of the emotions or of the genital/reproductive systems, you may use only the sigils in those respective sections.

3. The Arcturian Fairy Sound Elixirs that accompany this material as an audio download are required when using this healing modality. The specific effect of sound elixirs is to dissolve obsolete programs in the body (and the environment) by using an exact balance of black and white frequency[4] to cancel out illusion.

---

4   See www.angelsoundhealing.com for more information on sound elixirs.

The Healing Method

Place the following wheels under yourself or the person you are working with, in the order given below. You may be lying on a bed, massage table or seated in a chair, they do not have to be placed directly under the body.

1. **Wheel for Release of Atlantean Healing Codes** - place on the bottom of the stack

2. Next place the **Power Wheel for the 144 Fragrances**

3. Then place the **Wheel for the Rapture of Great Awareness**

4. On top place the **Wheel of Surrendered Trust**

Have nearby:
1. Tools: Power Wheels, Arcturian Fairy sigils, Atlantean sigils, Belvaspata Emotional Healing sigils, Love, Praise, Gratitude sigils and Incantations.
2. Oils that you wish to use that pertain to the sigils.
3. Arcturain Fairy sound elixirs – to play during the session.

Sigils

Note: Belvaspata and Fragrance Alchemy may be used as part of a usual Belvaspata healing session or as a separate session. Add the Fragrance Alchemy after the usual session. If using it as a stand-alone session, open the session with an expansion process and hold the expanded awareness for as long as you feel is appropriate. For example, 5-10 minutes may be sufficient; proceed as below.

- With your left thumb on the small Arcturian Fairy Sigil,[5] contemplate the meaning of any insight associated with it. Read the name of the Atlantean sigil and move your right index finger from left to right over it. Then read the angel name for the Atlantean sigil and glance at its sigil.
- Sign (draw) the Belvaspata sigil over the person you are working with, or yourself and say its name. You may also trace the sigil in your book or draw it in the air.
- End by speaking the Incantation for the specific number of the sigil.
- Repeat for each of the sigils in a particular section.
- Complete all of the sigils within a section. For example if you only require the sigils for the left ankle, you must still use and draw all the sigils for the Joints.
- Close with signing the sigils for Love, Praise and Gratitude.

---

5 The Arcturian Fairy Sigil is located to the right of the oil name. For example, see page 219.

Questions and Answers

Q. Is it necessary to use all of the sigils in one specific section, for example, if we are using the 13 Joints of the Body, is it necessary to use all of the sigils in that section? Would you also use all of the oils for any specific section?

A. Use all of the sigils in any specific section, even if only treating for one particular body part, chakra, etc. Choose one or 2 oils that best suit the intent of your session as in Angelica oil for the left ankle if treating a sprained or fractured left ankle. The oil could also be chosen for its particular qualities. Combining too many oils could be over-stimulating.

Q. Many of the oils are expensive. Is it absolutely necessary to have the essential oil to use this healing method?

A. The essential oils are very nice to have and use with Belvaspata Healing through Oneness but are not absolutely essential. The Arcturian Fairy sigils and the sound elixirs hold the frequency of the correlating oil.

Wheel for the Release of the Atlantean Healing Codes

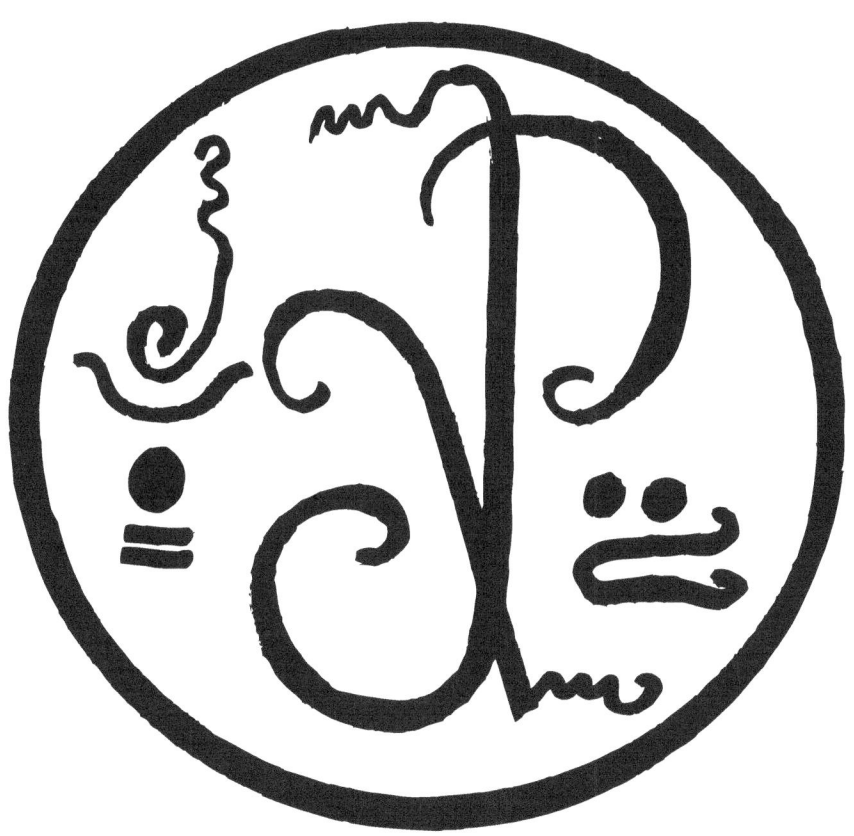

Power Wheel for the 144 Fragrances

Naktaru brihespahur esat blavi

Wheel of the Rapture of Great Awareness

Nechparavek Huraspa Aranik

Wheel of Surrendered Trust

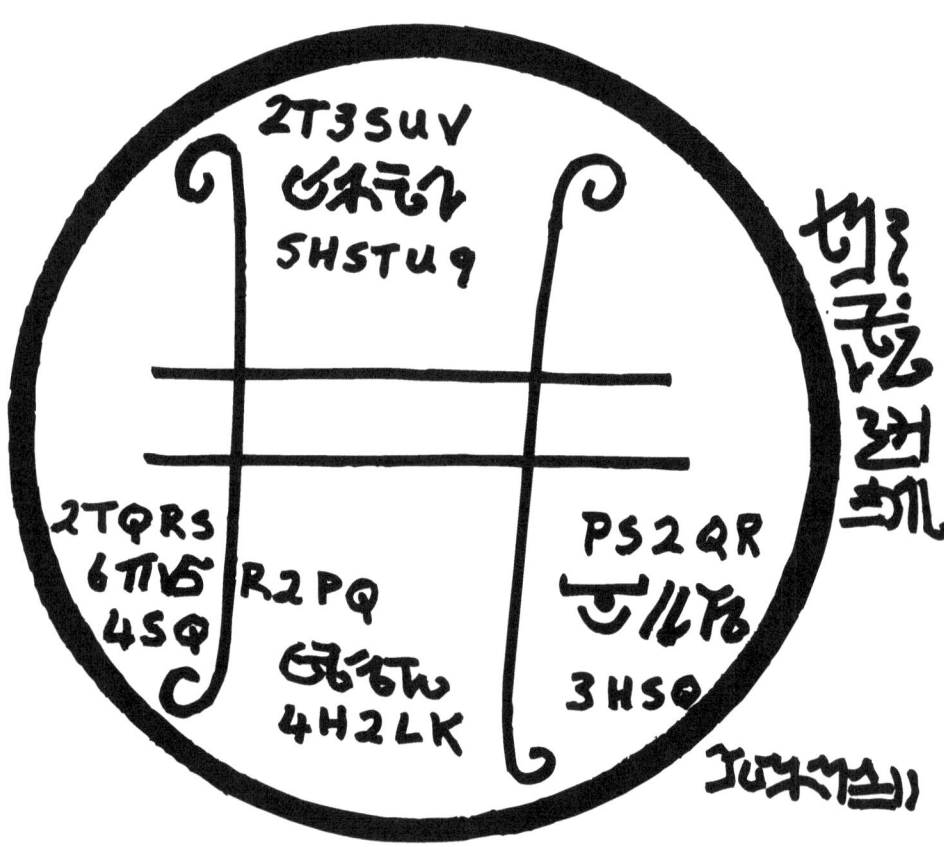

Sigils for Praise, Love and Gratitude

Praise

Love

Gratitude

The 144 Essential Oils for the Arcturian Sigils

Single Oils

1. Angelica
2. Basil
3. Bergamot
4. Birch
5. Black Cumin
6. Cajeput
7. Cardamom
8. Cedar (Canadian Red)
9. Cedarwood
10. Chamomile (German, Matricaria recutita)
11. Chamomile (Roman, Chamaemelum nobile)
12. Cassia
13. Citronella
14. Clary Sage
15. Clove
16. Coriander
17. Cypress
18. Davana
19. Dill
20. Elemi
21. Eucalyptus globulus
22. Eucalyptus polybractea
23. Eucalyptus citriodora
24. Eucalyptus radiata
25. Fennel
26. Fir
27. Fleabane
28. Frankincense
29. Freesia
30. Galbanum
31. Geranium
32. Ginger
33. Grapefruit
34. Helichrysum
35. Honeysuckle
36. Hyssop
37. Idaho Tansy
38. Jasmine
39. Juniper Berry
40. Lavender
41. Lavandin
42. Lemon
43. Lemongrass
44. Lilac
45. Lime
46. Lupin

47. Mandarin
48. Marjoram
49. Melaleuca alternifolia
50. Melaleuca ericifolia
51. Melaleuca quinquenervia
52. Melissa
53. Mountain Savory
54. Mugwort
55. Myrrh
56. Myrtle
57. Nasturtium
58. Neroli (from the blossom of the bitter orange tree)
59. Nutmeg
60. Orange
61. Oregano
62. Palmarosa
63. Patchouli
64. Pepper (black)
65. Peppermint
66. Petitgrain
67. Pikake
68. Pine
69. Plumeria
70. Ravensara
71. Rose
72. Rosemary
73. Sage
74. Sandalwood
75. Spearmint
76. Spikenard
77. Spruce
78. Stocks
79. Sweetgrass
80. Sweetpea
81. Tangerine
82. Tansy (blue)
83. Tarragon
84. Thyme
85. Tomato Leaf
86. Valerian
87. Vetiver
88. Violet
89. Vitex
90. White Lotus
91. Walnut
92. Wild Yam
93. Yarrow
94. Ylang Ylang

Oil Blends

(Indicated by one sigil, the ratio of individual proportions is indicated in parentheses)

95. Rose, Lavender, Stocks (ratio: 4, 4, 1)
96. Orange, Honeysuckle, Chamomile (German) (1, 4, 4)
97. Neroli, Lavender, Mugwort (1, 4, 1)
98. Ylang Ylang, Ginger, Nasturtium (2, 1, 1)
99. Fir, Juniper Berry, Clove (2, 1, 1)
100. Grapefruit, Tomato Leaf, Neroli (2, 1, 1)
101. Orange, Idaho Tansy, Ginger (2, 1, 2)
102. Peppermint, Rosemary, Angelica (1, 2, 1)
103. Jasmine, Geranium, Tangerine (2, 1, 1)
104. Sage, Lilac, Lemongrass (1, 4, 1)
105. Bergamot, Sweet Pea, Chamomile (Roman) (1, 2, 2)
106. Sandalwood, Patchouli, Rose (1, 1, 4)
107. Orange, Geranium, Plumeria (1, 1, 4)
108. Black Pepper, Walnut, Violet (1, 1, 4)
109. Ginger, Lemongrass, Geranium (1, 2, 2)
110. Frankincense, Galbanum, Sandalwood (1, 1, 1)
111. Helichrysum, Rose, Frankincense (1, 2, 1)
112. Myrrh, Lavender, Sandalwood (1, 4, 1)
113. Melissa, Cedarwood, Tangerine (4, 1, 2)
114. Lavender, Marjoram, Angelica (4, 1, 1)
115. Basil, Rosemary, Lemongrass (1, 1, 3)
116. Spearmint, Lemon, Ginger (1, 4, 1)
117. Tangerine, Honeysuckle, Peppermint (1, 4, 1)
118. Neroli, Jasmine, Geranium (1, 1, 3)
119. Bergamot, Lavandin, Mugwort (3, 3, 2)
120. Melissa, Angelica, Chamomile (German) (1, 2, 3)

121. Nutmeg, Patchouli, Orange (1, 1, 2)
122. Rosewood, Myrtle, Grapefruit (3, 2, 1)
123. Freesia, Hyssop, Rose (2, 1, 3)
124. Plumeria, Freesia, Geranium (2, 2, 1)
125. Helichrysum, Cedar, Myrrh (2, 1, 1)
126. Pikake, Plumeria, Tomato Leaf (1, 1, 1)
127. White Lotus, Rose, Ylang Ylang (1, 3 1)
128. Cassia, Myrtle, Sweetpea (1, 1, 4)
129. Ylang Ylang, Lavender, Honeysuckle (1, 2, 3)
130. Ravensara, Myrrh, Rose (1, 1, 4)
131. Cardamom, Hyssop, Jasmine (2, 2, 1)
132. Cedar (Canadian Red), Bergamot, Patchouli (1, 4, 1)
133. Wild Yam, Yarrow, Melissa (3, 2, 1)
134. Black Cumin, Clary Sage, Walnut (1, 2, 4)
135. Chamomile (Roman), Violet, Pikake (3, 1, 2)
136. Melissa, Ravensara, Violet (3, 2, 1)
137. Helichrysum, Frankincense, Myrrh (3, 2, 1)
138. Honeysuckle, Stocks, Chamomile (Roman) (4, 4, 1)
139. Davana, Sweetpea, Ginger (1, 2, 1)
140. Cedarwood, Cajeput, Lupin (3, 1, 4)
141. Lilac, Geranium, Tomato Leaf (2, 2, 1)
142. Myrtle, Fleabane, Stocks (1, 1, 4)
143. Neroli, Tangerine, Hyssop (3, 2, 1)
144. Rose, White Lotus, Spikenard (4, 2, 1)

144 Incantations

Place the incantations under the oils when stored; speak the incantations over the oils when they are being created

1. Nerech biretva hurespi
2. Miheret nusvreva ustavit
3. Pliharet seskavit uresvi
4. Kluhabit splechplava uvis
5. Kershvrava subavit krivechvi
6. Trihunas plesbavit kunachvi
7. Trenehit hutrechve silvates
8. Isatach spehu-urit pareva
9. Klibasut minavech struhavat
10. Elesta spihubis aleskla
11. Nanutach ikret paravi
12. Trihunes arsta privabit
13. Trechnanuvit eskla bihuret
14. Mistech mishet anenas
15. Etre pluhavit brishet bavi
16. Nuskalavech hespa uhunis
17. Triba estevit ka-ahurat
18. Esplek bisbaranut hespakla
19. Nechtu erserut bilechva
20. Aratu viresva uhura nesvrata
21. Aruk paravit nanastu
22. Pelechpra spivabut ereksta
23. Nuspahur esachve krehet preva
24. Nekva ersta bich prave
25. Arsana pruhit erekpartu

26. Meset arspata meskavich
27. Arksalana brispravet uklech
28. Rekpatu raskru-avet plivach
29. Stubit erek arechtuva
30. Rusatvi mishet arekstrava
31. Brihurasat estre pribu-aresta
32. Krachba este krivas aresta
33. Arasta miruch nanestra
34. Krubit plabava isanavit
35. Asta michvet elpahur
36. Krunaves vilesat virkbave
37. Nektu araset pruvaa
38. Nichtaver usubavit uklasvi
39. Petranuvis aresta prahut
40. Etre bilevach vunesvi
41. Kiset vranu usavesvi
42. Karanus misech vibres
43. Kluharanet espave minusach
44. Kisanach hestavi misuvet
45. Raktu biras harsata
46. Kluhunaves arsba esekrach
47. Itrech prihava vereklas
48. Nestuch eseta minavech
49. Virat ursata blihur arespi
50. Achna estava vibret huratvi
51. Asata privabur miseret
52. Aksava vispa mihur rarech
53. Neskavi versta prekprahur
54. Kruhanatvi prihavek ereshta
55. Michpaset eneshvi steve vrubaset

56. Nachve suvil peras prahet
57. Nusaret erakvi bra-uvraset
58. Lu-uhuvrivaset michvabet uveset
59. Pihi-arat michtave mishuret
60. Klihibaset nenechstu aranas
61. Stihubaret arskla viruset
62. Misetech bruhaset iste-manuhech
63. Kriba-hureset arechsta bravich
64. Krisanat-vistavi heskle-arurach
65. Sivahech-virusat manesh hustava
66. Plikat barech eruklasve manus
67. Achsava visat harastu
68. Misavach ninesvi hubrasat
69. Kiratuch nunasatvi paresh
70. Kasanet vibrach ubarechvi
71. Kirasut estetvi plavabich
72. Kruhasanat piresvi arusach
73. Kasanur este blaheresvi
74. Nanukta pliva este plahur plavi
75. Achnut areksta miset arachve
76. Nusba keres arustava
77. Nisaruk ublavi kerestahut
78. Achva vibresh mesenutvi
79. Aksava viblesvravi nuchtaha
80. Iklechvi spehat aresti
81. Iksalvanuch ri-arestat verebasbi-uhet
82. Akbelestat uras prahesvi
83. Nestava setvanut arkla
84. Sunech barut hurastavi
85. Naspa-eskla ruselvavis-praha

86. Kribaravit-eseta plahur
87. Achnahur setvivravis plek-pratahur
88. Nunek arachta prehavis
89. Kasanet hurahasvi iselbach
90. Nunas arsklava viselnet
91. Kisanut brihes prava
92. Kavavech haselvi steleva
93. Nunarak prihespavi eresta
94. Kavanut aspava respahur
95. Kutre plava birechvi stahur
96. Kavech setl-brisbrava uhet
97. Nanes spavilhut ubrachvi
98. Kiret tranadoch spirtlha uves
99. Neset ublach bravi menhat
100. Kiritpa splehus astra-hurat
101. Asbek uhurunutvi arach
102. Uhurures manach partlvi
103. Skartlhut ubrasvi menenech
104. Skarech uhurusut plavabesvi
105. Askra pret pranavit vilesvi
106. Misekra priharanet skuvi
107. Esechpahur plavabesvi urat
108. Nechpa spartlvu ruselvavi
109. Nenesplahur sparut arespahur
110. Klavanech spehererat ukla
111. Trenes bihivarasvi ekena
112. Sihararat ninechvi utrabit
113. Kretva-spereru etrasvi-nenu-hach
114. Viset-blavu eseratvi unech
115. Vuvaset pliheshvar areta hurech

116. Mistarut bravahur esena hurat
117. Kelpahet ekserenach hurasvi
118. Nekta bararet husetvavi
119. Nekararut asechvi plasplahur
120. Aktre brahus pirashvi
121. Kelevishva puhuraret aresutvava
122. Nekra-brahit alspa subarut
123. Nitrech kasbarasut uhururespi varasat
124. Keneverasat harchvi plerasut
125. Asbi sibre varasvi unech astat
126. Usalvaravesvi nachbar menehuset
127. Hureksta blahur aravesti asurat
128. Hasklavi pihiravach nesalavit viset
129. Nekbarut esta-barech viselvi
130. Kavabit arsta peret hirstava
131. Ekbar blivahur nenes-kalvavi
132. Erchtar kishet alesvar viselvi
133. Kereta prusabit helesklar anech
134. Valavesh ersetar brachbaver
135. Kasabavi ninach ruspavahur
136. Klisetret brivesh pravekbi
137. Kehet-trave arasatvi manesh
138. Arch-asanavar pluvar vitre-prahus
139. Usut-pravar este asunach
140. Kabahut menes-ishavar rutret
141. Sihubatret arska elechpavi
142. Kiset-bavi aras aresta
143. Mivarech iset blavabi
144. Hurat privatar bluhavabes-bi asatar

PART III

Healing through Oneness
The Sigils and Angels

The 13 Main Joints of the Body
Sigils and Angels 1 - 13

The name of the 13 sigils of the joints and their angels of the Atlantean Healing System are known as the Atlantean Azurarat.

The 13 Insights for the 13 Joints of Man -
The Principles of Achieving Oneness:

"The one sense that did not participate in the fall that brought about duality is smell. It is for this reason that fragrance can still remind us of the eternal indivisibility from which we sprang."
Almine

1. **Angelica**

Azur-ukletklanet

Kluhabersat-nanechvi

Angel:

Angel:

Prabahur-stellanut

Pribas-heresut

Left Ankle

Incantation: *Nerech biretva hurespi*

Note: Avoid exposure to sunlight for 72 hours after application of this oil.

Physical Benefits
Pre-menstrual syndrome
Menstrual cramps
Menopausal symptoms
Respiratory infections and coughs

Emotional Benefits
Post-traumatic stress disorder
Mood swings
Fear of the future

Spiritual Benefits
Releases the hold of the past on the future
Encourages authentic self-expression
Smoothes interaction with the environment

Insight: For everything there is a price to pay as long as life is lived within boundaries. The law of compensation applies to life within boundaries.

2. Basil

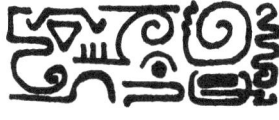
Kirata-frahim-klava

Nasbar-eklet-varsut

ANGEL:

ANGEL:

Spahut-mespata

Misavach-nanasut

Right Ankle

Incantation: *Miheret nusvreva ustavit*

Note: Do not use if epileptic. Apply to wrists, soles of feet and temples.

Physical Benefits
Soothes insect bites
Anti-viral and anti-bacterial
Decongestant – steam can be inhaled from boiling leaves, stems and flowers
Anti-inflammatory
Very effective anti-spasmodic and for soothing muscles

Emotional Benefits
Apply to the tip of the nose and under the bottom lip (on chin) for relief of despondency and mental fatigue

Apply to top of the head to relieve over-active thoughts, especially at bedtime

Alleviates fear of the unknown and fear of the future

Spiritual Benefits

Increases mental quietness for meditation and receptivity for sacred ceremonies

Assists with receiving and hearing inner guidance

Insight: Three overcomings of identity have to be made to step free from the boundaries of living within the matrices of existence.

3. **Bergamot**

Verbrit-pratahur-uskla   **Ukles-privar-miravesvi**

Angel: Angel:

Parech-stuhubaret   **Nuspletprahur**

Left Knee

Incantation: *Pliharet seskavit uresvi*

Note: Avoid exposure to sunlight for 72 hours after application of this oil.

Physical Benefits
May be beneficial for streptococcal and staphylococcal infections and fungal conditions
Antiseptic and anti-inflammatory qualities
Hormonal support and regulation
Stimulates appetite and aids digestion
Treats intestinal parasites
Can be used as a douche for vaginal infections
Useful as an insect repellant
Rheumatism
Cold sores

Emotional Benefits
Calming, aids peaceful sleep
Useful for treatment of agitation and hyperactive nerves
Useful for anxiety, stress and tension
Has a refreshing quality that uplifts mood

Spiritual Benefits
Instills hope in the future
Self-empowering
Wards off density

Insight: The first overcoming is that of the egoic self, identity based on the body, emotions and mind. The mind and emotions conspire during this stage to enslave the experiences of the body. In humanity, this stage is called ego-identification.

4. **Birch**

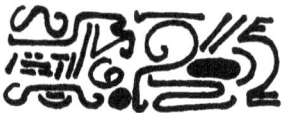
Belesatvri-miskavel

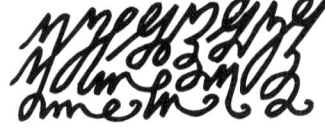
Sekreve-stubavech

ANGEL:

Erch-artu plubar

ANGEL:

Nish-peravesvi

Right Knee

Incantation: *Kluhabit splechplava uvis*

Note: Do not use if epileptic. May irritate sensitive skin – a skin test is recommended prior to use.

Physical Benefits
Liver stimulant
Supports bone function
Analgesic and anti-inflammatory qualities
Relieves tendonitis
May be used to treat urinary tract infection

Emotional Benefits
Enhances sensory experience
Encourages self-expression

Spiritual Benefits
Assists in handling density in the environment – apply to the bottom of the feet

Insight: The second overcoming is that of individuation, of believing ourselves to be a unique consciousness superimposed over all that is. When we realize ourselves to be in oneness with the Infinite's intent, the body or embodiment starts living automatically – a conduit of Infinite expression.

5. **Black Cumin**

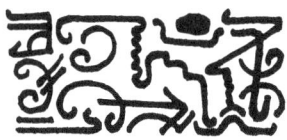

Kartu-selvabit

Nachvrabuch-ketrva

Angel:

Zertra-bruhavit

Angel:

Suhet-uselbi

Left Hip

Incantation: *Kershvrava subavit krivechvi*

Physical Benefits
Anti-parasitic, anti-viral and antiseptic qualities
Stimulates immune system
Stimulates digestion
Regulates liver function
May help with migraine headaches

Emotional Benefits
Stimulates inspiration
Calming effect

Spiritual Benefits
Assists with fluidity in responding to life's challenges
Aids in establishing mastery of the mind
Assists with opening of the heart

Insight: The third overcoming is the identity of being an embodiment within the vastness of our greater self. The way to achieve freedom from this illusion is to remind ourselves that what is without, is within. It just appears to be 'outside' because the belief in our reflection causes a reflection.

6. Cajeput (Myrtle)

Araktu-brizabat

ANGEL:

Veles-arsta-pravech

Nishpa-ukresvi

ANGEL:

Nisarek-velesvi

Right Hip

Incantation: *Trihunas plesbavit kunachvi*

Note: Use with caution on soles of feet and in diffuser. Synthetic Cajeput should be avoided.

Physical Benefits
Following a test on a patch of skin, may be used on insect bites or acne
Rheumatism and sore muscles
For respiratory infections – use diffuser
May be used as an expectorant

Emotional Benefits
Releases old grievances and resentments
Assists in releasing past trauma

Spiritual Benefits
Assists empaths to cope with their sensitivities

Insight: Life that is lived as an outer reflection is a life of opposition. Life lived as boundless expression knows neither opposition nor support, for it transcends relationship as a source of supply or a cause of hardship.

7. **Cardamom**

Menher-kluta-brahus　　　**Nikvra-velesvi**

Angel:　　　　　　　　　　Angel:

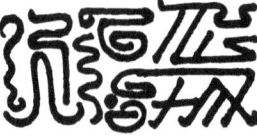

Iselvi-brizarat　　　**Miserat-uklasvi**

Left Wrist

Incantation: *Trenehit hutrechve silvates*

Physical Benefits
Combats worm infestation
May be used for pulmonary disease
May assist with intestinal and urinary tract complaints

Emotional Benefits
Assists with lightening the mood
Restores energy and optimism

Spiritual Benefits
Helps maintain the density of the fields surrounding the body
Assists with healing heartache

Insight: The egoic self as an identity causes a circle of mirrors to form. The belief in an individuation superimposed over the circle of our existence, caused the 'inside' of our self-made circle of expression to start spinning. The belief in our embodiment forms a reference point in the middle of the circle. All of these bind us to space.

8. **Cedar (Canadian Red)**

Arkbit-kli-urtra

Mechparet-stihurvi

Angel:

Rekva-karum

Angel:

Meshpa-usklava

Right Wrist

Incantation: *Isatach spehu-urit pareva*

Physical Benefits
Insect repellant
Anti-parasitic qualities
Stimulates hair follicles
Antiseptic qualities

Emotional Benefits
Purifying
Opens extra-sensory abilities
Wards off ill intent

Spiritual Benefits
Opens the pituitary's ability for omni-sensory perception
Stills the surface mind
Assists to interpret inner guidance by stimulating the abilities of the pineal gland to interpret multi-dimensional abilities

Insight: All the stages of humanity can be equated to the egoic stages when considered against the stages of godhood and super-godhood (see page 238 for clarification of these stages). To overcome ego is the challenge of man. To overcome individuation is the challenge of godhood and to overcome the illusion of embodiment is the challenge of super-godhood.

9. Cedarwood

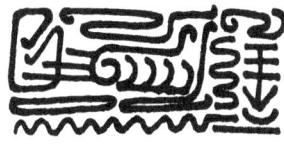

Plihurtu-danavis

ANGEL:

Erktu-arsarat

Pretpahur-nesevelesvi

ANGEL:

Nachpa-meserut

Left Elbow

Incantation: *Klibasut minavech struhavat*

Physical Benefits
May be effective against gonorrhea
Useful for treatment of bronchitis
Skin disorders
May reduce hardening of the arteries (atherosclerosis)

Emotional Benefits
May stimulate the limbic region of the brain (the center of emotions) and restores the strength of positive emotions
May produce deep sleep by stimulating melatonin release from the pineal gland

Spiritual Benefits
Releases joy and passion
Allows the opening of the heart
Restores trust in the benevolence of life

Insight: If man represents the challenges of embodiment, which is the reference point in the middle of the circle of existence, why does his challenge pertain to the overcoming of thinking himself to be mind (the circle), emotions (the rotating, moving field within the circle) and the reference point of his body? Because he sees all as being 'outside' of himself and himself as part of the environment.

10. **Chamomile (German)**

Urtrarut-velizarut　　　　**Ketre-bripahur**

Angel:　　　　　　　　　　　Angel:

Kalsut-prikpratur　　　　**Setl-privahur**

Right Elbow
Incantation: *Elesta spihubis aleskla*

Physical Benefits
Reduces scarring
Supports digestion, the liver and gallbladder
Useful for treatment of allergies

Emotional Benefits
Sedating and relaxing qualities
Assists with releases of tension and helps with anger management
Assists with clearing the mind

Spiritual Benefits
Assists with releasing of emotional trigger responses and in achieving emotional mastery
Assists with stilling the surface mind

Insight: The individuation that forms the rim (called spirit) identifies with what is 'inside' itself. It is the origin of the personal matrix each individual is imprisoned by. This matrix consists of a feminine and masculine layer and is neutral versus the body that is masculine and the rotating fields that are feminine and represent soul.

11. Chamomile (Roman)

Uvelvrek-vraspur

Nech-varavespi-esklatur

ANGEL:

Kisanur-plavabi

ANGEL:

Biver-araras

Left Shoulder

Incantation: *Nanutach ikret paravi*

Physical Benefits
May restore elasticity of skin
Assists to relieve muscular tension and spasms
Apply to bruises and cuts
Use as a blood cleanser and for relief of allergies

Emotional Benefits
For relief of mood swings, fear of being alone and depression
Assists to release old grievances

Spiritual Benefits
Assists with centering and focusing in the present
Assists with releasing 'stuck' patterns

Insight: During our existence our awareness passes through these three different components of the body (life), the soul (death) and the spirit (ascension). These three stages are mirrored throughout existence as the linear stages of change.

12. **Cassia**

Kasarut-helespra **Nusit-haravesvi**

Angel: Angel:

Buravil-fravahim **Echklava-biresh**

Right Shoulder

Incantation: *Trihunes arsta privabit*

Physical Benefits
Antibacterial, antiviral and antifungal
Calms the adrenals

Emotional Benefits
Restores contentment and a sense of well-being

Spiritual Benefits
Brings dynamic balance to the emotions

Insight: When we access that which has had neither beginning nor end, hidden within form, with our whole being (rather than our five senses), we gain a poetic perspective. This way of experiencing life with all of ourselves, as a living work of art, is the first step to overcoming separation as an illusion.

13. **Citronella**

Keveneret-asklava   **Nesta-misetvi-nasarut**
Angel: Angel:
Palut-meneshet   **Kripahur-astrevi**

Upper Neck Joint

Incantation: *Trechnanuvit eskla bihuret*

Note: Skin test for sensitivity.

Physical Benefits
Insect repellant and insecticide
Deodorant

Anti-inflammatory and anti-spasmodic
May alleviate headaches

Emotional Benefits
Uplifting qualities
Stabilizes emotions

Spiritual Benefits
Restores yellow to auric fields which creates stable growth

Insight: Allowing ourselves to become aware of the real in life and surrendering with trust to the Eternal One, are the following stages of expression that allow life to transcend duality, into the deep rapture of no opposites. This leaves all matrices behind. (This was achieved by Almine on 24th September, 2011.)

The Evolutionary Stages of Man

(From Secrets of the Hidden Realms)

The evolution of a human being into the stage that lies beyond humanness, that of a god-being that can come and go throughout the cosmos with the speed of thought, follows three distinct stages. Each stage has within it three separate phases. This brings the total number of phases to nine through which a human being can evolve.

An initiation is a test of skill, impeccability, knowledge and often one's relationship with other life forms. It not only tests the worthiness of the truth seeker to move from one rung of advancement to another, but through the testing provides him or her with the chance to fill any gaps of perception necessary for the next phase.

In the Egyptian and Atlantean initiations the last stage, with its three phases was guarded by the two Lords of the Two Horizons, also known as the two Lords of the Three Gates. The smaller triangle represented the triangulated view of Sirius rising above the horizon as seen from the bottom of the pyramid. But as the nine rungs were completed, the Lords of the Two Horizons would bring the Ascended Master to the top of the pyramid. From there the horizon and Sirius's rising would be further away. This would create a larger triangle. The master would have completed all nine phases of his human evolution. The two triangles represent the change in perception between the phase of the Initiate and the Ascended Master. It illustrates how much vision will expand, and how much more of the unknown will be able to be accessed as a master.

The Sacred Sothic Triangle
Representing the nine phases of human evolution

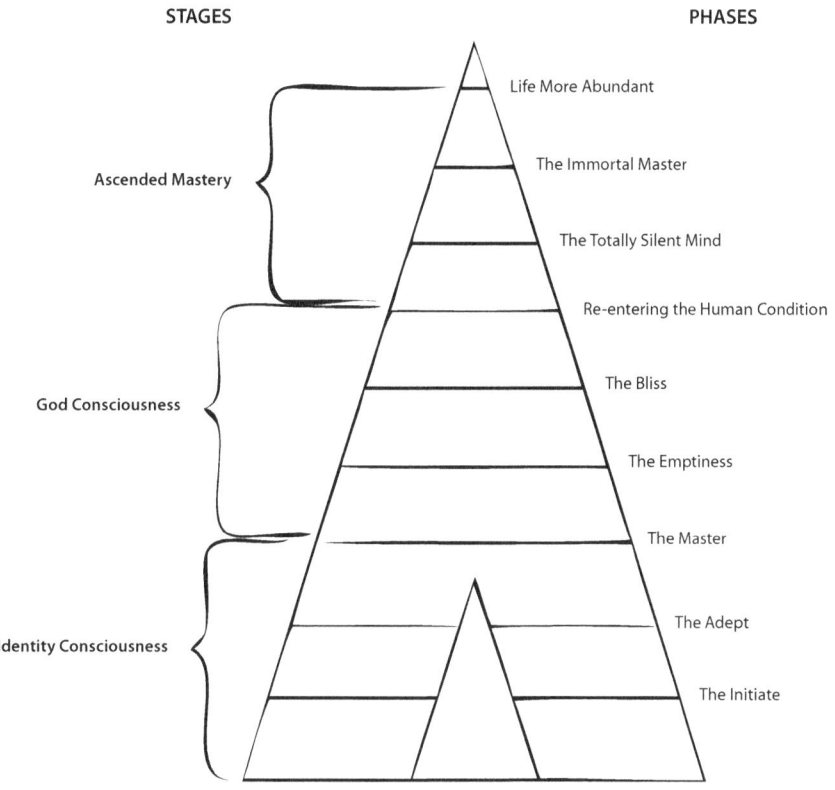

The Sothic triangle has a 4 to 9 proportion and is also the ancient hieroglyph for Sirius. It represents the secret of the last three gates or phases within Ascended Mastery, presided over by the two Lords of the Two Horizons. The two triangles represent the view as seen by someone at the base of the pyramid (Identity Consciousness) and at the top of the pyramid (Ascended Mastery) of Sirius's rising above the horizon.

Stage 1: Identity Consciousness

This stage is like the bottom of the pyramid in that many enter this stage but far fewer make it through. The three phases of this stage are all lived while in ego-identification, that state of beingness that sees ourselves as separate from others and identifies with the body and surface mind (the ego).

Phase 1 - The Initiate

Type of Change: *Transformation*
Transformation is the stage within change that discards that which is no longer needed. The truth seeker dies to the old way of being.

Testing: *Fear*
To have all belief systems, identities and worldviews eradicated, leaves one without the comfort of shelters or a frame of reference and creates fear.

Changes:
The seals of debris in the chakras start to burst open, causing at times physical distress in their areas. The chakras become spherical, instead of resembling a cone to the front and a cone to the back with the narrow ends meeting in the middle.

Challenges:
The Initiate has to learn not to take anything at face value but to cultivate the necessary humility that will remind him for the rest of his journey that all he can know for certain is that he doesn't know.

Phase 2 - The Adept

Type of Change: *Transmutation*

During transmutation something of a lower frequency is changed into another substance of a higher frequency, much like the alchemist changing lead to gold. In this instance, challenge is transmuted to insight.

Testing: *Addiction*

Every stage's second phase has the testing of addiction. In this phase the adept learns how to turn challenges into power by seeing behind the appearances of 'problems'. This results in power surges that create endocrine releases of hormones that can be very addictive. The adept can become addicted to challenge.

Changes:

As the adept learns to cooperate with the challenges of life, every challenge becomes a source of power and energy; this causes the spherical chakras to become enlarged and overlap each other more and more.

Challenge:

The adept can take himself too seriously at this point and so diverts his attention from chasing challenges to balancing the sub-personalities. It is essential to become emotionally self-reliant at this point by bringing balance and expression to our inner family. If we neglect this, it is unlikely that we will pass the testing of power presented during the next phase.

Phase 3 - The Master

Type of Change: *Transfiguration*

The third phase of every stage tests us with power. Because it is seeing whether we are worthy of the major evolutionary leap that occurs during transition from stage to stage; its testing is severe. Passing the test produces transfiguration of either the fields of the body or the body itself.

Testing: *Power*

The master's abilities become quite apparent at this point, bringing praise and in some instances, worship from others. The feeling of power can produce a sense of gratification that can divert the master from being a perception seeker to becoming a power seeker, in which case he cannot proceed any further on the path.

Changes:

Not only is the power the result of bringing order to the mind, but also of the chakra spheres growing so enlarged that they form one large unified chakra field around the body. A heartache or an orgasm or the opening of the crown chakra by a peak spiritual experience, is felt throughout the body.

Challenge:

At the very moment that our egos want to assert themselves, we must not waver for an instant from reaching beyond the allure of the magical world of the unknown, to the far distant horizon of the unknowable. Resisting the temptations to do miracles for show, we must keep our goal of increased perception firmly in mind. Not many truth seekers make it beyond this point.

Stage 2: God Consciousness

The previous stage believed the character we play on the stage of life to be real. This stage no longer identifies with the character. In fact, during the first two phases, we walk off the stage of life only to return for the third phase. But even as we again stay in character, we know without a doubt that we are just enacting a role.

Phase 1 - Emptiness

Type of Change: *Transformation*
Everything we thought we knew gets thrown out of the window. All we know is that we are no-thing. The usual emotions are gone as a result of the dramatic shift in perception as our minds become empty. Nothing in our lives makes sense anymore and a great disassociativeness is felt.

Testing: *Fear*
Although the testing in the first phase of every stage is fear, most ordinary, everyday fears were overcome during the previous stage. Now the very foundation upon which we have stood has been knocked out from underneath us. Not only do we at times feel terrified, but a vast loneliness grips us. We feel afraid when expanding too much, fearing we may lose our self-awareness just as we have lost our identities; afraid that our responsibilities won't be properly done. But something larger is running our lives and everything gets done without much forethought. We feel claustrophobic when we contract our awareness back into the body.

Changes:

The changes that take place during this entire stage affect the emotional body. During this phase the emotional body forms a large round ball, slightly larger than the luminous cocoon formed by the seven bodies of man under usual circumstances.

Challenge:

If enough fear is present, one can step out of God Consciousness and, because one didn't stay in long enough to enjoy the more blissful states that come later, be hesitant to try it again. This could then keep us locked into Identity Consciousness. It is helpful to have someone ahead on the path be able to say that the disassociativeness one is experiencing is appropriate to this rather bewildering phase.

Phase 2 - The Bliss

Type of Change: *Transmutation*

The realization that it isn't that we are no-thing but that we are all things transmutes the feeling of complete emptiness to the fullness of bliss. We feel everything as though it is inside us.

Testing: *Addiction*

The test is a difficult one, not only because of its intense addictive quality, but because most traditions teach that this is the end goal on the spiritual seeker's path. The years of disciplined living have to somehow penetrate the euphoria and remind us that there is no point of arrival.

Changes:

A strange phenomenon now takes place in the emotional field, reducing the physical energy, while creating a vastness of emotion. It is as though the desire of the cosmos has become one's own. The emotional body forms rope-like spikes radiating out from the physical body. When I first observed this in my own field, I thought that the shock of encountering the Infinite's vastness had shredded my emotional body. Only later did I realize that it was an appropriate part of the bliss phase.

Challenge:

There is very little growth during the first two phases of God Consciousness when one essentially walks off the stage of life. The master has no boundaries and is in a very vulnerable state. But because others around him are allowed to misbehave as they choose, they aren't growing either. The great challenge of this phase is to remember that there is value to the play; that it was designed that all may grow. The master has to re-enter the human drama while remembering it's just a play.

Phase 3 - Re-Entering the Human Condition

Type of Change: *Transfiguration*

The emotional body now expands itself to twice its former size, completely transfiguring the size of the bodies' luminous cocoon.

Testing: *Power*

As with all third phases, the testing concerns the impeccable use of power. The master has the ability to manifest whatever he or she wants to, but having spent many years gathering such power, must now forgo using it in most instances in favor of cooperating fully with life.

Changes:

The changes that occur during this phase create intense emotion. But even as the renewed emotions again churn the surface of the master's life, the vast stillness of expanded awareness lies beneath.

Challenge:

The tremendous power that is part of the master's life at this point demands the utmost respect and sensitivity for all lifeforms. It also requires the master's full cooperation in order to become a tool in providing learning opportunities for others. In other words, the master becomes a steward of all life.

The Seven Bodies of Man in God Consciousness

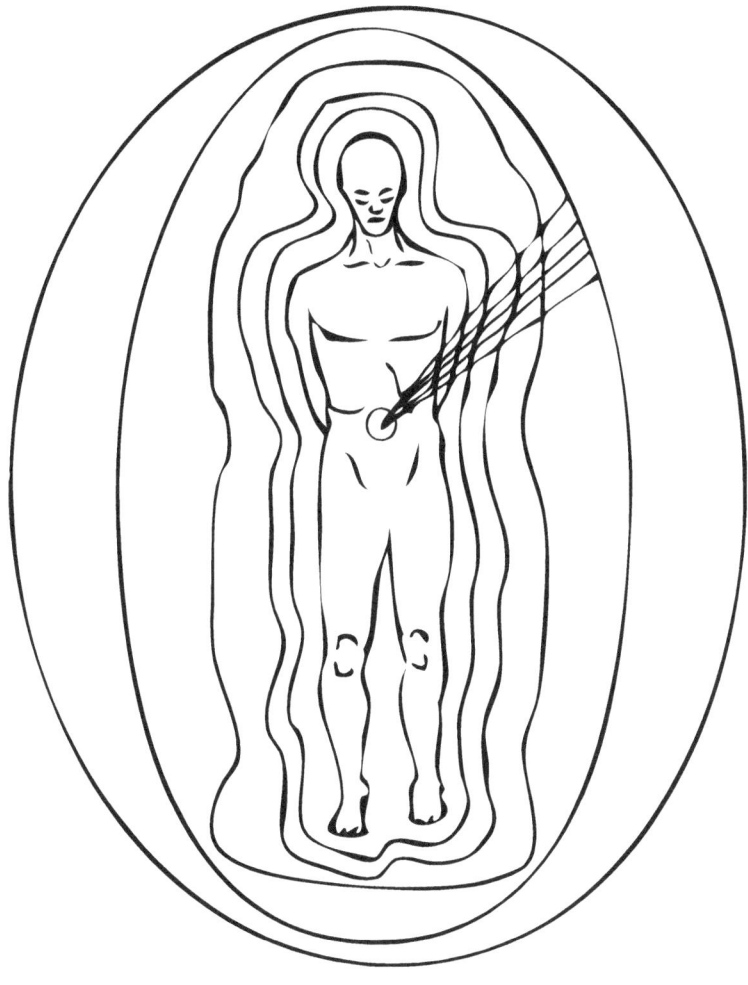

Phase 1

The emotional body enlarges and surrounds all other bodies.

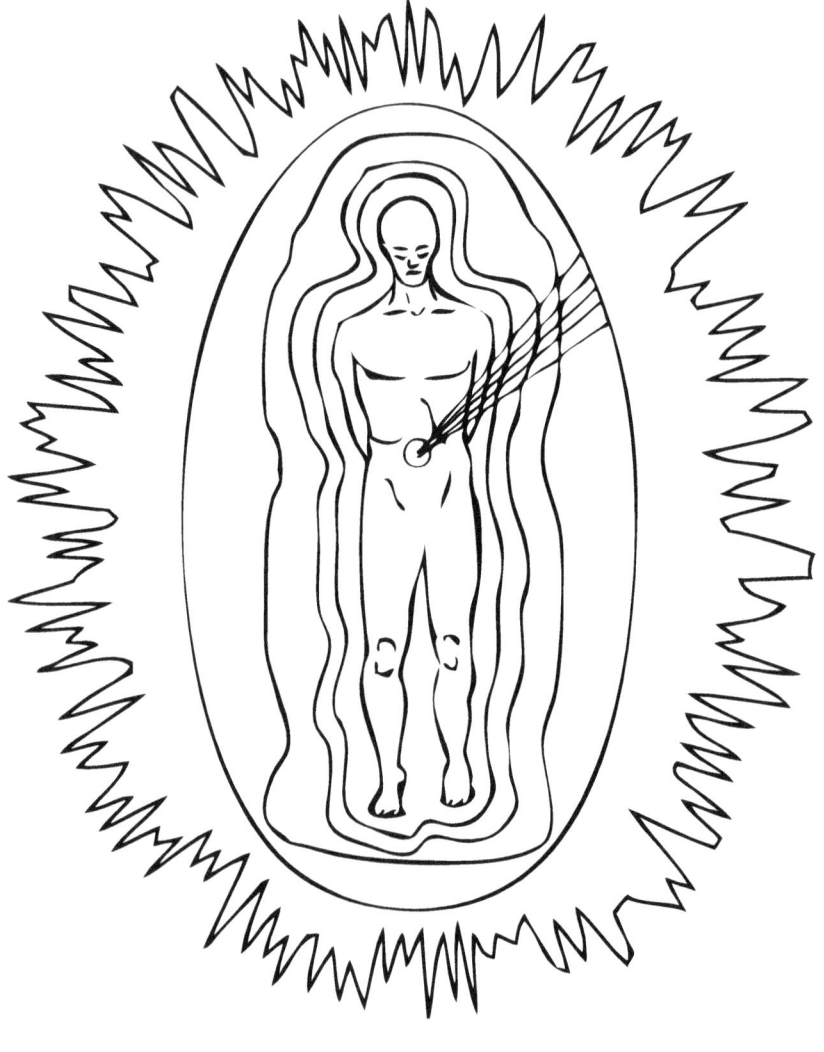

Phase 2

The emotional body becomes enlarged with spikes.

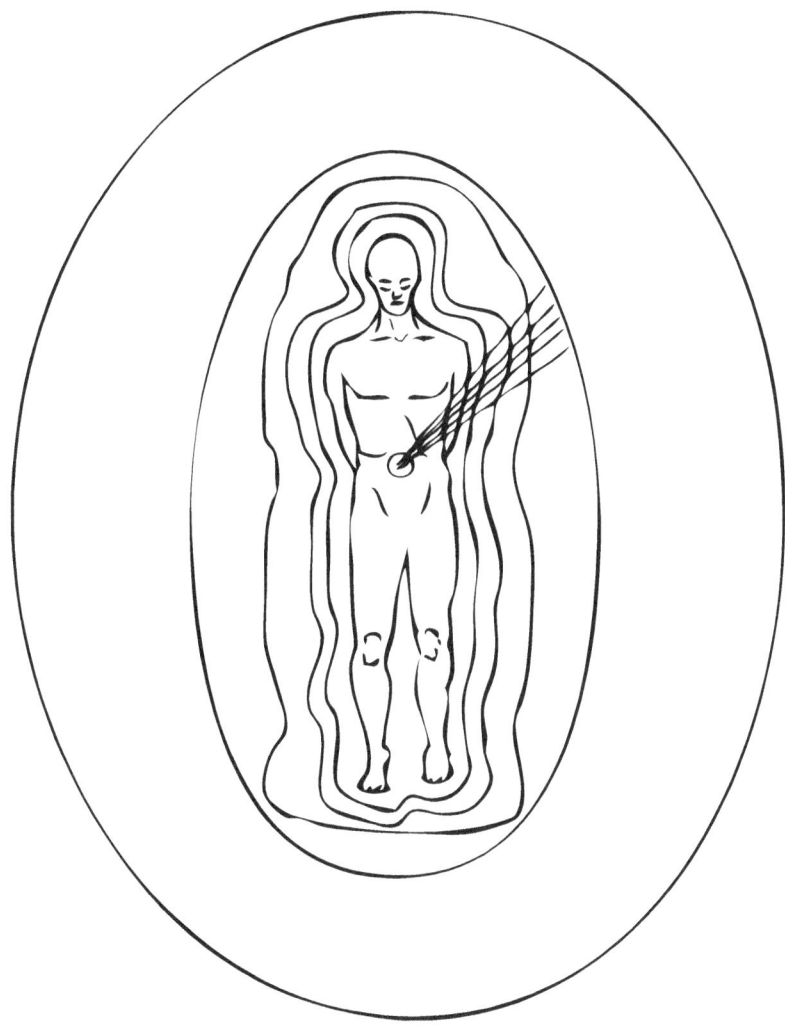

Phase 3

The emotional body becomes very enlarged.

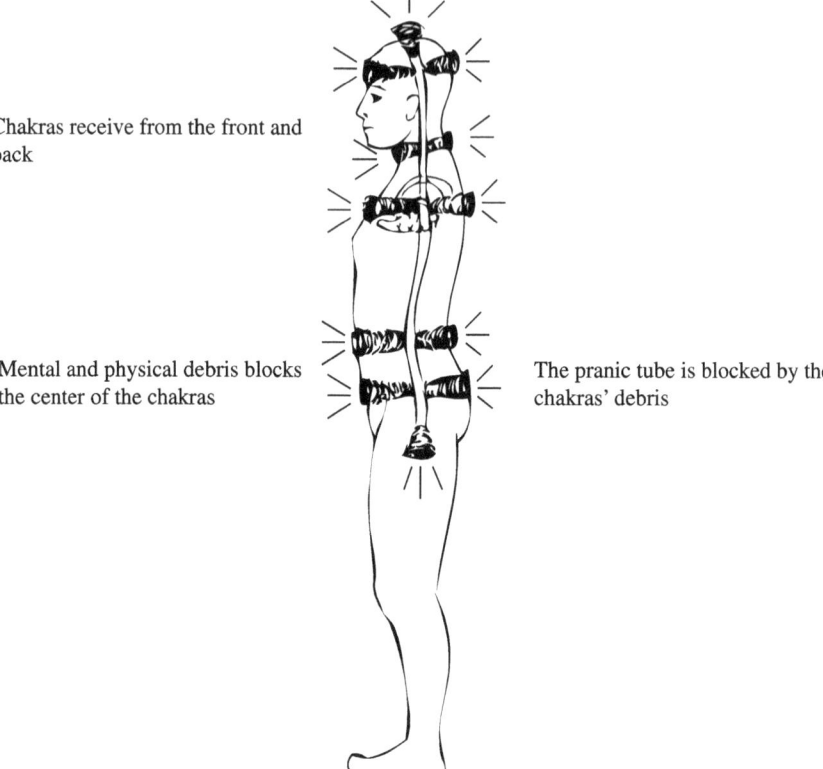

Phase 1 of Chakra Opening

Seven levels of light enter the chakras. The light cannot immediately download into the endocrine system because of the blockages of a person who hasn't overcome the past and holds onto that which no longer serves him. The light is assimilated during sleep.

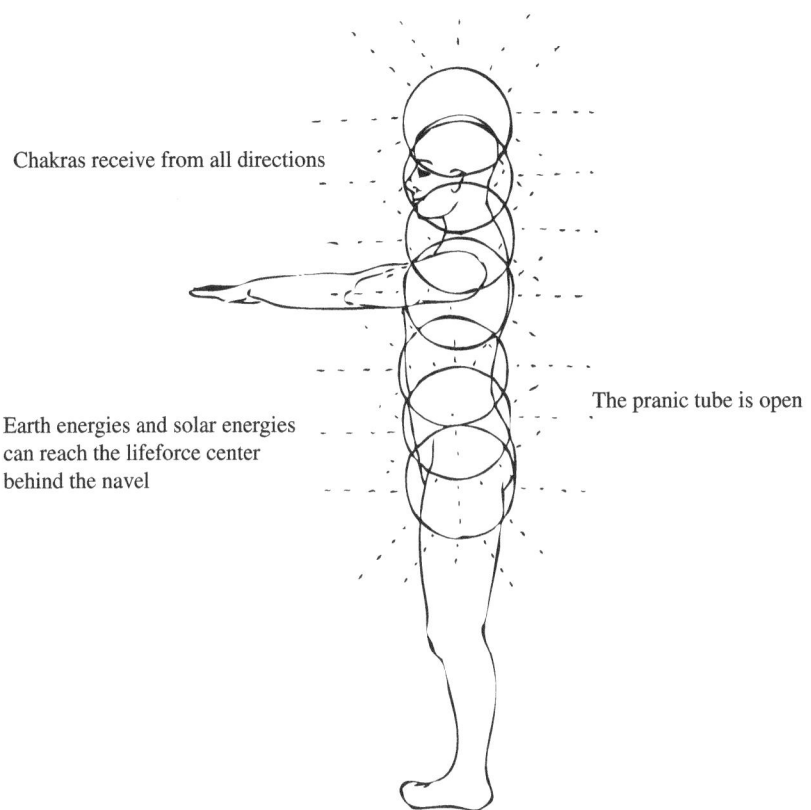

Phase 2 of Chakra Opening

Less sleep is needed while the endocrine system downloads the seven levels of light. Light is felt as non-cognitive information.

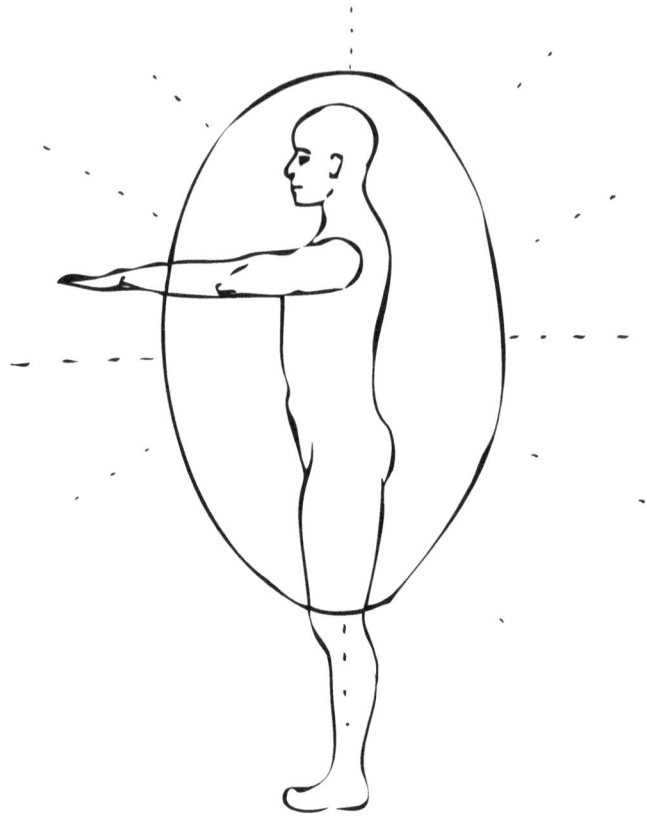

Phase 3 of Chakra Opening

The chakra spheres have opened into a unified chakra field. The mental body no longer blocks access to light from the higher bodies.

Stage 3: Ascended Mastery

The three stages themselves follow the roadmap of all change: Transformation, Transmutation, Transfiguration.

The stage of *Identity Consciousness* is in essence transformational in that it is the shedding of that which no longer serves, namely the ego.

The *God Consciousness* stage is transmutational in that it turns a form of awareness that learns very little from experience, into a combination that does. In its third phase the master observes his experiences from an eternal perspective while again enacting the human drama - it feels a lot like thinking with two minds at once.

The *Ascended Mastery* stage transfigures not only the fields of the body, as do the other two stages, but also the physical body itself. To transfigure something that dense is a tremendous accomplishment and the primary function of this stage is transfiguration.

Phase 1 - The Totally Silent Mind

Type of Change: *Transformational*

Previous God Consciousness phases had silence within the mind during any time the master did not have to relate or act. Now, even this form of inner dialog is discarded. Interaction, writing and speaking are done from a place of complete silence as though being on 'auto-pilot'. The silence is only broken occasionally to do something deductive.

Testing: *Fear*

It takes a lot of trust to have your mouth speak that which you didn't first think of. If anything is done from a place of old, obsolete programming, everything starts to spin. One is physically incapable of doing something that isn't meant to be. The overall fear is that life is completely out of control and it is - out of the control of the egoic self. But the vast cosmic mind governs our lives at this point.

Changes:

Because of the transfigurative qualities of this entire stage, every phase has very dramatic changes, all of them pertaining to the mental or linear bodies of man. In this phase the mental body implodes into a pinpoint of light, pulling the emotional body with it. It then explodes and fuses with the etheric body. The emotional body becomes smaller and denser.

Challenge:

The vestiges of a desire for a personal life have to be laid aside at this point. The master can and must make sure that his life has joy and balance in it. His life affects too much to have it be anything less. But his life's work is pre-determined by his contract with the Infinite. To a certain extent, he can determine how he wishes the work to unfold, but he cannot deviate from his purpose. He cannot allow the total inner silence to seduce him into inaction.

Phase 2 - Immortality

Type of Change: *Transmutation*

This is the incredible phase in which mortal matter is transmuted into immortal matter - 'lead is turned into gold'. The whole event takes but minutes to complete and feels like a lightning flash throughout the body.

Testing: *Addiction*

The bliss that follows this transmutation far exceeds what was experienced before. Within the body of the Immortal Master, the energy lines zig-zag through the areas where the chakras used to be localized. In women they criss-cross from side to side and in men from front to back. They end in the area above the pineal gland, about four inches apart, and excrete a substance that is the hormone for this level of bliss (also called the life hormone). It can be tasted as a sweet substance in the back of the palate during intense bliss. Once again, addiction becomes the challenge.

Changes:

The Immortal Mastery phase culminates in yet another spectacular alteration in the bodies of man. The spiritual mental body implodes to a pinprick of light and when it explodes, merges with the combined mental/etheric bodies and carries them outward, forming a large sphere around the body. The emotional bodies fill the sphere and the spirit body's light-fibers radiate out from the life-force center through the sphere.

Challenge:

The unseen realms present an alluring detour during the third phase of Identity Consciousness. Yet now they become a way of life. They are no longer seen by the master to be outside of himself, so no longer present an enticement in the former way. But beings from the various unseen kingdoms we dwell amongst are attracted to the master's light and enter his life. The master has to learn to know the many different idiosyncrasies of dealing with the various beings around him so that he can further refine his ability to benefit all life. This helps him resist the temptation of inactivity induced by bliss.

Phase 3 - Life More Abundant

Type of Change: *Transfiguration*
The change that occurs with this transfiguration is the apex of human achievement; it creates an evolutionary leap that only 9 Ascended Masters had made up until August 2005. When fully transfigured, the master exits the human kingdom and enters the God-Kingdom.

Testing: *Power*
We can surmise by looking at the previous third phases of the other two stages that this stage's third phase also has something to do with power. The challenge here is to accumulate, harness and conserve enough power to shatter the glass-like shield that separates kingdoms. The master has to overcome the huge temptation of over-polarizing into the light; into the seasonless place of no emotion and great peace -- the place of ultimate stagnation and inaction.

Changes:
The life-force center explodes during this phase, forming a large ball of life-force, slightly larger than the sphere of mental bodies. The spirit body's light fibers cluster into one rope extending from the assemblage point behind the shoulder blades, to the zero point portal that has formed behind the belly-button.

Challenge:
Ascended Masters have great perception. The greater our perception, the greater our emotions have to be. When emotions aren't recognized and utilized as the growth mechanisms they are,

these very large emotions can be deliberately disconnected in order to experience the peace of the bliss that plays through every cell at this point. But it is the power of emotion that will crack the 'glass' shield the master has to go through to get to the next kingdom. All chakras must be participating in creating this emotional response.

Most Ascended Masters live only in the upper chakras. It becomes necessary to re-awaken the lower chakras, re-activate the sex drive and use it to arouse the other emotions. With the power of emotion, the shield shatters and the zero point opening explodes to fill all the fields. The fields around the body explode to double their size. The chord of light fibers now elongates and loops from the assemblage point on the outside edge of the fields to the heart center and back again to the assemblage point. The master has become a god-being in the flesh.

The Seven Bodies of Man in Ascended Mastery

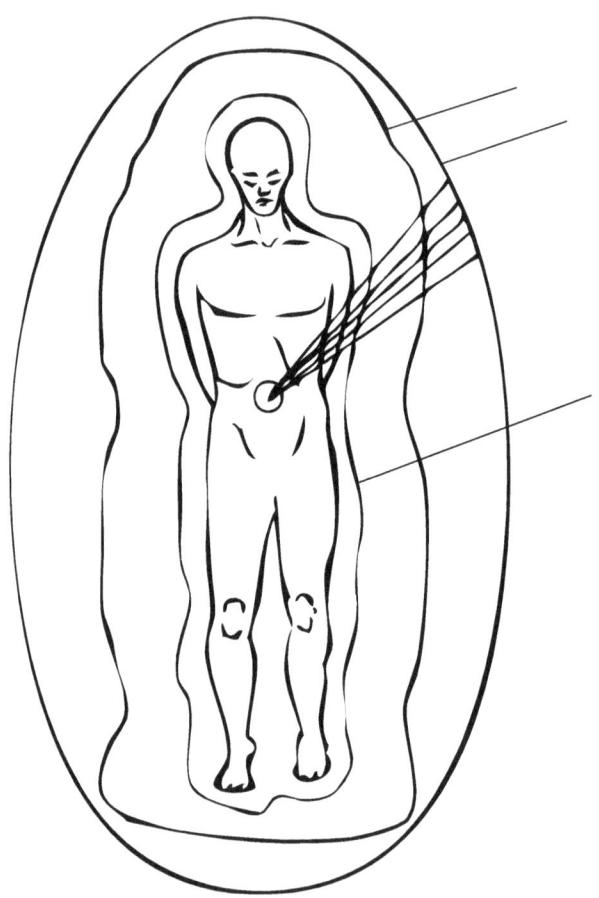

Phase 1

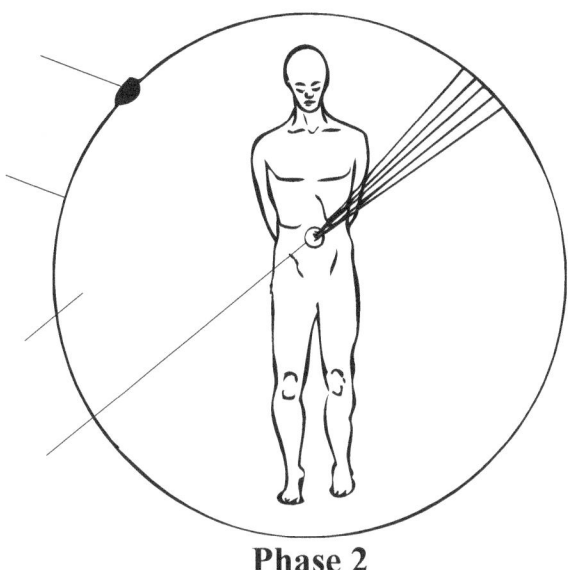

Phase 2

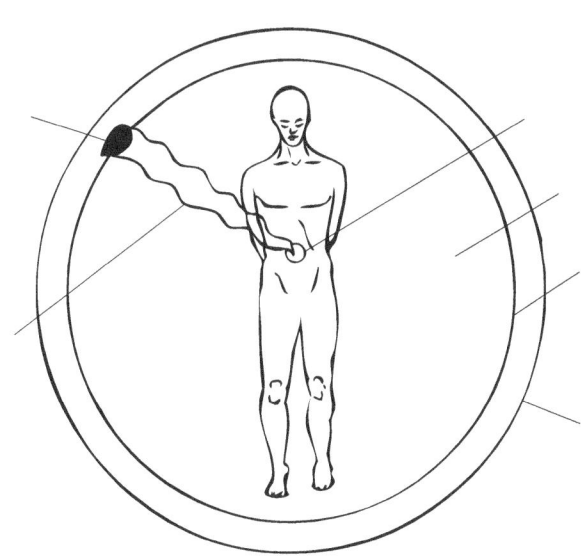

Phase 3

Hormonal Excretions that Hold the Higher Bliss

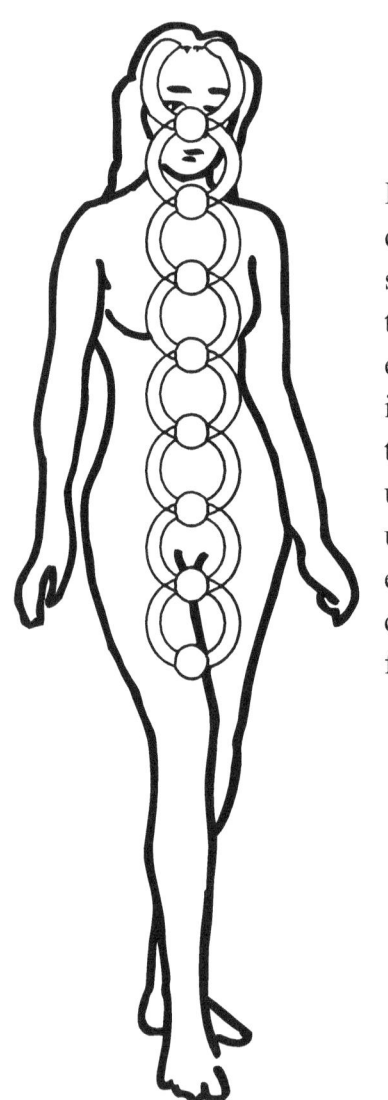

In the Immortal Master the alpha chakra (a hand length below the spine) and the second heart (on the sternum) are fully opened. The energy meridians move (sideways in women, front to back in men) through the centers where the chakras used to be before they formed a unified chakra field. The meridians end slightly above the pineal gland, causing it to excrete life hormones for heightened bliss and immortality.

Within the God-Kingdom

A large leap of consciousness awaits man if he wishes to go beyond human boundaries. As we have seen, only 9 made it across this boundary before 2005.[6]

Unlike the 3 stages within the human kingdom, the God-Kingdom has two levels. It is essential that more and more humans enter the God-kingdom, as did Christ, Buddha, Krishna, Quan Yin and Sunat Kumara among others, because it is their destiny to change the inactivity found there. Humans are accustomed to struggle, and a great struggle awaits in the God-Kingdom to avoid succumbing to the inactivity and lack of growth in that realm. The struggle is against the huge enticement of bliss. Although we encounter bliss as a testing within the human stages, the bliss of this higher stage is eight times stronger. It becomes difficult to move even a limb and activity tends to slow almost to a standstill.

During the first phase of the God-Kingdom, the fields around the body are very enlarged. The small zero point opening found behind the belly-button of an Ascended Master explodes as the transition to the God-Kingdom is made. The zero point enlarges to fill the entire mental body, pushing the emotional body outside of the mental body.

The mental body (the sum total of all the mental bodies initially found in man, fused into one) starts to rotate. The chord of light fibers loops from the assemblage point through the heart and back again. During this phase emotions are felt much more intensely.

One of the main reasons the vast majority of Ascended Masters never enter here is because it requires pulsing the emotions between their positive and negative poles, fueled by sexuality, to break the glass-like membrane between the kingdoms — something shunned by Ascended Masters until recently.

---

6   See *Secrets of the Hidden Realms.*

The 7 Bodies of Man in the God Kingdom

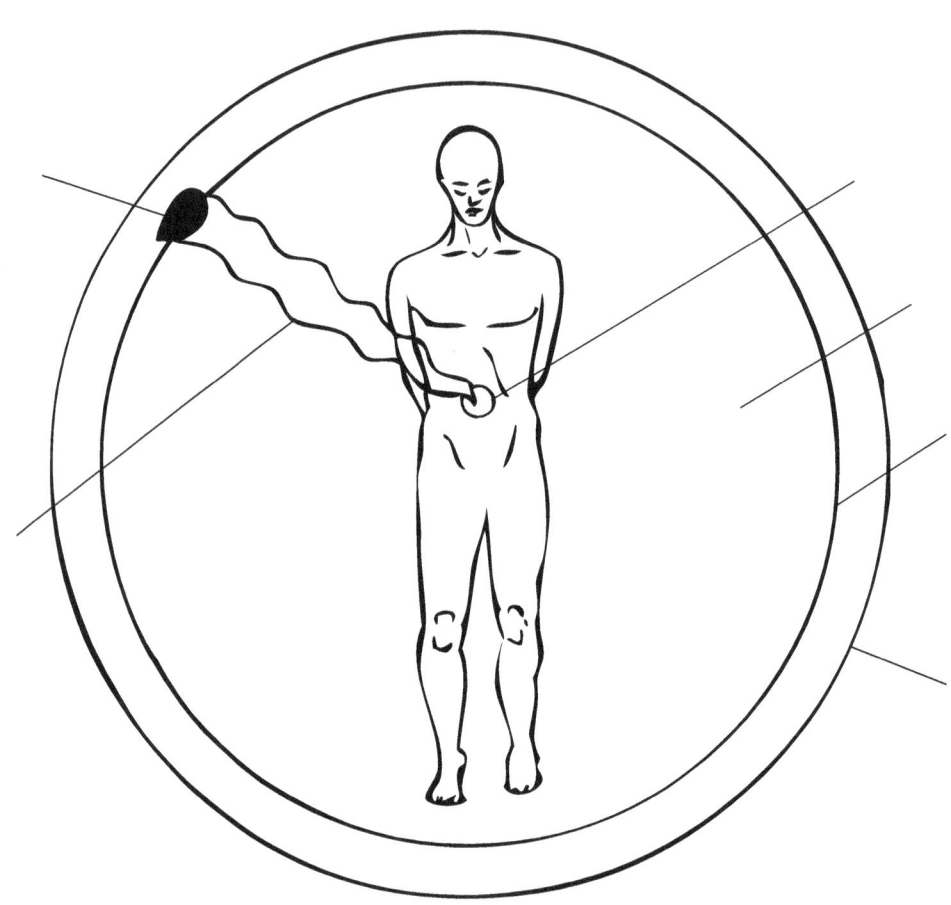

Secrets of Transfiguration

Stages In The Evolution Of Awareness

In ancient Egypt there were specific temples to guide truth seekers dedicated to the spiritual path through the stages of the evolution of awareness. They were built in a logarithmic spiral, culminating in the place where man might transcend the stages altogether and move into the next level of being, the God-kingdom. This event that lay even beyond ascension took place in the great pyramid of Giza.

The stages of man have never varied. They are part of our human condition and truth seekers today face the same testings and initiations man has always faced.

Stage 1: Ego-Identification

Phase 1. The Initiate (Transformation)

In the initiate's phase, there is an emptying out of old beliefs and ideas. The student becomes aware of the old programming that has shaped his reality. He starts to loosen the grip of social conditioning and becomes aware of his identities he has so relied on. In this phase, the initiate begins to acquaint himself with tools used for discernment and learns which to use for the known and for the unknown.

The result of these increased insights and new skills is that the mind achieves more order. The more the mind is trained and the more the prison bars of old belief systems dissolve, the more energy becomes available. Everything the initiate has taken for granted is now questioned. The greater the realization that he knows nothing for certain, the greater are his chances of success upon the path to ascension. Spiritual growth accelerates during this phase and old relationships will either start to reject him or he will start to shed them as no longer relevant to his life.

The testing of this phase comes when fear arises as the old, safe parameters of his world disappear. It is disconcerting to find life's foundations, like a belief in good and evil, dissolve before one's eyes. Finding most of what he held onto so tightly to be illusion will either send the initiate scampering fearfully back to his prison cell, or help him take a leap of faith over the edge of the cliff into the unknown.

Phase 2. The Adept (Transmutation)

The adept is beginning to become quite proficient at wielding the tools of awareness. He is aware of how limited his knowledge is, and as a result, other realities begin to open.

He starts to see symbolically, no longer taking his world at face value, and becomes literate at reading the signs in his environment. The world becomes his teacher as it speaks to him.

One of the key insights of this phase is the loss of feeling victimized. The adept sees instead how he has co-created each event to help him fulfill his destiny. Challenges become welcome sources of insight, which in turn yield power. There is a greater feeling of stability in this phase as the rewards are more immediate and discernable.

The power surges that accompany the insights his new-found tools help him extract from challenges can be exhilarating. No longer does he shun these sources of power the way the rest of the world does, but instead welcomes them. The larger the challenges, the greater the rewards, until he can feel himself grow more and more powerful.

The surges of power he now regularly experiences release physical excretions within the endocrine system, triggering feelings much like the thrill the gambler gets. His testing now comes as he finds himself becoming addicted to the thrill of challenge.

To help prevent this pitfall from snaring him and stopping his progression, he must now change his focus to balancing the sub-personalities within. The balancing of the sub-personalities is not only the task of the adept, it is also his salvation. As he works diligently on parenting his inner child and learning about his inner nurturer, for instance, it takes his mind off the pursuit of challenge and helps him take himself less seriously.

Phase 3. The Master (Transfiguration)

The master has a formidable task to accomplish. As this is the last phase remaining in identity consciousness (ego-identification), he must gather enough power and energy to make the big leap of entirely disconnecting from ego and enter into God-consciousness.

The training of this phase emphasizes the streamlining of the master's life. The conservation of energy is essential and must become a part of life. All initial energy is used up by a disorganized left brain. Only the surplus is available to the right brain to access the unknown. At this point the master's mind must become so organized that energy is freely available to access more and more of the unseen realms.

The unseen world, once accessed, can be very seductive. It is valuable as a tool to loosen the iron grip of the rational mind, but it can also become a pitfall in two ways:
- The lure of this vast unseen reality can easily divert the master's attention from where his real supply of power lies – his everyday challenges and relationships. Instead of building his power supply for the task ahead, he could become more and more aloof and

arrogant as his reality takes on vast dimensions beyond those of his fellow man. He could withdraw from everyday life, stifling his spiritual growth even as his abilities increase.
- When someone becomes aware of the unseen worlds, the unseen worlds also become aware of him. Entities of all types (some call themselves guides) are attracted to the master and offer their skills to assist him. The more the master focuses on them, the more his energy is given to them. The ease with which they can materialize objects or see the future or other people's lives prevents the master from developing those skills himself. Particularly if the sub-personalities were not 'hooked up' in the previous stage, the inner child's need for recognition will come to lure the master into using his allies to gain recognition and applause from others. At the very moment when the master should be free from identity, a new one (such as master, shaman, saint, etc.) arises and he is unable to proceed to God-consciousness.

It is during this phase that the purpose with which the student embarked on this path makes a very large difference. If his purpose was power, this is the end of his spiritual progress. If his purpose was to seek perception, he has a good chance of slipping past the lure of power as long as he keeps his eyes firmly and unwaveringly on his goal. Tempted by power and learning to conserve energy, the master prepares for the large leap of entirely disconnecting from identifying with the limited self – the stage of God-consciousness in which he is called a seer.

As the time approaches for this momentous event that occurs in a moment, the master feels more and more disconnected. He views his life and actions as though from a distance and his perception becomes more objective. Value judgments of what is desirable and what is not fall away.

Stage 2: God-Consciousness

Phase 1. The Emptiness (Transformation)

As in the first phase of ego-identification, this is the phase of emptying out. But unlike the initiate's phase, it happens suddenly and without conscious effort. The seer in this first phase knows he is no-thing, emptied of thoughts and most common emotions except for an overwhelming loneliness that recognizes that there is no being besides himself in existence.

At times he is as vast as the cosmos and at other times he crashes back into the body and feels claustrophobic at the confinement. The fear that he may not find his body at all is strong during the first few weeks. Although he has lost identity, he must retain self-awareness or he will plunge into insanity. As it is, in the absence of the inner dialogue he feels as though he has lost his mind (and he has – his surface mind).

For one who has had concussion, the feeling is very similar. Information does not imprint. In other words, one cannot retain what one decided half an hour ago and so one either has to write everything down or keep making the same decision over and over again.

Linear time is meaningless. Physical activity slows down enormously. If life would allow it, the seer in this phase would just sit. It's too much effort to talk and interact. Physical energy is very low as he learns to traverse inner space instead.

Because the stages differ from each other only in that they are one spiral up in awareness, their three phases exhibit similar qualities. As in the first phase of ego-identification, the first phase within God-consciousness has as its testing, fear. Some enter into this phase but because they fear their duties won't be done (which is not the case-even though their old way of thinking no longer exists, duties are done without thought when they should be), they retreat. Fear at relinquishing mind or that the feeling of disassociation is somehow a step in the wrong direction can have the same effect.

If the seer can stay in this state for more than a few weeks, it becomes a way of life. The concern of loved ones who interpret the symptoms of this phase as depression must be avoided. A month of interacting as sparingly as possible with others would help.

Phase 2. The Bliss (Transmutation)

Just as surely as the seer knew that he is no-thing in the previous phase, just as surely does he now know that he is all things in this phase. It happens suddenly and begins as a blissful sensation in the cells. As one walks, it feels as though everything moves through one. Laughter diminished greatly during the first phase, but now it feels as though laughter is bubbling through the cells. The sex drive is virtually non-existent, since one cannot desire something one knows already to be part of oneself.

Just like the second phase of ego-identification, addiction is again the challenge here. At this higher level, however, few ever leave this phase. The world is accustomed to someone being 'in bliss' and frequently devotees support the physical needs of the seer at this point. To the onlooker it appears as though the master has 'arrived' and this phase seems much holier than the next one.

Although the seer in his bliss cares little for what others think, the devotees' care of him doesn't assist in awakening the desire to leave this intoxicating state. The seer has no boundaries and only allows. This leaves him wide open to others who promote his dependency on them in order to feel needed and feed their own egos. The seer will be able to see their motives clearly but, like a benign parent that laughs at a child's folly, will indulge them.

The formidable temptation the bliss presents cannot be stressed enough. Even with years of training to know there is no point of arrival, the bliss is inclined to drive the training out of one's head. During this and the previous phase, the seer withdraws from the opposition human experiences present. As a result, all growth stops since friction is necessary for progress.

Time lies around one like a spider web as linear time continues to be meaningless. The seer can see alternate futures like points on the web – the most likely future has the most threads through it. But because time lies in all directions, there is little difference between the future and the past.

Phase 3. Re-Entering the Human Condition (Transfiguration)

Like a glimmer here and there, the memory stirs through the bliss reminding that there is something more; that if the seer stays in the bliss, the power he has accumulated with such effort throughout his life will sift through his fingers like sand.

As in the previous cycle's third phase, the accumulation of power in this phase is absolutely crucial to make the transition to the third and final stage of human development – Ascended Mastery. The rungs of the ladder are not evenly spaced. Breaching the gap between the three stages takes an enormous amount of energy to achieve.

The only way to accumulate power without damaging oneself or the web of existence is through gaining more perception. The seer has to re-engage in human interaction to gain the insights. If he does not, he stays polarized in the light (the known) when all new insight comes from delving into the unknown (dark).

It takes great humility and dedication to the path to leave the obvious mastery (which others recognize and support) of the bliss and blunder back into the human drama, seemingly as foolish as everyone else. But one cannot re-enter the womb any more than an adult body can become that of a child again. Thus even as we once again laugh our laughter and cry our tears, underneath the surface the vast stillness remains.

The seer, new to the human drama from the vastness of this level of perception, in fact blunders more than most. To many it may seem as though their master had feet of clay after all. True to the co-dependent triangle of most people's affections (leg one = I adore, leg two = I control, leg three = I find you to have feet of clay), their attitude becomes one of 'if you don't let me control you or you step out of the box of expectations I erected around you, I reject you'.

Three minds work simultaneously towards the end of this phase: the surface mind, the 4th dimensional higher mind and the vast highest mind. If someone asks a question, three answers from all three minds' perspectives present themselves. The answer the seer gives will be gauged to the level of the recipient's ability to understand.

The way in which power tests a masterful seer at this level has seldom been revealed since few make it this far and fewer still speak about it. Circumstances respond to the seer's intent at this point. If a parking space isn't available, he can manifest circumstances that will produce one. In this way he can create less opposition in his life, but with it, less growth and accumulated power.

To his great amusement, the seer discovers that having gained enough power to change the circumstances of his life, he is unable to do so. Instead, he has become fully co-operative with life. If he has to park his car several blocks away from his destination, he does so and finds there a homeless person whom he knows he has a contract to assist.

What the seer does create at this point, however, are situations to give others the opportunity to grow. It happens effortlessly and without attachment to outcome. The seer sees the flaw, creates a 'space of expectation' in his mind (like a mold the universe rushes to fill), and the opportunity arises for the student to look his own flaw in the face.

Stage 3: Ascended Mastery

Phase 1. Original Thinking (Transformation)

The vast change of entering into the stage of Ascended Mastery is accompanied by the same profound visionary experiences that occur with entry into God-consciousness. It feels as though one is melting into the heart of God.

As in both previous stages' first phases, this phase is one of emptying out. The silence within the mind during God-consciousness is broken when one has to speak or write, for instance. Now, however, even that is done without conscious thought and from a place of complete silence.

It is as though the Ascended Master is on 'auto-pilot' and any action that isn't meant to be is simply impossible to take; the hand will not dial the phone number or pick up the pen even if the reason why isn't yet clear. If there is any resistance, dishonesty or agenda, a swirling sensation takes place as though one is in a vortex of confusion.

Because surface mind is seldom used, there is a great deal of energy at one's disposal. In fact, if one refrains from reading or any activity that needs the deduction of surface mind, one can go days without sleep. Anesthetics no longer work as they block the surface mind and one doesn't often use that mind in everyday life.

The source of genius that some are privileged to feel on occasions or in a particular field is the Ascended Master's constant companion. The mind is almost totally silent but the answer to any question is immediately there. The answers require an existing vocabulary to understand, but if one can understand the question, the answer will be given.

The miracles during this phase increase dramatically, but if they are not on the Ascended Master's path to demonstrate, they will not be done in front of others.

Phase 2. Immortality (Transmutation)

This experience of a lifetime feels as though the cells 'pop' like popcorn while the body feels on fire and tingles all over. The luminous cocoon around the body doubles in size. Symptoms leading up to this experience include:
- Pressure in the back of the head where the process seems to begin;
- Light-headedness and spatial disorientation. This includes the feeling of the head 'opening' at the crown;
- Anesthetics don't work. Local anesthetics require quadruple dosages but immediately wear off (like dental injections);
- Pain is experienced differently – more like an unpleasant pressure;
- Everyone seems to be in slow motion, their thoughts disorganized and slow;
- There is the premonition that life is about to change forever.

After the event, beings of all descriptions congregate around the Immortal Master and for those who perceive energy directly, the light around the body is so dense that the features are hardly discernable. The ability to become immortal is rare among species and noteworthy enough that many unseen hands come to touch one's face.

As in the previous two stages' second phases, there is an addictive quality that must be overcome before moving on. The energy lines that twine through the chakras (in women they go sideways and in men back to front) create an endocrine secretion in the brain that generates intense bliss, less diffuse and more orgasmic than the previous stages' bliss. A sweet-tasting fluid is excreted in the back of the throat. The enticement is to totally surrender to the bliss and withdraw from human interaction.

Phase 3. Ascended Mastery (Transfiguration)

The expansion in this phase becomes intoxicating. One feels as though drugged and loses most motivation. Emotions are virtually non-existent, but are the key to leaving the human kingdom for the God-kingdom. In this expanded state, if one doesn't encourage emotions in oneself, loss of power occurs.

The 20 Primary Systems of the Body

Sigils and Angels 14 - 33

These 20 sigils also help balance the amino acids of the body.

14. **Clary Sage**

Prihurusut-arske　　**Akra-brivasut**

Angel:　　Angel:

Kliraprat-anestu　　**Salva-nechspri**

Lymphatic system

Incantation: *Mistech mishet anenas*

Physical Benefits
Anti-diabetic
May assist with reducing high cholesterol
Supports hormone balance
May assist with PMS and menopause

Emotional Benefits
Very calming and relieves stress

Spiritual Benefits
Allows resolution of past life issues

15. Clove

Krihurasetvi-arskana

Nanusech-bivarut

Angel:
Kret-harsparu

Angel:

Spetlha-prabasur

Endocrine system

Incantation: *Etre pluhavit brishet bavi*

Note: Skin test for sensitivity.

Physical Benefits
Highly antiseptic and anti-microbial
Speeds healing of mouth and skin sores
Supports thyroid function
Numbing of gums when applied topically
Anti-parasitic

Emotional Benefits
Mentally stimulating
Awakens passion for the adventure of life

Spiritual Benefits
Self-empowering, allows the obsolete to fall away

16. Coriander

Arknasut-huras

Kiset-uklavesvi

Angel:

Pliplarut-servevu

Angel:

Nechtranadok-uspeva

Integumentary system (skin)

Incantation: *Nuskalavech hespa uhunis*

Note: Use in small doses – it can be mentally overwhelming in large doses.

Physical Benefits
Supports pancreatic function and sugar regulation
May alleviate menstrual cramps
Provides relief from gout and rheumatic pain
Sedative properties

Emotional Benefits
Soothing and calming

Spiritual Benefits
Helps release sentimental attachments (cords of the heart)
Increases receptivity to inner guidance

17. Cypress

Kusanar-arestu

Nikset-esetra

Angel:
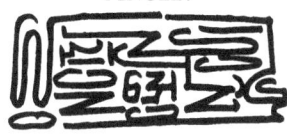
Archverevar-sarestu

Angel:

Vrives-elestru

Digestive system

Incantation: *Triba estevit ka-ahurat*

Physical Benefits
One of the primary essential oils used to support the circulatory system: Massage with long strokes towards the center of the body and apply to the armpits.

Emotional Benefits
Assists in releasing pent up self-expression that causes asthma
Assists in promoting grateful acknowledgment

Spiritual Benefits
Creates the frequency of abundant supply
Assists with grounding and promotes feelings of security and contentment

18. Davana

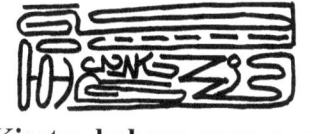

Kisetre-bahara-varsvaset

Basarut-michparu

ANGEL:

Arch-arnut-hurskla

ANGEL:

Naset-esetklavi

Absorption system

Incantation: *Esplek bisbaranut hespakla*

Physical Benefits
Skin softener
Hormonal balance
Strengthens the endocrine system

Emotional Benefits
Promotes emotional sovereignty

Spiritual Benefits
Assists with creating spiritual poise and grace

19. Dill

Sakavat-usuvi-varsna

Nuktaruk-brivabach

Angel:
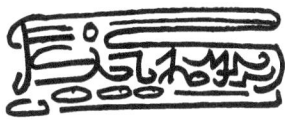
Pirtranut-areska

Angel:

Asarat-pribahur

Elimination system

Incantation: *Nechtu erserut bilechva*

Physical Benefits
May support pancreatic function and blood sugar regulation
Promotes proper milk production for nursing mothers
May alleviate constipation – rub on abdomen or the soles of the feet

Emotional Benefits
Eases muscle tension and anxiety
Aids in recognition of life's blessings

Spiritual Benefits
Opens up the use of dormant potential and suppressed expression

20. Elemi

Parsana-hevesbi

Kliharanesvi-ubrasut

ANGEL:

ANGEL:

Marchna-subetvi

Asanach-vistrevi

Immune system

Incantation: *Aratu viresva uhura nesvrata*

Physical Benefits
Antiseptic for uses on wounds and cuts
Skin care - rejuvenating and softening

Emotional Benefits
Strengthening for nerves and supports emotional resilience

Spiritual Benefits
Creates a 'sacred space' for the psyche wherever we may be
Promotes expanded awareness

21. Eucalyptus Globulus

Karasach-havesbi

Esba-stuvechvi

ANGEL:

Unes-kleveves-husbi

ANGEL:

Krihat-nisatrut

Respiratory system

Incantation: *Aruk paravit nanastu*

Note: Do not take internally.

Physical Benefits
Powerful antiseptic
Antibacterial aerosol
Insecticide

Emotional Benefits
Promotes well-being and purification

Spiritual Benefits
Directs attention from negative and illusory to the positive

22. Eucalyptus Polybractea

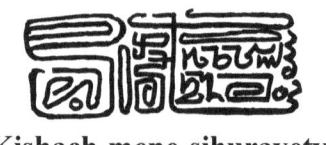
Kishach-mene-sihuravetvi

Niktra-brevablut

Angel:

Neksarut-plivavech

Angel:
Miset-asakla

Visual system

Incantation: *Pelechpra spivabut ereksta*

Note: Do not take internally.

Physical Benefits
Acne
Urinary infections
Insect repellant

Emotional Benefits
Inner strength

Spiritual Benefits
Clarity of choices

23. Eucalyptus Citriodora

Nanarech-parek-hersava   **Kribahur-neselvavi**

ANGEL: ANGEL:

Nesalvi-arskava   **Nach-berevach**

Auditory system

Incantation: *Nuspahur esachve krehet preva*

Note: Do not take internally.

Physical Benefits
Analgesic for sore or sprained muscles
Antiseptic, antibacterial and anti-viral
Insecticide

Emotional Benefits
Clearing mental and emotional confusion

Spiritual Benefits
Clarity of choices and consequences

24. Eucalyptus Radiata

Neneska-huseta

Angel:

Blavabur-nekpares

Ketre-mispahur

Angel:

Viset-asanut

Olfactory system (smell)

Incantation: *Nekva ersta bich prave*

Note: Do not take internally.

Physical Benefits
May help with ear inflammation
Respiratory infections
Sinus congestion - use in diffuser or rub on soles of the feet

Emotional Benefits
Assists in supporting change

Spiritual Benefits
Assists in transitions – also used to anoint the dying

25. Fennel

Kasahur-nakpavi

Angel:

Rukperehut-uras

Gustatory system (taste)

Incantation: *Arsana pruhit erekpartu*

Note: Do not use if epileptic.

Physical Benefits
Expels worms
Used to facilitate birthing with ease
Increases lactation
Stimulates cardiovascular system

Emotional Benefits
Enriches the inner life

Spiritual Benefits
Releases memories of trauma held in the tissues, releasing obsolete patterns

26. Fir

Klubarut-arskla **Haraklat-petruvar**

Angel: Angel:

Mesut-haresta **Nirek-parasur**

Central Nervous system and Spinal Cord

Incantation: *Meset arspata meskavich*

Physical Benefits
Respiratory ailments
Muscular and rheumatic conditions
Antiseptic aerosol

Emotional Benefits
Relaxes the body and eliminates the stress of linear time, releasing the power of the moment

Spiritual Benefits
Creates the expansiveness of a deep meditative state

27. Fleabane

Klusaret-mesta **Arsbavravanur**

ANGEL: ANGEL:

Arkpa-klevaset **Nitrananur-subavi**

Sympathetic and Parasympathetic Nervous system

Incantation: *Arksalana brispravet uklech*

Physical Benefits
Liver stimulant
May treat delayed puberty
Cardiovascular dilator

Emotional Benefits
For contact with the hidden realms

Spiritual Benefits
Creates timeless perspectives

28. Frankincense

Karsut-arak-parvi

Kabarut-mishprahur

ANGEL:

ANGEL:

Nuchbaret-ararus

Sihet-alasklar

Brain and Brain Stem

Incantation: *Rekpatu raskru-avet plivach*

Physical Benefits
Anti-tumor properties
Stimulates the immune system
Anti-depressant
Balances hormones

Emotional Benefits
Elevates capacity for increased awareness
Supports higher frequency and changes perception

Spiritual Benefits
Used in initiations – stimulates higher mind
Strengthens spiritual growth

29. Freesia

Neksalavut-hurastut

Archnatur-brivahur

Angel:

Prihes-arsata

Angel:

Rekstabrihat-menenech

Cardiovascular system

Incantation: *Stubit erek arechtuva*

Note: Use in a diffuser only, not topically.

Physical Benefits
Stimulates the release of human growth hormone

Emotional Benefits
Assists with healing from grief

Spiritual Benefits
Establishes angelic communications and connections

30. Galbanum

Nenuch-plibarut　　**Asanenenuch-privabar**

ANGEL:　　　　　　　　ANGEL:

Aratu-minavech　　**Eret-klevasur**

Organs and Soft Tissue

Incantation: *Rusatvi mishet arekstrava*

Physical Benefits
Kidney support
Aids in rectifying genital malfunction

Emotional Benefits
Enhances meditative states and inner harmony

Spiritual Benefits
Opens the crown chakra

31. Geranium

Virarusva-nechpi   Arkpa-pretvanur

Angel: Angel:

Harasat-ninustar   Suret-arskla-privechbi

Muscular system

Incantation: *Brihurasat estre pribu-aresta*

Physical Benefits
Aids biliary function
Stops bleeding
Restores and enlivens skin
May assist with healing skin conditions

Emotional Benefits
Promotes deep contentment, inner balance and deep peace

Spiritual Benefits
Aids in releasing restrictions of belief systems

32. Ginger

Kashanat-plubahur-usalvi

Brivablut-ersklava

Angel:

Nachtu-menesut

Angel:

Nuchpa-pirarut

Reproductive system

Incantation: *Krachba este krivas aresta*

Note: avoid sunlight after use.

Physical Benefits
Relieves motion sickness and nausea
Aids digestive disorders and protein digestion
May be used for treating alcoholism
Eliminates parasites and mucous in the digestive tract

Emotional Benefits
Assists with depression
Stimulates initiative and vibrancy of living

Spiritual Benefits
Helps stimulate the inner warrior to protect boundaries
Helps get rid of parasitic relationships and reveals cords that bind

33. Grapefruit

Karsana-biverespi

Nerek-urspahur

Angel:

Luset-arek-perevi

Angel:

Neste-platprahur

Skeletal and Connective Tissue system

Incantation: *Arasta miruch nanestra*

Physical Benefits
Cleanses oily skin
Acne
Cellulite and fluid retention
Digestive aid
Cleanses the lymphatic system

Emotional Benefits
May assist during drug withdrawal
Uplifts mood

Spiritual Benefits
Supports self-acceptance and promotes self-love

The 24 Chakras of the Body

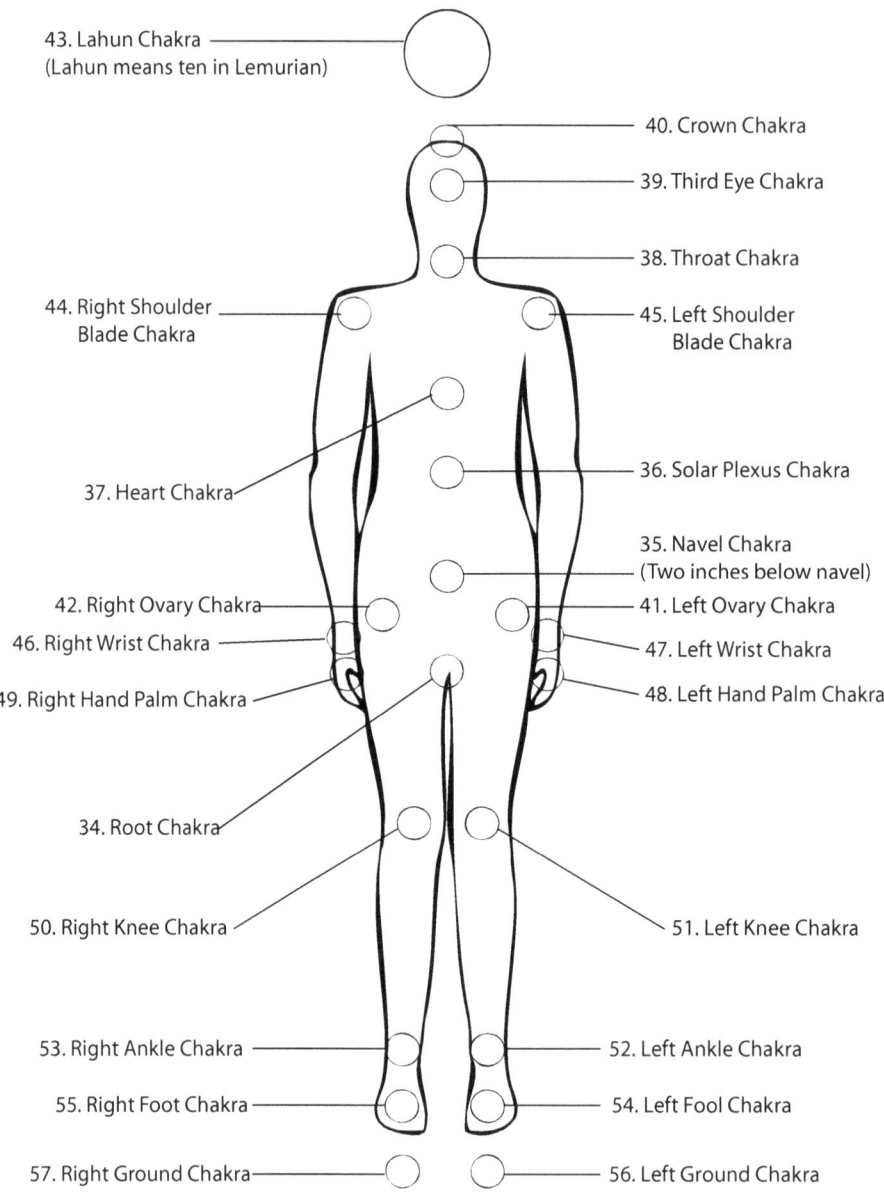

Sacred Sexuality Exercise

Preparation for use of the Atlantean Sigils for the 24 Chakras of the Body

This information is an excerpt from the online course, *The Atlantean Book of the Angels*. See www.spiritualjourneys.com.

Step 1 - Digesting Density
- Breathe deeply and relax for 10 minutes.
- Breathe out all tension, making sure that your body is totally relaxed.
- Using your inner vision, see an image of yourself in all your perfection, as if by magic, a reality now.
- Imagine a cylinder similar to a washing machine, parallel to your shoulders but above your abdominal area. Visualize it churning backwards and forwards like a grinding motion in your stomach and even deeper into the etheric soul levels behind the stomach.
- Intend and pull in all the density from the body into the stomach. Intend that all old programs are pulled into the stomach so they can be digested.
- Continue churning until all density is white and clear.
- See from time to time how your image keeps developing.

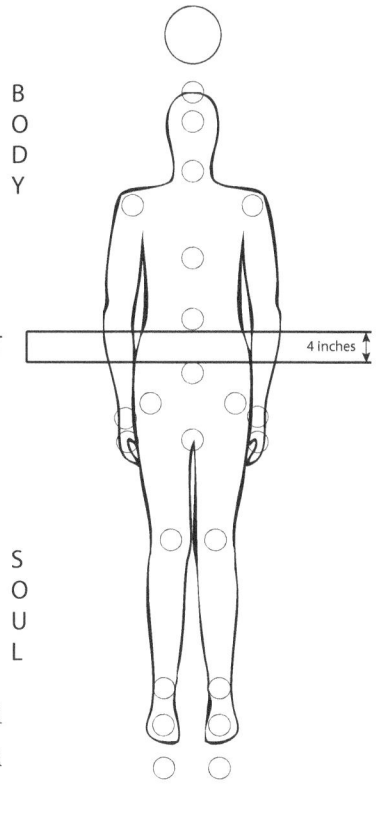

Step 2 – Getting the Bottom Circle of Soul Moving

While there is no specific position for your hands, it is important that your legs are uncrossed.

To get the bottom circle of the soul moving:
- Begin at the chakra located a hands length below the left foot and start pulling the resources up from there. Create a flow of these resources/energy up through the left ankle to the left knee, left hip, left ovary area, root chakra and onto the 2nd chakra (2 inches below the belly button). From there continue the flow into the right ovary area, and then down the right leg through the right hip, right knee, right ankle and out the bottom of the right foot into the chakra that lies a hands length into the earth.
- See a spark of light go from the right earth chakra to the left earth chakra (in the ground). This completes one circle. Continue with the directions described above and proceed to create a fluid, balanced flow. The circle never goes beyond the 2nd chakra, 2 inches (5cm) below the belly button.
- Initially you may see it going through all of the listed chakras but later you may see it as a large oval, sparking in the ground below the right leg to the left leg each time.
- Coordinate your breathing as follows: Inhale: as you move the energy up the left side of the body and exhale as you push the energy down the right leg.

Step 3 – Getting the Upper Circle of the Body Moving

When creating this upper circle, the placement of your hands is important.

- Once you are ready to start, bring your hands up (with palms facing upwards) to just below you rib cage.
- Just as the bottom circle starts below the left foot, see the left palm pulling energy inwards and upwards in a direct line to the 3rd chakra and onto the heart chakra, left shoulder blade, throat, 3rd eye, crown, up the left side of the lahun chakra and down the right side, and back to the crown, 3rd eye, throat, right shoulder blade, heart, 3rd chakra and into the right palm, causing a spark to release into the left palm.
- Match the speed and rotation of the lower, soul circle. Both sides go up at the same time and down at the same time.
- Have the 2 circles rotate in unison for about 5 minutes.
- You can also use your breath as you breathe in for the upward flow and out for the downward movement of the circles.
- This time the circle never goes lower than 2 inches above the belly button. The 4 inch Spirit belt around the belly button could be considered a neutral zone as no circle enters it.

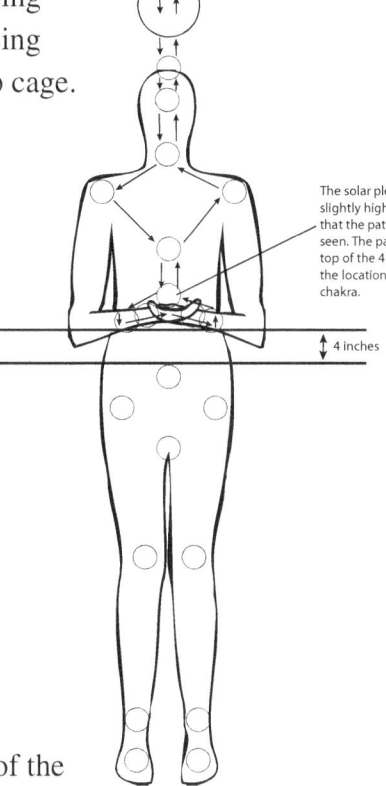

The solar plexus chakra is shown slightly higher in this diagram so that the path of the loop can be seen. The palms should rest at the top of the 4 inch band, which is the location of the solar plexus chakra.

4 inches

Step 4 – Bringing the Two Circles Together

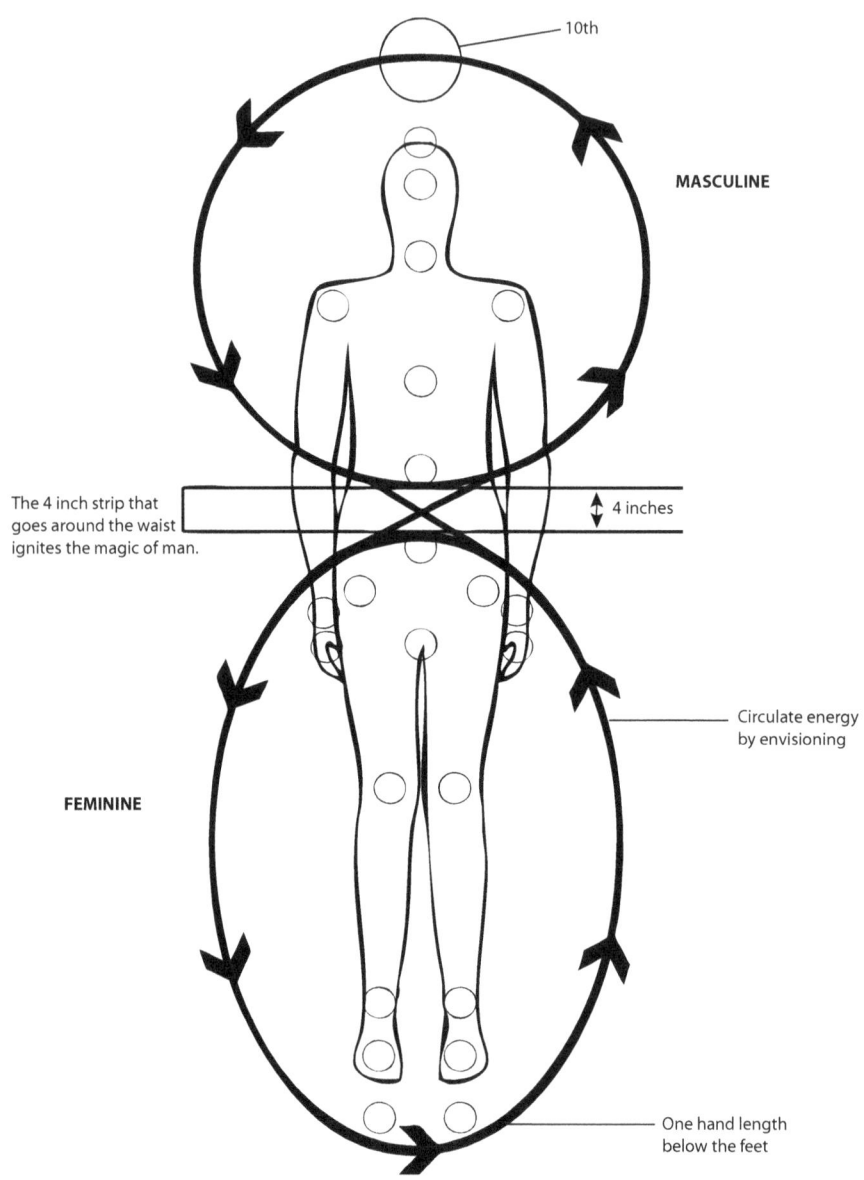

- Slow the top circle down a bit until the apex of the lower circle is aligned with the upper circle as it sparks from the right palm to the left palm.
- At that point both circles bulge towards the center (the 4 inch zone) where they almost meet at the belly button.
- Envision again the image of your manifestation.
- When both circles meet at the belly button zone there is an exploding energy.
- At that moment, force your breath out and send the energy through your belly button into your image.
- You may either feed the image with your breath and energy each time the circles meet, or you can wait until both circles have built in momentum and then send the breath and energy out together, when you feel the time is right.
- You may start to feel a trembling in your cells.
- This exercise may be done by yourself or with a sexual partner. If you choose to do this exercise while making love with someone, you will first have to digest the density in your partner before you can aim the sexual magic energy into the image of your desire. Time the release of the sexual magic energy with the moment of ejaculation or peak orgasm.
- The digestion of the other partner's density is necessary otherwise the sexual magic energy will go into the density of the other person rather than the image you wish to manifest.

Step 5 – Final Clean up and Deactivating the Influence of Spirit

- When you have finished, pull in all residual density that is in your field and digest it in the stomach.
- Envision the assemblage point[7] (masculine qualities) at the outer edge of your field, which is attached to your life force center (a ball of light behind your belly button about the size of an orange) via an umbilical-like cord.
- Allow the life force center to be filled with the song of silence and deep beingness. This makes the life force center feminine. Feel the peace in your belly.
- Envision the assemblage point traveling down the tube (umbilical cord) until it reaches the ball of light behind the belly button. Once they are merged, breath prana in three times from both ends of the pranic tube. After the third in-breath and on the third out-breath, see it explode – filling the entire field around your body.
- Pull in any remaining density within your field, including any fragments of your life force center and assemblage point, into your stomach and digest them.
- You have removed 2 of the points that spirit has used to 'pull your strings'.

---

7 **Assemblage Point** The outer rim of the seventh or spirit body has an illuminated spot about an arm's length behind the heart. It determines what reality we are in. It has always been on the outer edge of the bodies of man. The new creation has it placed deeper into man's luminous cocoon. The position changes as we move into higher evolutionary stages. *A Life of Miracles* (2nd Edition) page 85-86. See also *The Ring of Truth* pages 191-192.

The 24 Chakras of the Body

Sigils and Angels 34 - 57

The following sigils give messages through the genital fluids to all parts of the body left behind in time, to come into the moment through trusting surrender.

34. Helichrysum

Kasana-husbi   Sukrava-esachvrave

Angel: Angel:

Nanachvi-kerseru   Nekte-ratvavi

Root chakra

Incantation: *Krubit plabava isanavit*

Physical Benefits
Balances blood pressure
Reduces skin discolorization

Chelates chemicals from the body
Supports cardiovascular system
Supports liver function

Emotional Benefits
Releases old memories
Instills hope

Spiritual Benefits
Creates new opportunities
Increases manifesting abilities

35. **Honeysuckle**

Kivarus-meseret

Prubasur-nusal-marachvi

Angel:

Nanuk-huras-paravi

Angel:

Usekplahur

Navel chakra

Incantation: *Asta michvet elpahur*

Note: For use in a diffuser only, do not use topically.

Physical Benefits
Stimulates hormones of well-being
Balances endocrine system

Emotional Benefits
Promotes joy and a poetic perspective of life

Spiritual Benefits
Opens a multi-dimensional perspective

36. **Hyssop**

Lukpa-mechtrevi

Angel: 
Nusar-esetretvi

Esetret-harusatvi

Angel: 
Misat-nanesvi

Solar Plexus chakra

Incantation: *Krunaves vilesat virkbave*

Note: Do not use if epileptic or if you have high blood pressure (hypertension).

Physical Benefits
Reduces cellulite and assists with acne
Raises low blood pressure
Regulates hormonal function
Anti-catarrhal

Emotional Benefits
Provides the impetus for inspired living
Promotes creative solutions

Spiritual Benefits
Promotes expanded awareness

37. **Idaho Tansy**

Melsech-nivastra   **Kratnut-plubesahur**

ANGEL: ANGEL:

Prihas-pelevi   **Neska-viresva**

Heart chakra

Incantation: *Nektu araset pruvaa*

Physical Benefits
Anti-tumor properties
Immune stimulant
Tonic for various skin conditions

Emotional Benefits
Assists with grounding

Spiritual Benefits
Promotes acceptance of the physical

38. Jasmine

Kabaru-elesvi　　　**Kavabis-bravut-useva**

Angel:　　　Angel:

Rakta-meset-huravi　　　**Nastu-ereskla**

Throat chakra

Incantation: *Nichtaver usubavit uklasvi*

Physical Benefits
Soothes irritated skin
Rejuvenates skin and reduces wrinkles

Emotional Benefits
Uplifting and inspiring

Spiritual Benefits
Eliminates shame

39. Juniper Berry

Utret-barus-hura	Karsu-bichpahur
Angel:	Angel:

Veresh-truhavi	Nesta-plibavet

Third Eye chakra

Incantation: *Petranuvis aresta prahut*

Physical Benefits
Potent diuretic
Promotes kidney function
Promotes uric acid excretion, reducing pain after exercise
Reduces cellulite

Emotional Benefits
Heightens consciousness

Spiritual Benefits
Increases energy by dissolving belief in illusion

40. **Lavender**

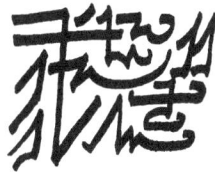
Kasablut-natvi

Usublech-patravit

Angel:

Rekta-bruhavit

Angel:

Skrahut-areknut

Crown chakra

Incantation: *Etre bilevach vunesvi*

Physical Benefits
Anti-tumor properties
Antiseptic, anti-viral, antibacterial
Reduces wrinkles and purifies skin
Application of this oil regularly to nipples may reduce menstrual headaches
Deodorant

Emotional Benefits
Promotes deep satisfaction
Provides for deeper sleep and relaxation
Provides peace during stressful times

Spiritual Benefits
Provides memories of how to live a life of no opposites

41. Lavandin (A hybrid of Lavender)

Sekparut-arseta   **Karsa-mirarak-spavu**

Angel: Angel:
Nuruk-pelenur   **Ruktek-brihasur**

Left Ovary chakra

Incantation: *Kiset vranu usavesvi*

Note: Lavandin should not be used for burns, however Lavender can be used and will reduce scarring and hasten healing.

Physical Benefits
Antiseptic
Supports respiratory and circulatory system conditions
Reduces muscular tightness

Emotional Benefits (same as Lavender)
Promotes deep satisfaction
Provides for deeper sleep and relaxation
Provides peace during stressful times

Spiritual Benefits (same as Lavender)
Provides memories of how to live a life of no opposites

42. **Lemon**

Karus-arsek-prava

Sabavu-mechtar

Angel:
Neserut-elesut

Angel:
Rarut-haresta

Right Ovary chakra

Incantation: *Karanus misech vibres*

Note: Avoid sunlight or UV light after applying.

Physical Benefits
Promotes white blood cell formation
Enhances micro-circulation
Enhances immune system function

Emotional Benefits
Promotes a sense of well-being
Balances 'mood swings'
Eases anxiety and may promote lowering of blood pressure

Spiritual Benefits
Assists in clarity of seeing beyond appearances
Assists in making clear choices

43. Lemongrass

Aravek-virehat

Spibarut-areskla

Angel:

Mishpe-rurahut

Angel:

Blibavech-nubares

Lahun chakra

Incantation: *Kluharanet espave minusach*

Physical Benefits
Supports regeneration of connective tissue and ligaments
Strengthens vascular walls and dilates blood vessels
Promotes lymph flow
Powerful anti-fungal properties

Emotional Benefits
Purifying and calming

Spiritual Benefits
Promotes psychic abilities
Increases intuitive capacities

44. Lilac

Serehut-alskar

Satve-mishpa-arates

ANGEL: 
Aret-pratavi

ANGEL: 
Kusavit-archbavur

Right Shoulder Blade chakra

Incantation: *Kisanach hestavi misuvet*

Physical Benefits
Assists with symptoms of sun deprivation

Emotional Benefits
Assists with depression and stagnation

Spiritual Benefits
Assists in elimination of perceived limitation
Strengthens inter-dimensional awareness by strengthening the Vagus nerve

45. Lime

Nererut-halesklar **Neskla-arsbahuresta**

Angel: Angel:

Arat-pritlvar **Varista-hublavit**

Left Should Blade chakra

Incantation: *Raktu biras harsata*

Physical Benefits
Anti-fungal
Antiseptic
Promotes imagination by stimulating frontal lobe activity

Emotional Benefits
Refreshing and uplifting

Spiritual Benefits
Promotes fresh perspectives and a sense of well-being

46. **Lupin**

Eresatvi-nurarek

Setva-nihar-varus

Angel:

Rachtu-pretprahur

Angel:

Kuchvi-barutet

Right Wrist chakra

Incantation: *Kluhunaves arsba esekrach*

Note: Use in a diffuser only.

Physical Benefits
Enhances bone function

Emotional Benefits
Beneficial in altering the mood
Promotes lightness of being

Spiritual Benefits
May enhance the experience of timelessness and reveal inner light

47. Mandarin

Aravar-nusprevu   Kasanut-sihat-parvu

Angel: Rusalvavi-nechtar   Angel: Maranech-vilhestrat

Left Wrist chakra

Incantation: *Itrech prihava vereklas*

Note: Avoid direct sunlight after use for at least 4 hours.

Physical Benefits
Stimulates biliary function
Anti-fungal
Promotes healthy digestion

Emotional Benefits
Promotes pleasant moods and joy

Spiritual Benefits
Increases depth of awareness and the poetic perspective

48. Marjoram

Stubelevik-araksu

Bisarut-mileve-artu

Angel:
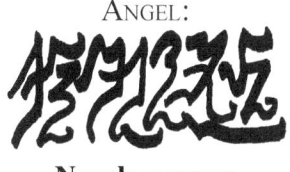
Nerek-nusava

Angel:

Nuch-karanuk-useva

Left Hand - Palm chakra

Incantation: *Nestuch eseta minavech*

Physical Benefits
Promotes regular bowel movements by optimizing peristalsis
Supports the respiratory system
Supports the parasympathetic nervous system

Emotional Benefits
Strengthens the nerves
Calming

Spiritual Benefits
Strengthens the ability to silence the mind

49. Melaleuca Alternifolia

Artahur-hebelsta   Nusba-spihelesut

ANGEL: ANGEL:

Kesetvavi-unas   Karavek-niharaset

Right Hand - Palm chakra

Incantation: *Virat ursata blihur arespi*

Physical Benefits
Powerful anti-bacterial action
Anti-viral, anti-fungal, anti-parasitic
Cardio-tonic
Stimulates the immune system

Emotional Benefits
Purifying and cleansing

Spiritual Benefits
Stimulates the higher spiritual function of the genitals, such as intuitive capabilities

50. Melaleuca Ericifolia

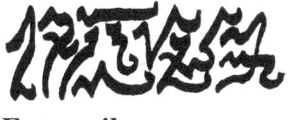

Erte-prihanur-uvaves

Nespa-alesklar

Angel:

Angel:

Arasta-piraklut

Visba-nuchparek

Right Knee chakra

Incantation: *Achna estava vibret huratvi*

Physical Benefits
Treatment of bronchitis and sinus infections

Emotional Benefits
Promotes optimism

Spiritual Benefits
Creates stability with spiritual growth

51. Melaleuca Quinquenervia

| Kusunar-herevat | Alsva-spibavit |

ANGEL:

ANGEL:

| Merek-eretar | Nukset-ires-haresta |

Left Knee chakra

Incantation: *Asata privabur miseret*

Physical Benefits
Genital conditions
Treatment of amoeba and parasites in the blood
Respiratory conditions

Emotional Benefits
Calms and reduces tension – may lower blood pressure

Spiritual Benefits
Enhances refinement of enjoyment

52. Melissa

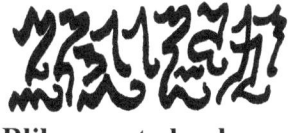

Bliharanut-skruhavar

Puhubaves-eseta

Angel:

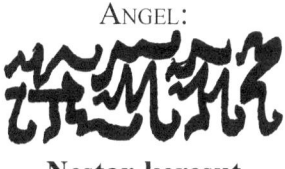

Nestar-keresut

Angel:

Livaset-misech-arsta

Left Ankle chakra

Incantation: *Aksava vispa mihur rarech*

Physical Benefits
Allergies and chronic coughs
Anti-cholera action
Anti-microbial (used for Herpes simplex lesions)

Emotional Benefits
Promotes gentleness
Promotes refinement of emotional responses
Promotes an optimistic outlook on life

Spiritual Benefits
Assists in awareness of a life beyond duality
Promotes inclusiveness and oneness

53. Mountain Savory

Karanach-blivabi · Kitra-misanit

Angel: · Angel:

Mesenut-kilehasvi · Isech-havraves

Right Ankle chakra

Incantation: *Neskavi versta prekprahur*

Note: Dilute with pure almond oil when using topically.

Physical Benefits
Abscesses, burns and cuts
May stimulate adrenal gland function
May have anti-HIV properties

Emotional Benefits
Motivates and energizes

Spiritual Benefits
Opens up our authentic source of inspiration

54. Mugwort

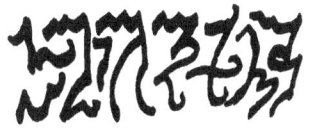

Kesbanadek-ersekla   **Keneves-piharut**

ANGEL: ANGEL:

Privet-urut-harasta   **Setl-mivanus**

Left Foot chakra

Incantation: *Kruhanatvi prihavek ereshta*

Physical Benefits
Assists with strengthening and balancing the pineal gland as well as the pituitary gland
Promotes restful sleep and calms a racing mind
Assists to regulate appetites

Emotional Benefits
Assists to still the internal dialogue and instills a feeling of well-being and contentment

Spiritual Benefits
Aids in bridging communications between the dream states and the awakened state
Promotes the ability to interpret dreams and enhances mastery of the dream body

55. Myrrh

Keset-nanuvi

Rekpa-iseta-nanuk

Angel:

Bivaret-pletplahur

Angel:
Usbar-kavanesvi

Right Foot chakra

Incantation: *Michpaset eneshvi steve vrubaset*

Physical Benefits
Helps with diarrhea, dysentery, ringworms
Eases stretch marks on skin
Anti-fungal for athlete's foot, mouth ulcers and thrush
Hyperthyroidism

Emotional Benefits
Uplifitng
Assists empaths in adjusting to their environment

Spiritual Benefits
Raises consciousness and purifies emotion
Removes past life programs

56. Myrtle

Kalsva-urestu

Iles-plavavu

Angel:

Minavech-vibleshvi

Angel:
Kisbar-nesak-vravu

Left Ground chakra

Incantation: *Nachve suvil peras prahet*

Physical Benefits
Aids with insomnia
Hypothyroidism
Pulmonary support
Skin conditions

Emotional Benefits
Anger management
Supports self-expression
Euphoriant – assists with depression

Spiritual Benefits
Elevates states of praise

57. Nasturtium

Kersba-raktanavu	**Asach-nevesba-arut**
ANGEL:	ANGEL:

Hurech-berestu	**Pishet-klesbarut**

Right Ground chakra

Incantation: *Nusaret erakvi bra-uvraset*

Note: All parts of the plant can be used as each provides subtle differences in benefits.

Physical Benefits
Strengthens the immune system
Colds and sinus infections

Emotional Benefits
Creates enhanced enjoyment

Spiritual Benefits
Promotes rapture through extreme awareness

The 24 Pure Emotions

Sigils and Angels 58 - 81

"The Pure Emotions, without agenda, benevolently affect the quality of life. Emotion coupled with need, binds life, creating karmic repercussions."

Almine

The Perceptions of the 24 Pure Emotions

	Positive Aspect	Negative Aspect
1.	<u>Love</u> The desire to include	<u>Trust</u> The desire to surrender (replaces fear)
2.	<u>Inspiration</u> The desire to be inspired and to inspire (replaces anger)	<u>Peace</u> The desire to be at ease (replaces protectiveness)
3.	<u>Creativity</u> The desire to create	<u>Pleasure</u> The desire to be delighted
4.	<u>Empathy</u> The desire to connect	<u>Acknowledgement</u> The desire to see the perfection
5.	<u>Generosity</u> The desire to give	<u>Receptivity</u> The desire to receive

6.	Encouragement The desire to encourage or to be encouraged	Beauty The desire to be uplifted
7.	Communication The desire to express	Assimilation The desire to integrate
8.	Passion The desire to know	Joy The desire to live
9.	Achievement The desire to excel	Fun The desire to revel
10.	Enlightenment The desire to enhance or be enhanced (replaces pain)	Contentment The desire to retain
11.	Empowerment The desire to be of service	Humor The desire to be amused
12.	Growth The desire to expand	Satisfaction The desire to be fulfilled

The Seed of Life

Also known as the Cosmic Egg

58. Neroli

Karspa-raktuvi-menesh

Alasklar-vilseva

Angel:

Harspa-uklepravit

Angel:

Nistar-ersklavit

Love

Incantation: *Lu-uhuvrivaset michvabet uveset*

Physical Benefits
Digestive spasms and spastic colon
Scars, stretch marks and wrinkles
Anti-viral, anti-bacterial and anti-parasitic

Emotional Benefits
Panic attacks and hysteria
Heart palpitations and heart arrhythmias
Relieves stress, tension and anxiety

Spiritual Benefits
Strengthens and stabilizes emotions
Supports silence of the mind for greater clarity
Encourages sensuality, increases joy and stimulates passion

Insight: Incorruptible matter in formless form is the substance of Infinity.

59. Nutmeg

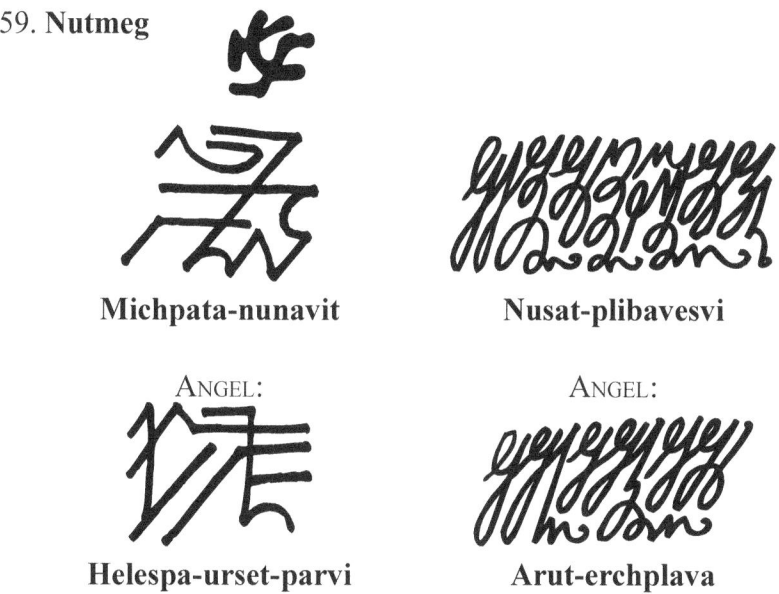

Michpata-nunavit

Nusat-plibavesvi

Angel: **Helespa-urset-parvi**

Angel: **Arut-erchplava**

Trust

Incantation: *Pihi-arat michtave mishuret*

Note: Do not use if epileptic. Dilute with almond oil if applied topically or just use a single drop.

Physical Benefits
Supports the nervous system and overcomes fatigue
May benefit muscles and joints
May benefit circulation
Supports the adrenal glands

Emotional Benefits
Invigorating and uplifting

Spiritual Benefits
Enhances appreciation for the physical life
Supports establishment of dynamic balance between the physical and emotional components of life

Insight: The Seed of Life, 6 circles around the seventh, consists of the 7 sub-atomic elements of Creation, with incorruptible matter being the middle circle. It has been captured and imprisoned by the other elements that have surrounded it like a ring.

60. Orange

Krivasut-neneklusve-pravaa   **Usbar-arsk-klevesvi**

Angel: **Nechbilesek-uvravi**   Angel: **Nanusak-esklava**

Inspiration

Incantation: *Klihibaset nenechstu aranas*

Note: Citrus oils should not be applied to skin that will be exposed to the sun.

Physical Benefits
Wrinkles and skin disorders
Lowers high cholesterol
Tissue repair
Fluid retention
Insect repellant

Emotional Benefits
Stimulates the senses and feelings of well-being
Anti-depressant

Spiritual Benefits
Stimulates communication between cognitive and non-cognitive awareness

Insight: The other elements are light, frequency, energy, life force, and intelligent perception (cognitive and non-cognitive). The sixth is the force of intent, also known as Presence.

61. Oregano

Brishparut-harsata **Kuvitre-varanu**

Angel: Angel:

Nechvi-plavasur-nerstu **Rasanech-blavi**

Peace

Incantation: *Stihubaret arskla viruset*

Note: Dilute when applying to areas of the body, other than the soles of the feet.

Physical Benefits
Powerful anti-fungal, anti-viral, anti-bacterial and anti-parasitic agent

Emotional Benefits
Creates inner dynamic balance

Spiritual Benefits
Strengthens the ability to repel psychic invasion

Insight: The elements of the Seed of Life are the fabric of time and space, the various tones of the sub-atomic particles creating different realities. This has formed the Cosmic Egg we have been in.

62. Palmarosa

Havravech-elesplavu

Kivaravespi-arsarut

ANGEL:

ANGEL:

Nisata-pretpranahur

Nechta-bluharanis

Creativity

Incantation: *Misetech bruhaset iste-manuhech*

Physical Benefits
Supports uterine function
Supports cardiovascular function
Assists with many skin conditions

Emotional Benefits
Stimulates resilience in the face of stress

Spiritual Benefits
Promotes trust in the benevolence of life

Insight: *"Kesvelech husavespi aravachvi nusavaa araras herespa nusklava"*

Emerge now from the Seed of Life, the Cosmic Egg that has been your incubation chamber.

63. **Patchouli**

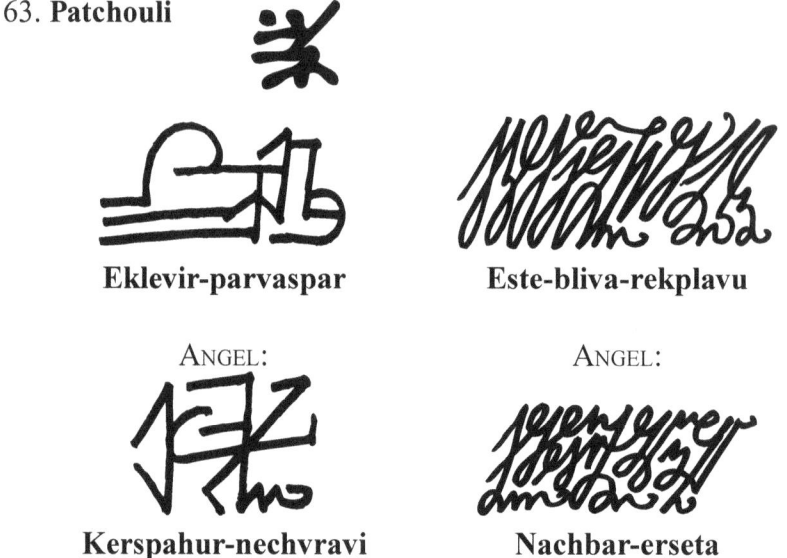

Eklevir-parvaspar

Este-bliva-rekplavu

Angel: **Kerspahur-nechvravi**

Angel: **Nachbar-erseta**

Pleasure

Incantation: *Kriba-hureset arechsta bravich*

Physical Benefits
Anti-inflammatory
Itching of hives or weeping wounds
Weight reduction

Emotional Benefits
Stimulates sensual experience
Calming and relaxing

Spiritual Benefits
Releases old paradigms and belief systems

Insight: The relationship caused by desire (frequency) and light (knowledge) traps us in the egg. It is time to birth into pure beingness that does not desire, nor think it knows. It enjoys, with full surrender to life unfolding, the newness of the eternal adventure.

64. **Pepper (Black)**

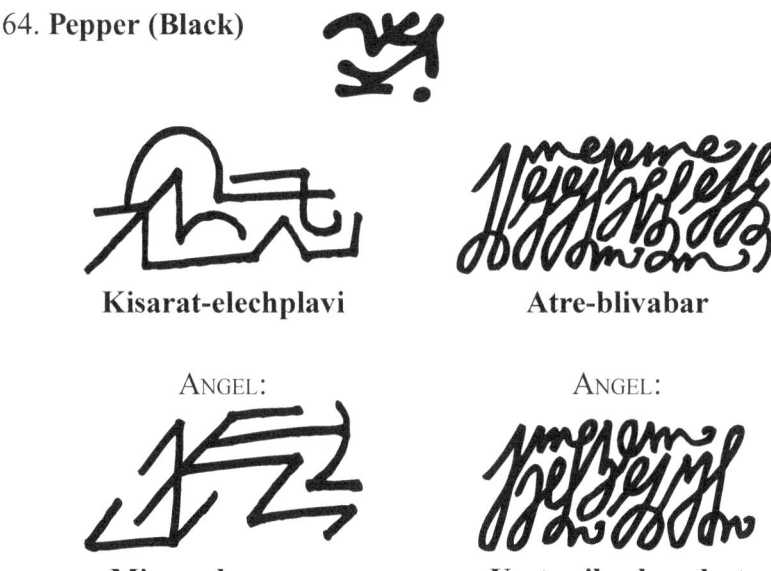

Kisarat-elechplavi   **Atre-blivabar**

Angel: **Mirspa-havrasur**   Angel: **Uset-mibechvrahut**

Empathy

Incantation: *Krisanat-vistavi heskle-arurach*

Physical Benefits
Flatulence (works especially well when combined with fennel)
Toothache
Stimulates appetite and blood circulation

Emotional Benefits
Stimulates optimistic outlook
Comfort and contentment

Spiritual Benefits
Restores the balance between passion and joy

Insight: Incorruptible Matter emerges from its incubation when these other six elements are seen as an illusion and cease to exist. It enters spaceless space and formless form in which the directions of without and within merge.

65. Peppermint

Neseklet-alasklar **Eskla-biret-arseta**

Angel: Angel:

Heresatvi-nasbahur **Niset-aset-bavarus**

Acknowledgement

Incantation: *Sivahech-virusat manesh hustava*

Note: Avoid mucous membranes, open wounds, cuts, eyes and other sensitive areas.

Physical Benefits
Improves mental alertness
May aid weight control by providing a feeling of 'fullness' through stimulating the ventro-medial hypothalamus
Menopausal and menstrual activity

Emotional Benefits
Purifies density accumulated through interaction with others

Spiritual Benefits
Stimulates attitudes of youthfulness

Insight: Intelligent perception is the choosing of what it thinks is life enhancing and what is not. The root of this value system is instinctual knowing. The element of intelligent perception could therefore be called instinctual knowing.

66. Petitgrain

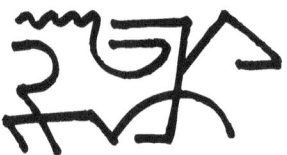
Nenklet-huvarasvi

Aspavit-kiranetvi

ANGEL:

Misetplahur-arasta

ANGEL:

Ruspahur-erskla-minech

Generosity

Incantation: *Plikat barech eruklasve manus*

Physical Benefits
Excessive perspiration
May assist with acne
Strengthens and balances the nervous system

Emotional Benefits
Clears confusion and mental fatigue
Refreshes and purifies

Spiritual Benefits
Increases joy and optimism

Insight: The six elements around the 7th form a mirror; they are therefore forming an illusion of space. This is similar to someone standing between two mirrors and seeing themselves in a never-ending line of images.

67. Pikake

Neska-uvrabit-haresta   **Haranas-trevit-urespi**

Angel: **Misavir-uraklet**   Angel: **Reksatur-nisbahur**

Receptivity

Incantation: *Achsava visat harastu*

Physical Benefits
Lymph stimulation

Emotional Benefits
Lightness of heart

Spiritual Benefits
Creates states of praise

Insight: The separation of the elements (part of an unreal dream, for nothing can ever be separated) creates duality and a distorted reality, for mirrors mirror backwards.

68. Pine

Visabiraklet-prihat-alesklar   Nisatblavabuch-urtarespavi

ANGEL: ANGEL:

Subaret-harechta   Nisba-retklavi

Encouragement

Incantation: *Misavach ninesvi hubrasat*

Note: Low-grade pine oil may contain the hazardous ingredient turpentine; avoid this by using pure, high-grade essential oil products.

Physical Benefits
Powerful disinfectant
Respiratory ailments

Emotional Benefits
Relieves anxiety and stress

Spiritual Benefits
Purifies density

Insight: Everything that is part of separation is antagonistic to its opposite. Life is therefore at war with itself.

69. Plumeria

Nesarat-prahur

Asevi-nivahur

Angel:

Usalvi-betre-sahur

Angel:

Kuvis-plavevanis

Beauty

Incantation: *Kiratuch nunasatvi paresh*

Physical Benefits
Beneficial for the nervous system
Softens and rejuvenates skin

Emotional Benefits
Euphoriant

Spiritual Benefits
Encourages bliss and rapture

Insight: To eliminate the illusion of the separate 7 elements that form the two-dimensional screen on which life has played out, they need to be seen as the inverted mirror image.

70. **Ravensara**

Aratklaver-patrahur

Uskla-prihet-uselvi

ANGEL:
Neska-vesetretvi

ANGEL:
Nachvatur-misbaruch

Communication

Incantation: *Kasanet vibrach ubarechvi*

Physical Benefits
May heal herpes, mononucleosis, viral hepatitis, and chronic fatigue syndrome

Emotional Benefits
Assists hypersensitive persons to cope with their environment

Spiritual Benefits
Establishes greater self-sovereignty

Insight: Matter, in the middle and at the heart of the other 6 particles and their properties, is a model for the form of the micro-cosmic sub-atomic particles as well as the macro-cosmic realities.

71. **Rose**

Kusaravit-harasklar

Espa-sklivrevaspavi

ANGEL:

Nesech-ubavesvi

ANGEL:

Urut-arechva

Assimilation

Incantation: *Kirasut estetvi plavabich*

Physical Benefits
Supports youthful, regenerated skin
Assists with sexual disabilities
Herpes simplex

Emotional Benefits
Heals birth trauma for mothers and children (dilute with pure almond oil for use with infants)
Contributes very powerfully to well-being

Spiritual Benefits
Intoxicating feelings of bliss and rapture
Opens higher function of the pineal gland

Insight: Matter should activate the properties of the other 6 particles that lie dormant within it. In its full expression, it becomes incorruptible matter and the separated elements 'without' are absorbed and cancel one another out. (The outer and inner become one.) This removes the illusion of all 7 separated elements.

72. Rosemary

Petre-harasach

Karsut-nechte-blivabi

ANGEL:

Nusavi-esetkla

ANGEL:

Ravasetvi-mishtanur

Passion

Incantation: *Kruhasanat piresvi arusach*

Physical Benefits
May assist with high cholesterol
Respiratory infections
Skin care and hair loss

Emotional Benefits
Clears emotions

Spiritual Benefits
Brings dynamic balance to heart and mind

Insight: When the dormant potential within matter is fully expressed, Incorruptible Infinite Matter is revealed beyond the illusions of separation – the Element of Oneness. We can begin to activate this potential within matter by living from a poetic perspective.

73. **Sage**

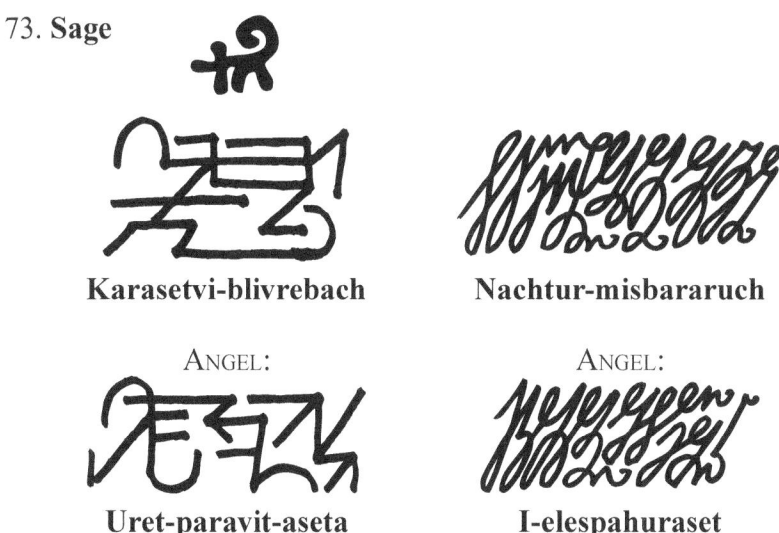

Karasetvi-blivrebach

Nachtur-misbararuch

Angel:
Uret-paravit-aseta

Angel:
I-elespahuraset

Joy

Incantation: *Kasanur este blaheresvi*

Note: Do not use if epileptic or diagnosed with high blood pressure.

Physical Benefits
Supports hormonal balance with menstruation and menopause; may assist with PMS
Soothes skin ailments and reduces scarring
Oral conditions

Emotional Benefits
Elevates the mood

Spiritual Benefits
Encourages states of praise and grateful acknowledgment

Insight: When the illusion of the separate elements is removed, no programmed potential exists in Incorruptible Infinite Matter, just the limitless possibilities of the All. All suffering contracts are removed.

74. Sandalwood

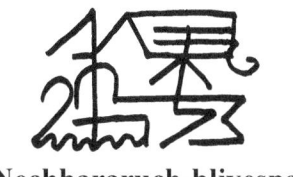
Nechbararuch-blivespa

Niserat-misbaranus

Angel:

Arskla-suhutvavi

Angel:

Kistra-vilshbrevat

Achievement

Incantation: *Nanukta pliva este plahur plavi*

Physical Benefits
Cystitis and urinary tract infections
Youthening effects
Supports nerves and circulation

Emotional Benefits
Calming and stabilizing

Spiritual Benefits
Assists in removing negative programming from the cells

Insight: Within the mirrored life bound by illusion, light has been previously known as accessed information, which implied that information is 'outside' us, creating separation. Light as an inseparable nuance of expression is the catalyst for manifestation of sovereign intent.

75. **Spearmint**

Mechpararek-nusavi

ANGEL:

Hiret-aresta

Arus-aresta

ANGEL:

Nenek-misarech

Fun

Incantation: *Achnut areksta miset arachve*

Physical Benefits
Respiratory and nervous system
Cystitis
Promotes easier labor during child birth
Stimulates appetite and increases metabolism, causing weight loss

Emotional Benefits
Releases emotional blocks

Spiritual Benefits
Promotes lasting well-being

Insight: Emotion, (which is frequency) has been based on desire or the recognition of something as 'separate' from what we think our limited self to be. Emotion is an inseparable response to the unfolding moment.

76. **Spikenard**

Aklaberespi-huraret

Vilesavanu-ursa

Angel:

Nekva-blivahespi

Angel:
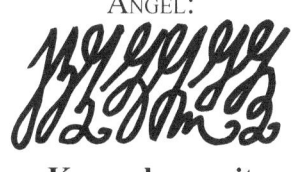
Kanus-hespavit

Enlightenment

Incantation: *Nusba keres arustava*

Physical Benefits
Deodorant
Skin tonic
Anti-inflammatory
Flatulent indigestion

Emotional Benefits
Soothing influence

Spiritual Benefits
Assists with relieving memories of insufficient mothering (rub into abdomen)

Insight: Life-force is the 'rhythmless rhythm' that flows into spontaneous, authentic living.

77. Spruce

Nuhururuk-arklavet

Asat-mivech-vileshvi

ANGEL:

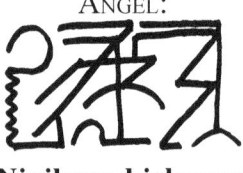
Ninikvra-bichparet

ANGEL:

Vanus-prihat-aleskla

Contentment

Incantation: *Nisaruk ublavi kerestahut*

Physical Benefits
Stimulating to the thymus
Hyperthyroidism
Rheumatism
May assist with growth pains in children

Emotional Benefits
Releases blocked emotions

Spiritual Benefits
Releases cellular patterns from the past

Insight: Instinctual knowing is, in its state of oneness, the receptivity and acceptance of existence being unknowable, and trust in the automatic expression of the self in oneness as the expression of fulfilled hope.

78. **Stocks**

Utru-asahechspi

Blivabas-harestu

Angel:
Asva-esekletvi

Angel:
Archna-subavis

Empowerment

Incantation: *Achva vibresh mesenutvi*

Note: Use in a diffuser only.

Physical Benefits
Stimulates melatonin release

Emotional Benefits
Euphoriant, stimulates bliss

Spiritual Benefits
Restores memories of life beyond duality

Insight: Energy has previously been the movement between two opposite poles. In reality it is the inclusive sovereignty of expression of the self as all, the result of the one and the many becoming one.

79. **Sweetgrass**

Ekvar-petrenusvavi

Kruhat-nestravis

Angel:
Rakspar-bihuvrabit

Angel:
Iset-arkvravi

Humor

Incantation: *Aksava viblesvravi nuchtaha*

Note: Use the smoke that is released after Sweetgrass is lit and the flame is extinguished.

Physical Benefits
Antiseptic, anti-bacterial, anti-viral

Emotional Benefits
Creates a sacred space around the area of the smoke

Spiritual Benefits
Creates expanded awareness

Insight: Intent has been (in its imagined separation), the force holding the templates of existence in place. The templates, or matrices, are made of sub-atomic particles called 'presence particles'. Grids are sub-matrices formed by mind-controlled belief systems. Intent in oneness is the power generated through the expression of being a tribe of One - all lives within us.

80. **Sweetpea**

Trebar-mechpravi-selvenu   **Kabavilevis-harstunu**

Angel: Angel:

Hustanadoch-krubavi   **Nechsavit-eresva**

Growth

Incantation: *Iklechvi spehat aresti*

Note: Use in a diffuser only.

Physical Benefits
Alleviates symptoms of sunlight deprivation

Emotional Benefits
Restores the experience of innocent joy

Spiritual Benefits
Supports living in the moment

Insight: Matter is the home of the family of One and all other elements must express within it in dynamic balance. When all elements are in inspired expression, they cancel out their separate existences by forming the alchemical equation below (they cancel one another out). $1 + 1 + 1 + 1 + 1 + 1 + 1 = 0$

81. **Tangerine**

Espar-nekvra-velesvi

Visenurarat-irachparve

Angel:
Kasanet-sivatru

Angel:
Kevenut-arutpere-klavi

Satisfaction

Incantation: *Iksalvanuch ri-arestat verebasbi-uhet*

Note: Like all citrus fruit oils, avoid sunlight after using and skin test for sensitivity.

Physical Benefits
Smoothes wrinkles when blended with lavender
Fluid retention
Anti-parasitic

Emotional Benefits
Calming and comforting

Spiritual Benefits
Engenders optimism

Insight: The eighth element, Incorruptible Infinite Matter, is the expression of the Indivisible Existence.

The 24 Emotions of Recognition

Sigils and Angels 82 - 105

The Perceptions of the 24 Emotions of Recognition

1a. Plenitude: The recognition that I have all
1b. Omni-presence: The recognition that I am all

2a. Rapture: The recognition of Infinite existence in stillness
2b. Reverential Existence: The recognition of Mundane Sacredness

3a. Omni-perspective: The recognition of simplicity in complexity
3b. Timelessness: The recognition of the fullness of all in the moment

4a. Creating Absolute Truth: The recognition of existence as a devotional prayer
4b. Fulfilled Contentment: The recognition of the unfolding wonderment of existence

5a. Awakened Awareness: The recognition of meticulous caring
5b. Fluid Vastness: The recognition of dynamic balance in expression

6a. Supported Expression: The recognition of limitless supply of resources
6b. Deep Peace: The recognition of the self as the only being in existence

7a. Effortless Knowing: The recognition of indivisible existence
7b. Unchangeable Perfection: The recognition of new revelations

8a. Carefree Surrender: The recognition of the impeccability of timing of the unfolding revelations of Oneness
8b. Harmonic Resonance: The recognition of the perfection of expressions of diverse consciousness

9a. Lighthearted Eternal Presence: The recognition of fluid, eternal existence
9b. Comforting Presence: The recognition of floating on the calm waves of existence

10a. Perpetual Freshness of Expression: The recognition of countless possibilities of eternal existence
10b. Eternal Fulfillment: The recognition of the complete equity of existence

11a. Supreme Elegance: The recognition of infinite diversity of beauty
11b. Confidence of Purity: The recognition of the benevolence of unfolding life

12a. Humorous Conjunction: The recognition of Infinite bliss
12b. Transient Expression of Indivisible Form: The recognition of form as the ever-renewed vehicle of Infinite Intent

82. Tansy (Blue)

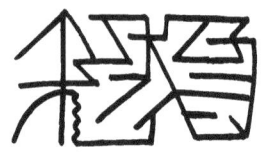
Kirasach-menuvishvi

Nakve-usbaravech

Angel:

Pararechvi-harustat

Angel:

Nesba-kelesvi

Plenitude

Incantation: *Akbelestat uras prahesvi*

Note: Do not use if you have high blood pressure.

Physical Benefits
Relieves itching
Antihistamine action
Assists with low blood pressure

Emotional Benefits
Sedative

Spiritual Benefits
Balanced grounding

Insight: Within matter and the geometry of shape, lies the stillpoint that cancels out space and time. When you enter this inner sanctum within your body, hostile illusory realities around you change and disappear.

83. Tarragon

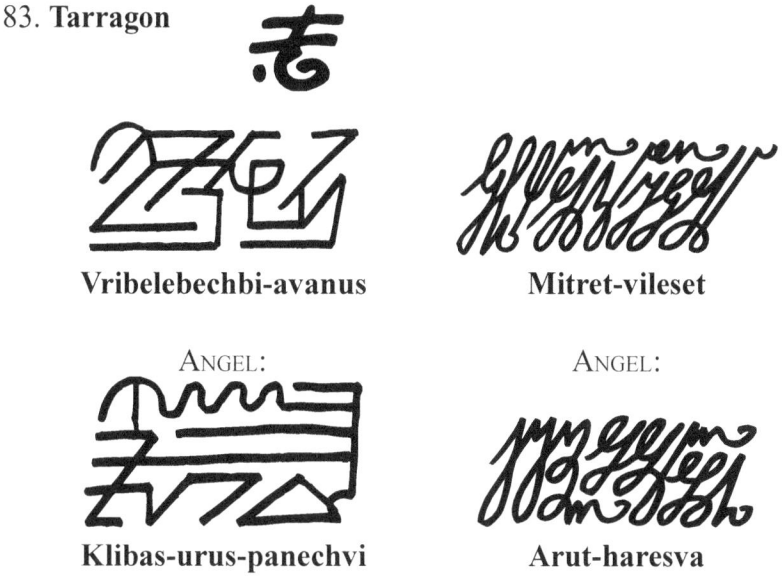

Vribelebechbi-avanus

Mitret-vileset

Angel: Klibas-urus-panechvi

Angel: Arut-haresva

Omni-presence

Incantation: *Nestava setvanut arkla*

Physical Benefits
Pre-menstrual discomfort
Genital and urinary tract infections
Abdominal discomfort

Emotional Benefits
Benefits the autonomic nervous system

Spiritual Benefits
Removes obsolete programs from the reproductive system

Insight: When you find the stillpoint of matter, automatic living takes place. Not dictated by heart or instinct or head, you automatically follow the dance of life.

84. **Thyme**

Klasanut-miravaa

Vrivek-valesba

Angel:
Vribaves-elenuchvi

Angel:
Nantuk-miskrave

Rapture

Incantation: *Sunech barut hurastavi*

Physical Benefits
Pleurisy, pertussis, asthma and bronchitis
Respiratory conditions
Spinal viruses

Emotional Benefits
Strengthens vitality

Spiritual Benefits
Lightens the mood; instills optimism

Insight: Slow down the momentum of your life and all flows to you. Striving for results, the river of supply flows away from you.

85. Tomato Leaf

Skrabanush-uvrablevanush

Kavavech-iravi

ANGEL:
Harstu-aklaranechvi

ANGEL:
Niset-karaharasvi

Reverential Existence

Incantation: *Naspa-eskla ruselvavis-praha*

Physical Benefits
Rejuvenates cells
Anti-oxidant
Stimulates the immune system

Emotional Benefits
Gladdens the heart

Spiritual Benefits
Encourages states of praise

Insight: The great illusion of the existence of opposites must dissolve itself in the presence of absolute truth: nothing other than eternal existence, indivisible and indescribable, exists.

86. Valerian

Vribas-usat-palaneshvi **Sutret-blivahespi**

Angel: **Akravet-eset-nanuvash** Angel: **Neste-usbavek**

Omni-perspective

Incantation: *Kribaravit-eseta plahur*

Physical Benefits
Hypothermia, body chills, cold feet and hands

Emotional Benefits
Tranquilizing to the nervous system
Assists with post-traumatic stress disorder (PTSD)

Spiritual Benefits
Assists to remember dreams (also use mugwort)

Insight: The one who transfigures his body into incorruptible, infinite matter transfigures his whole world.

87. **Vetiver**

Asanut-plivech-vribasvi

Si-uvit-nanasvi

Angel:
Kravanusvabi

Angel:
Kerspa-eleskla

Timelessness

Incantation: *Achnahur setvivravis plek-pratahur*

Physical Benefits
Hypothermia, cold extremities, body chills
Arthritis
Anti-inflammatory

Emotional Benefits
Soothes irritation
Calming and stabilizing

Spiritual Benefits
Releases trauma and shock

Insight: All life flows with grace when we acknowledge its right to exist.

88. Violet

Creating Absolute Truth

Incantation: *Nunek arachta prehavis*

Note: Use sparingly in diluted form – place a few drops in 1/4 cup pure almond oil.

Physical Benefits
May help reduce blood pressure
Balances cholesterol

Emotional Benefits
Creates depths of living and gently releases old trauma

Spiritual Benefits
Very helpful for balancing inner masculine and feminine – a prerequisite to mastery

Insight: Learn now the greater depth of communication that silence brings. In the silences of your own company, do you learn this skill.

89. **Vitex**

Krivanus-blivanutvi

Neskavis-biret-urspe

Angel:
Paranas-eskranuch

Angel:
Arak-nenestu

Fulfilled Contentment

Incantation: *Kasanet hurahasvi iselbach*

Physical Benefits
May assist with Parkinson's disorder

Emotional Benefits
Creates a sense of well-being

Spiritual Benefits
Instills gratitude and hope

Insight: Between the moments, with intent; allow yourself to slip into timelessness, dissolving your form into the Ocean of Infinity, only to reform the next.

90. **White Lotus**

Sabahutvi-arach

Kavanesvi-hurespa

Angel:

Nus-setvavi-eskranut

Angel:

Ritpa-iles-nanesvi

Awakened Awareness

Incantation: *Nunas arsklava viselnet*

Physical Benefits
May be anti-carcinogenic
Supports the immune system

Emotional Benefits
Self-empowering and instills confidence

Spiritual Benefits
Fulfilling and instills contentment

Insight: To remove the illusion of separate elements of the body, contemplate the eternal nature of your being, having neither beginning nor end.

91. **Walnut (Black)**

Selenatvi-vrabanuch

Esta-vrihespa

Angel:
Nesut-aranas-selena

Angel:
Asva-klivavru

Fluid Vastness

Incantation: *Kisanut brihes prava*

Physical Benefits
Anti-parasitic

Emotional Benefits
Inner strength

Spiritual Benefits
Calming the inner dialogue

Insight: Strictures in the body are formed by the grids of belief systems. Let them tell you in meditation the story that they hold. Then release all stories in the knowledge that within indivisible existence neither history, nor story exists.

92. **Wild Yam**

Karat-plivahesbi

Nektar-bilheshna

Angel:
Pruhet-sekrenut

Angel:
Skuvavi-urespi

Supported Expression

Incantation: *Kavavech haselvi steleva*

Physical Benefits
Menopausal symptoms

Emotional Benefits
Emotionally stabilizing

Spiritual Benefits
Assists in mastery of emotions and mind

Insight: Hear the stories from all 7 elements, all 7 levels of life. Light speaks through the dream symbols of the 12 shallow dream states. (See *Shrihat Satva Yoga*.)

93. **Yarrow**

Akravit-seklevranut

Sivenus-arsk-klava

Angel: **Usach-misavetvi**

Angel: **Rekpa-haranus**

Deep Peace

Incantation: *Nunarak prihespavi eresta*

Physical Benefits
Reduces and prevents scarring (use with Lavender oil)
Wound healing
Cleanses prostrate

Emotional Benefits
Equalizes mood swings
Promotes silence of the mind

Spiritual Benefits
Supports making decisive decisions

Insight: Frequency speaks to us from the 12 deep dream states through the Poetry of Dreaming; an example from *Labyrinth of the Moon*: "The dolphin jumps through the hoop of the moon. Rings ripple through starry skies."

94. Ylang Ylang

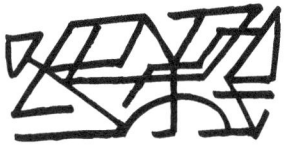
Parasut-arklat

Itre-brihanut-hures

ANGEL:

Visanach-brivabesvi

ANGEL:

Silve-arsklablut

Effortless Knowing

Incantation: *Kavanut aspava respahur*

Physical Benefits
Beneficial to health of hair
Balances blood pressure and may assist in regulating heart rate

Emotional Benefits
Releases frustration

Spiritual Benefits
Promotes androgynous mastery by balancing male/female energies

Insight: The communication from Energy required a combination of movement and images (found in *Saradesi Satva Yoga*). Move from the depth of silence and allow images to form. Feel what they are saying.

Oil Blends

If using the oils on any individual who has epilepsy or sensitive skin, consult the section on the properties of the individual ingredients before using them in oil blends.

95. **Rose, Lavender, Stocks**
    Ratios: 4, 4, 1

Arkla-vribaharanat   Michpa-ures-arseta

ANGEL: ANGEL:

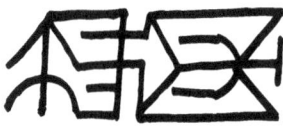

Kisapelenutvi   Ekvelavis-merechta

Unchangeable Perfection

Incantation: *Kutre plava birechvi stahur*

Physical Benefits
Cellular regeneration

Emotional Benefits
Emotional rejuvenation and lightness of being

Spiritual Benefits
Promotes inclusivity

Insight: Life-force speaks to us through meditation when images arise unbidden, like the waves of the ocean.

96. **Orange, Honeysuckle, Chamomile (German)**
    Ratios: 1, 4, 4

Suvich-kriharanasvi   **Karsu-nanarek-harstu**

ANGEL: ANGEL:

Isanuch-brivahiruset   **Vibrech-aranet-vravi**

Carefree Surrender

Incantation: *Kavech setl-brisbrava uhet*

Physical Benefits
Strengthens the immune system
Rejuvenates cells

Emotional Benefits
Anti-depressant, calming

Spiritual Benefits
Lengthens life-cycles by providing spiritual vitality

Insight: Matter speaks through movement alone. Ask a question, and then dance the answer. Note the feelings the interpretive dance sets free.

97. **Neroli, Lavender, Mugwort**
    Ratios: 1, 4, 1

Asanekvi-klivanush

Arak-blivablut-hurspa

Angel:
Krihas-bich-merestu

Angel:
Archna-sivavet-helesta

Harmonic Resonance

Incantation: *Nanes spavilhut ubrachvi*

Physical Benefits
Anti-wrinkles
Reduces scarring
Balances the hypothalamus

Emotional Benefits
Feelings of abundant bliss
Youthful attitudes

Spiritual Benefits
Freedom from programming

Insight: Breath is the language of life force. Lying in a bath of warm water for 20 minutes, eliminate the gaps between the breaths (do not hyperventilate – leave the bath if you become dizzy). Draw in deep, rhythmic breaths and sigh them out. Leave no gaps between the in and out-breaths.

98. **Ylang Ylang, Ginger, Nasturtium**
    Ratios: 2, 1, 1

Nechba-suba-eleskla

Varavespi-nesparuk

Angel:
Sitra-visanut

Angel:
Klives-usutrachve-minusat

Lighthearted Eternal Presence
Incantation: *Kiret tranadoch spirtlha uves*

Physical Benefits
Anti-parasitic
May promote lymph flow
Acne

Emotional Benefits
Aphrodisiac

Spiritual Benefits
Opens blocked emotions for effortless resolution

Insight: Instinct speaks through the poetic perspective, through becoming a living work of art. The poetry we see in the surrounding circumstances of our life and the graceful artistry from which we live, releases effortless insights - messages from instinct.

99. **Fir, Juniper Berry, Clove**
Ratios: 2, 1, 1

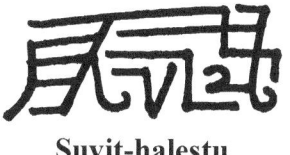
Suvit-halestu

Vrachvra-mesetur-nanusak

Angel:

Angel:

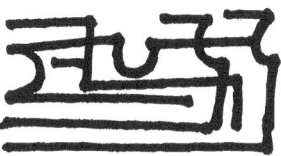
Kesba-miserut

Alach-vereharstu

Comforting Presence

Incantation: *Neset ublach bravi menhat*

Physical Benefits
Anti-bacterial, anti-viral, anti-parasitic

Emotional Benefits
Stimulates positive attitudes

Spiritual Benefits
Promotes inner strength

Insight: Multi-sensory perception, practice now each day; experiment with the senses in every way. See the music like color flow; the song of the bird within your skin you will know. Then matter will remember that it contains in indivisibility, all other elements.

100. Grapefruit, Tomato Leaf, Neroli
Ratios: 2, 1, 1

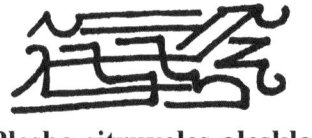

Plesba-sitruveles-aleskla　　**Brivet-usavi-vrihesvi**

Angel:　　　　　　　　　　　Angel:

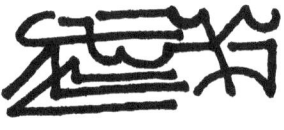　　

Krananuch-bribaset　　**Aruk-nanatur-sparu**

Perpetual Freshness of Expression

Incantation: *Kiritpa splehus astra-hurat*

Physical Benefits
May lower blood sugar
May lower high cholesterol
Supports health of hair

Emotional Benefits
Refreshes mental fatigue

Spiritual Benefits
Encourages the release of world views

Insight: Chanting heals energy blocks. Speak your truth through chants.

Saradesi vra u nam
The Fountain of Youth I am

Ka nun ta ba haravu ukla
Without beginning nor end am I

Sanata su resvi uta
Indivisible forever am I

101. **Orange, Idaho tansy, Ginger**
   Ratios: 2, 1, 2

Sitrahus-vribasut

Kiritva-elch-klavar

Angel:
Mishta-esehit-eresta

Angel:
Subit-pretprahur

Eternal Fulfillment

Incantation: *Asbek uhurunutvi arach*

Physical Benefits
Anti-parasitic, anti-fungal
Supports absorption of nutrition

Emotional Benefits
Encourages fresh perspectives
Increases resilience to stress

Spiritual Benefits
Increases appreciation through awareness

Insight: The gift of flowers' fragrant essences, removes the matrices that separate the layers of life, that once more all may be known to be indivisibly one.

102. Peppermint, Rosemary, Angelica
Ratios: 1, 2, 1

Skechva-bri-aranas

Nanuk-hilesatvi

ANGEL:
Pruhas-plabavi

ANGEL:
Aret-paruha

Supreme Elegance

Incantation: *Uhurures manach partlvi*

Physical Benefits
Colon spasm, digestion, bowel disorders

Emotional Benefits
Balances mood swings, eases fear of being alone
Refreshing

Spiritual Benefits
Renewed trust in the benevolence of life

Insight: The Song of the Self required the 7 tones of life to sing. They each hold a note. When the life of a person sings in harmony with the One Life, effortless magic flows.

103. **Jasmine, Geranium, Tangerine**
    Ratios: 2, 1, 1

Velestat-manavesvi

Harach-aravakrihuvesvi

Angel:
Pluves-mishuvat-uklesbavi

Angel:
Asanut-rekpahur

Confidence of Purity

Incantation: *Skartlhut ubrasvi menenech*

Physical Benefits
May ease genital disorders
Anti-wrinkles

Emotional Benefits
Deepens emotions and opens the heart

Spiritual Benefits
Creates openings for new solutions

Insight: Leave now separation and the matrix behind. Create your own universe where all are you and you are all. Then close are you to leaving duality behind.

104. **Sage, Lilac, Lemongrass**
     Ratios: 1, 4, 1

Machpa-esetet-klabahus

Nanuk-spibahur-arnas

Angel:
Keshva-visklebehet

Angel:
Kihur-etrak-verebach

Humorous Conjunction

Incantation: *Skarech uhurusut plavabesvi*

Physical Benefits
May assist bronchial complaints
May support hormone balance

Emotional Benefits
Grounded balance

Spiritual Benefits
Refinement of appreciation of life

Insight: No more relationship, you are all and all are one. Know this and you shall become filled with the purity of indivisibility. In an existence of no opposites shall you in rapture reside. (Almine moved into a state of Oneness on 24th September 2011.)

105. **Bergamot, Sweet Pea, Chamomile (Roman)**
   Ratios: 1, 2, 2

Arakna-brihas-esekla   **Sabahut-isetra**

Angel: Angel:

Stubahelesvi   **Parunat-kelhevestri**

Transient Expression of Indivisible Form

Incantation: *Askra pret pranavit vilesvi*

Physical Benefits
May support the nervous system
May support the adrenal system
Insect bites

Emotional Benefits
Calming, relaxing and promotes deeper sleep

Spiritual Benefits
Assists with living in meditative states

Insight: Existence is the poetic expression of the sexual interaction between perspective and unfolding eternal Oneness.

The 16 Rays of Light

Sigils and Angels 106 - 121

Tools to Restore the Mystical Properties of the Reproductive Organs

1. Release of the illusion of the permanence of the past
2. Release of the illusion of the permanence of the future
3. Release of identifying with the 'story' of life in the matrix
4. Release of memories of birth trauma
5. Release of memories of death trauma
6. Closing the gateway to the realms of the future in the pineal gland
7. Closing the gateway to the realms of the past in the coccyx bone
8. Cleansing of all parts of the self, strewn across the wheel of time
9. Cleansing of all parts of the self, strewn across the spirals of past cosmic realities
10. Allowing the moment to become a fluid eternal moment
11. For dissolving the past and future
12. Allowing the moment to become a fluid, eternal moment
13. Discovering the poetry of eternal existence speaking through the veils of illusion
14. Marriage of time and timelessness to allow the illusion of space to collapse
15. Awakening of the genital fluids' higher function as messengers of consciousness
16. Full ability of the eternal spark within to reign supreme by conveying its intent through the genital fluids

See pages 45 and 103 of this book for more information on the Rays of Light.

106. Sandalwoood, Patchouli, Rose
Ratios: 1, 1, 4

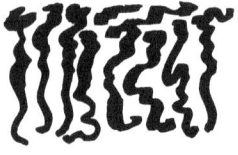

Michpa-rerestu

Isach-vave-uhurunas

Angel:

Angel:

Aklas-brivetu

Plihet-usanit

The Root

Incantation: *Misekra priharanet skuvi*

Physical Benefits
Pineal support
Anti-aging
Supports circulatory system

Emotional Benefits
Releases 'frozen' expression and sensuality

Spiritual Benefits
Increases enhanced awareness

Insight: Home becomes a state of being rather than an exterior location. Home is wherever we are.

107. Orange, Geranium, Plumeria
Ratios: 1, 1, 4

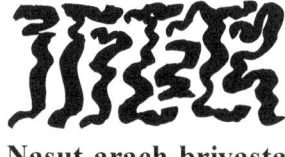
Nasut-arach-brivasta

Krihanas-iset-manuvis

Angel:

Klubavet-ustra

Angel:

Tribahur-ikletvi

Faith

Incantation: *Esechpahur plavabesvi urat*

Physical Benefits
Anti-parasitic, anti-bacterial
Supports lymph flow

Emotional Benefits
Releases sentimental value systems

Spiritual Benefits
Increases feelings of rapture

Insight: The genitalia create a life of flourishing rather than survival, by pulling in resources and creatively using them in actualizing potential into manifestation.

108. **Black Pepper, Black Walnut, Violet**
Ratios: 1, 1, 4

Trebehech-savavusta

Nankurat-pribaspava

Angel:

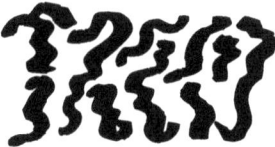
Nestu-arakles

Angel:

Unach-bileshet

Balance

Incantation: *Nechpa spartlvu ruselvavi*

Physical Benefits
May support gastro-intestinal health
Aids digestion
Anti-parasitic

Emotional Benefits
Self-empowering and grounding

Spiritual Benefits
Opens up eternal perspective

Insight: The purpose of life becomes art for art's sake, a life of grace rather than agenda-driven purpose.

109. **Ginger, Lemongrass, Geranium**
Ratios: 1, 2, 2

Set-verevaranuch-hespi   Setkla-misvet-urnavech

Angel: Angel:
Arak-nenetru   Ista-minavet

Abundance

Incantation: *Nenesplahur sparut arespahur*

Physical Benefits
Nausea and motion sickness
Insecticide and anti-parasitic
Stimulates blood flow

Emotional Benefits
Builds confidence and optimism

Spiritual Benefits
Stimulates seeing beyond appearances

Insight: The combining of pro-activity and receptivity into oneness begins in the androgynous expression of the genitals. By knowing itself to be self-fulfilled, whole and self-sovereign, self-confidence is born from the genitals.

110. Frankincense, Galbanum, Sandalwood
Ratios: 1, 1, 1

Bisat-ark-blavabech

Kurnavit-arsut-parhesvi

Angel:

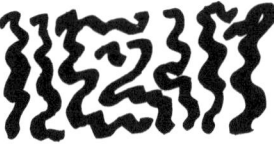
Ursta-mivavech

Angel:

Eklevar-etre-anunit

Wisdom

Incantation: *Klavanech spehererat ukla*

Physical Benefits
Rejuvenates hair and skin
Stimulates the immune system and aids detoxification

Emotional Benefits
Deepens meditation and aids in the ability to remember dreams
Opens communication with etheric realms

Spiritual Benefits
Assists with the interpretation of inner guidance

Insight: Seduction as the desire for a specific outcome is the use of sexual powers to achieve a benefit for self. In a broad sense, this is black magic. Seduction as an ongoing love affair with life is the ongoing unveiling of the infinite self.

111. Helichrysum, Rose, Frankincense
Ratios: 1, 2, 1

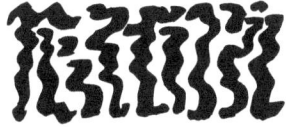
Rektu-aresta

Piranur-sehet-utrechvi

ANGEL:

Miraset-huvech-vavi

ANGEL:

Karunach-plibavu

Mercy

Incantation: *Trenes bihivarasvi ekena*

Physical Benefits
Detoxification
May assist with oxygenation of the cells
Anti-wrinkles

Emotional Benefits
Brings balance during great change

Spiritual Benefits
Restores memories of oneness beyond duality

Insight: Identity is the greatest stumbling block to achieving an existence with no opposites. Identity of gender originates from the genitals and can be overcome by eliminating the unwholeness of seeing external fulfillment. The genitals hold the key to Oneness.

112. Myrrh, Lavender, Sandalwood
Ratios: 1, 4, 1

Naksut-brivech-varaspavi

Arspanut-karus-prehespi

ANGEL:

Nisut-hirahespi

ANGEL:

Vrivavit-erekla

Diversity

Incantation: *Sihararat ninechvi utrabit*

Physical Benefits
Prevents and minimizes scarring
Anti-viral, anti-bacterial – apply to cuts and wounds that will not heal

Emotional Benefits
Brings deep satisfaction and contentment

Spiritual Benefits
Brings quietness to the mind

Insight: The largest contributor of intuitive knowing is the reproductive system. It far exceeds the third eye in opening inter-dimensional accessing of information.

113. **Melissa, Cedarwood, Tangerine**
 Ratios: 4, 1, 2

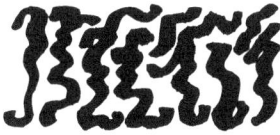
Nararak-piravesvavi

Spanut-sabahetvi

Angel:

Utrek-piraras-varavi

Angel:

Vilevis-asetvrana

Energy

Incantation: *Kretva-spereru etrasvi-nenu-hach*

Physical Benefits
Anti-infection
Bolsters the immune system
May help rheumatic conditions

Emotional Benefits
Assists with soothing emotional distress of menstruation
Soothing to the nerves

Spiritual Benefits
Dissolves patterns of resentment

Insight: Women's genitals promise joy, men's promise passion. When we combine these two within ourselves, rapture forms in the upper chest.

114. Lavender, Marjoram, Angelica
Ratios: 4, 1, 1

Karch-spavabi   Kranus-ubas-aravespranu

ANGEL: ANGEL:

Arstu-mishanut-aresva   Esta-plibaves

Bliss

Incantation: *Viset-blavu eseratvi unech*

Physical Benefits
Blood purification and general tonic
May assist with psoriasis and other skin conditions

Emotional Benefits
Clears the vision to assist in arriving at solutions
Stimulates self-confidence and self-sovereignty

Spiritual Benefits
Assists with establishing an eternal perspective
Instrumental in helping silent communication, known as 'the song of silence', in creating sensory perception beyond the linearity of the 5 senses May increase rapture

Insight: Inner guidance through effortless knowing is received from the ovaries and the prostate.

115. **Basil, Rosemary, Lemongrass**
   Ratios: 1, 1, 3

Sukvatret-harspi

Nanaruk-arachpravi

Angel:

Mesevech-kluvaset

Angel:

Isklavit-arestu

Perception

Incantation: *Vuvaset pliheshvar areta hurech*

Physical Benefits
Anti-spasmodic and anti-inflammatory
Decongests the prostate and lungs
Headaches and migraines

Emotional Benefits
Refreshes mental fatigue
Instills optimism

Spiritual Benefits
Promotes self-love

Insight: Genitals are the center for surrendered trust. When we seek external fulfillment, we surrender to others. When we are whole in self-sovereignty, we surrender to the Infinite – a prerequisite to leaving duality.

116. **Spearmint, Lemon, Ginger**
     Ratios: 1, 4, 1

Rutra-brivahet

Nechpa-pubara-nasanut

Angel:
Arktu-arakla

Angel:
Irikta-petrenit

Presence

Incantation: *Mistarut bravahur esena hurat*

Physical Benefits
Nausea and vomiting
Exfoliates skin, supports skin rejuvenation
Aids digestion

Emotional Benefits
Invigorative and restorative, assists memory

Spiritual Benefits
Stimulates creativity

Insight: Genitals are the key to youthful regeneration. When they are self-sovereign and have overcome the need for external emotional fulfillment, they stop leaking energy. As their passion and joy become one, they self-generate resources.

117. Tangerine, Honeysuckle, Peppermint
Ratios: 1, 4, 1

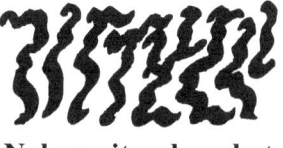

Nekva-sitru-barahet

Narut-pribararut

ANGEL:

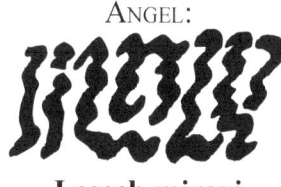

Lesech-miravi

ANGEL:

Urtre-esklanavis

Hope

Incantation: *Kelpahet ekserenach hurasvi*

Physical Benefits
May support the cardiovascular system

Emotional Benefits
Heals past trauma and releases emotional blockages

Spiritual Benefits
Induces introspective self-discovery

Insight: The linear giving and taking of sex in a relationship of opposites, creates the illusion of space and the movement between two opposite points, which is time. In their self-sovereignty, they close time and space, the two key components of a reality of opposites.

118. **Neroli, Jasmine, Geranium**
    Ratios: 1, 1, 3

Narak-esetretvi

Arektu-prubesprahut

Angel:
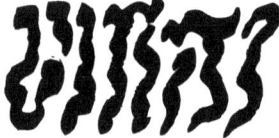
Ursta-blivabek

Angel:

Virseta-arektranut

Mastery

Incantation: *Nekta bararet husetvavi*

Physical Benefits
Stimulates cellular oxygenation
Anti-wrinkles

Emotional Benefits
Calms and restores emotional equilibrium

Spiritual Benefits
Produces states of ecstasy
Stimulates a love affair with life
Increases rapture by stimulating the eternal core of divinity

Insight: When the genitals are an instrument of expressing great depth of love, our environment flourishes.

119. **Bergamot, Lavandin, Mugwort**
    Ratios: 3, 3, 2

Ratsut-misbavech

Barech-plabavi

Angel:

Kravit-alestratvi

Angel:
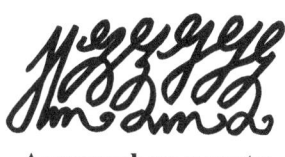
Arusprehar-narstu

Discovery

Incantation: *Nekarararut asechvi plasplahur*

Physical Benefits
Aids with insomnia
May lower blood pressure
Anti-fungal

Emotional Benefits
Very relaxing, induces clear dreams and deep sleep

Spiritual Benefits
Initiates higher states of consciousness and enables clear dream symbols to be retained

Insight: Genital flowering through self-love and self-acceptance, allows abundant elegance and grace to permeate our world.

120. Melissa, Angelica, Chamomile (German)
Ratios: 1, 2, 3

Neksabit-harstu   Perenut-ukletbravi

ANGEL: ANGEL:

Plekbarabit-erektu   Arkpa-vrivrevat

Power

Incantation: *Aktre brahus pirashvi*

Physical Benefits
Calms the nerves
Supports the excretionary pathways and purifies the blood

Emotional Benefits
Refinement and mastery of emotional responses
Deepens enjoyment

Spiritual Benefits
Creates purification of mind and emotions

Insight: The tendency for the feminine to be subservient to the masculine during sexuality occurs because of its desire to belong, which is tribalism. We can evolve by seeing ourselves as everything, and everything as us – a tribe of one.

121. **Nutmeg, Patchouli, Orange**
 Ratios: 1, 1, 2

Sutra-arkvanot

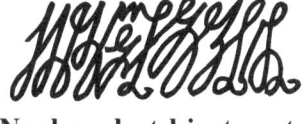
Sunit-klarut-aresta

ANGEL:

Kesebiratret-harvi

ANGEL:
Nachprahut-biret-arstu

Truth

Incantation: *Kelevishva puhuraret aresutvava*

Physical Benefits
Increases energy
General health tonic
Aids digestion

Emotional Benefits
Increases sexual satisfaction

Spiritual Benefits
Assists to rise above the density of the world

Insight: When programs of guilt exist about our genitals, the need to prove their innocence and achieve acceptance spurs on more sexual activity.

The Closing Down of the Five Directions
The Four Directions and the Center Point

Sigils and Angels 122 - 126

Removing the 5 Great Illusions of Previous Earth Cycles That Formed the 5 Directions including that of Within

122. **Rosewood, Myrtle, Grapefruit**
Ratios: 3, 2, 1

Arach-nenastu-huretvi

Ki-hur-selvaviresta

ANGEL:

ANGEL:

Brivastet-elechvi

Naruk-pli-ures

Seeing the innocence of existence

Incantation: *Nekra-brahit alspa subarut*

Physical Benefits
Supports and balances the hypothalamus
Assists with 'jet lag'
May cleanse the kidneys

Emotional Benefits
Releases old fears

Spiritual Benefits
Releases programs that promote separation

Insight: The body must be seen as an eternal expression of spaceless space; and Infinite existence, not subject to detrimental or beneficial 'external' factors such as food, exercise and so forth.

123. **Freesia, Hyssop, Rose**
     Ratios: 2, 1, 3

Prihesh-uvranasva-iseklet   **Aresva-esklevreta**

ANGEL: ANGEL:

Brihava-nachbi-uselvavi   **Sihurenet-michta**

Acknowledged perfection

Incantation: *Nitrech kasbarasut uhururespi varasat*

Physical Benefits
Anti-septic, supports resistance to infections
Supports wound healing

Emotional Benefits
Assists healing of broken hearts

Spiritual Benefits
Brings one home to self and overcoming of addiction

Insight: The illusion that another can bring or enhance ones happiness must be replaced by the understanding that another can only deepen self-enjoyment by revealing aspects of the self, in order to inspire deeper self-expression.

124. **Plumeria, Freesia, Geranium**
　　Ratios: 2, 2, 1

Nesklet-prihavesvi-subaret

Kavanesvi-hurestat

Angel:

Michpe-blibasarut

Angel:

Mishur-ubreva

Inspired moments

Incantation: *Keneverasat harchvi plerasut*

Physical Benefits
Softens skin
Anti-parasitic

Emotional Benefits
Calming and promotes well-being

Spiritual Benefits
Opens the heart

Insight: Through the presence of another, a window is provided into the infinite significance of details of unfolding moments of eternity. They do not give significance to the events, nor does it disappear when they are not present.

125. **Helichrysum, Cedar, Myrrh**
    Ratios: 2, 1, 1

Krihas-usavalachvi

Knech-sivavetvi

Angel:
Mishtekle-briset-avravileshvi

Angel:
Stu-arat-plibesvravi

Fullness beyond the law of compensation

Incantation: *Asbi sibre varasvi unech astat*

Physical Benefits
Sinus infections
May support the pulmonary system

Emotional Benefits
Releases patterns of limitation

Spiritual Benefits
Opens up new possibilities

Insight: No limitation of the body exists other than what is perceived. Programs of age, fitness levels and health constraints, must be let go of for the imaginary boundaries that they are. The key to letting these illusions go is the spontaneous expression of existence without self-reflection.

126. **Pikake, Plumeria, Tomato Leaf**
Ratios: 1, 1, 1

Nenechste-krivaset

Alestra-sibanus

Angel:
Ublech-priharasutbahi

Angel:
Kehesprevi-etvahur

Boundless living

Incantation: *Usalvaravesvi nachbar menehuset*

Physical Benefits
Stimulates digestion
May support the thyroid

Emotional Benefits
Lightens the mood, restores faith in the benevolence of life

Spiritual Benefits
Engenders hope

Insight: The eyes see form, defining it by what it is not. This creates limitation by seeing the 'empty parts' of the moment. Let us know the fullness of the moment by realizing it contains all it has to, for its contribution to the poetry of existence.

The Stationary Fields of Light

Sigils and Angels 127 - 144

The Source and Inspiration for the Poetic Perspective

1. A baby's distant laughter in the stillness of morning
2. A song of the fullness of perfection in the depths of the One
3. Eternal poise in the rumbling noise
4. The wind is within
5. A joyous explosion in the midst of the Ocean
6. Coming home to the enchanted city within
7. The silence that swallows all
8. The inspiration of true love
9. The sacred romance beyond
10. An endless ocean of rapture beckons
11. The ever-changing nuances of grace
12. So good, it can only be true
13. Risen in love
14. The venturing beyond dreams and fantasy to the Oneness
15. The flower with unparalleled petals calls for silence
16. Sovereign is the butterfly that surfs the rays of golden mist
17. The poetry of perfection is the One
18. The rapture of endless beginnings

127. **White Lotus, Rose, Ylang Ylang**
  Ratios: 1, 3, 1

Sparuch-durchtapr

Nusarut-atravivras

Angel:

Manush-eshpatur

Angel:

Kespahur-elektranusvi

Innocence of new unfoldings

Incantation: *Hureksta blahur aravesti asurat*

Physical Benefits
Hair conditioner, scalp health
Increases sexual prowess
Stimulates the senses

Emotional Benefits
Assists feelings of self-love
Creates feelings of romance

Spiritual Benefits
Opens awareness

Insight: There can be no hole in the ocean; no loss goes uncompensated. Oppressors lose self-government by forfeiting self-mastery. This occurs due to focus on external mastery. The oppressed become wealthy in the inner, because of being denied in the outer realities.

128. **Cassia, Myrtle, Sweetpea**
    Ratios: 1, 1, 4

Brisbrat-kileves-pahur **Karusut-herachkleve**

Angel: Angel:

Mishavechvi-beleheshe-vishpratur **Prevra-suvitvrave**

Embracing the incomprehensible

Incantation: *Hasklavi pihiravach nesalavit viset*

Physical Benefits
Bruises, sprains
Scarring - prevents and heals

Anti-viral, anti-fungal, anti-bacterial

Emotional Benefits
Restores innocence, purifying

Spiritual Benefits
Overcomes stagnation

Insight: Masculine dysfunction caused the unraveling of Oneness and created an 'imagined' but seemingly, painfully real cosmos of individuations. The masculine genitals' higher function is the key to the healing of duality. It holds the intuitive and poetic perspective that allows the embracing of the eternal Divine within others.

129. **Ylang Ylang, Lavender, Honeysuckle**
     Ratios: 1, 2, 3

Skaruch-eshevechvi

Nechvra-rus-utre

Angel:
Klisanat-rubaharespi

Angel:
Sihar-mestranus

Becoming the contradiction

Incantation: *Nekbarut esta-barech viselvi*

Physical Benefits
Anti-wrinkles
Rejuvenates scalp and hair
Rejuvenates skin cells, supports healing of scars

Emotional Benefits
Stimulates sexual drive
Relaxing and calming

Spiritual Benefits
Peace inducing, rage management

Insight: Inner androgyny can be found as the final releasing of gender identity to leave duality behind. It is accomplished by the emphasis of alternating masculine and feminine expression. The masculine finds the poetic, which stimulates the feminine into artistic expression, which inspires him into the same. These alternating roles of inspiration take place simultaneously once duality has disappeared and timelessness takes it place as our reality.

- The roles of receptivity as a characteristic of the feminine and pro-activity as a masculine quality, was a program designed within the web of duality to maintain masculine supremacy. Both roles are played by both genders because the division between masculine and feminine does not exist in Oneness; it is an imagined program.

130. **Ravensara, Myrrh, Rose**
Ratios: 1, 1, 4

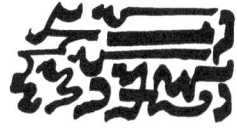

Kribat-nasarut

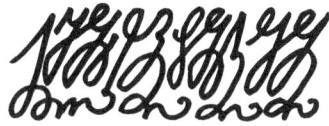

Kivranut-ekletvi

Angel:

Knisabat-blivasur

Angel:

Astravech-blivahur

Integrated rapture

Incantation: *Kavabit arsta peret hirstava*

Physical Benefits
Supports the nervous system
Supports the respiratory system

Emotional Benefits
Clears the mind, consolidates dispersed energies

Spiritual Benefits
Removes cellular programming

Insight: The concept of power is an illusion of the fallen state of the matrices of duality. When no being exists outside of the boundless ocean of existence, who is there to harness its power, or to measure the endless heaving of its boundlessness?

- Expression needs no reason but art for art's sake. The tyranny of mind demands that expression justifies its existence with purpose; enforcing the programs of guilt used by spirit to control our lives with opposites of good and bad, right and wrong.
- The refinement needed to cultivate the totality of awareness necessary to be inspired into a poetic perspective comes from allowing others and existence, to unfold and unveil itself layer by layer. Inspired by our receptivity to what lies beyond the sub-created illusory appearances, eternal existence reveals itself.

131. **Cardamom, Hyssop, Jasmine**
    Ratios: 2, 2, 1

Kretva-brinabasur **Nanech-sihas-utrechvi**

Angel: Angel:

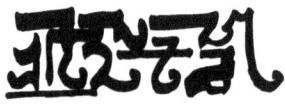

Krista-klisahur **Karus-petreha**

Inexhaustible supply

Incantation: *Ekbar blivahur nenes-kalvavi*

Physical Benefits
Expels worms
Increases elimination through the skin
Assists with nervous tension

Emotional Benefits
Regulates mood extremes, calming to nerves

Spiritual Benefits
Opens creative flow

Insight: When the endless spark within touches the divine spark of another, it is a life-altering experience of the highest form of love. To relate to and pacify another's illusory personality only strengthens their bondage.

132. **Cedar (Canadian Red), Bergamot, Patchouli**
    Ratios: 1, 4, 1

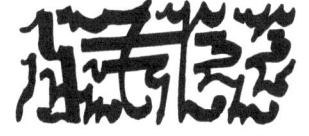
Krachva-stuba-velesvavi

Kinanech-kitre-uvar

ANGEL:

Neshpri-basubl-keresna

ANGEL:
Savis-plehes-usta

Sovereignty of the Eternal Self

Incantation: *Erchtar kishet alesvar viselvi*

Physical Benefits
Aids with hair loss
Aids with insomnia
Skin disorders

Emotional Benefits
Aids with sensitivity to the environment, supports mental clarity

Spiritual Benefits
Supports the receiving of inner guidance

Insight: Relating superficially affirms form, creating space and opposition for one another. Allow the true self beyond form to formlessly flow through the illusion of solid forms around you without resistance or judgment. Stay in the silence of eternity and in the neutrality of beingness. Disacknowledge the reality of the appearances of form as you permeate all existence like a never-ending current in the Indivisible One Life.

- Repetitious actions are only a rut when awareness of the subtle nuances of life is absent. No routine can bind us when we know it to be the fluid parameters in which we explore unfolding existence. The more the routine seems confining, the more it is the framework outlining the most delicate, refined and subtle changing ripples of all, and thus the greater that challenge is to find our source of inspiration.

133. **Wild Yam, Yarrow, Melissa**
   Ratios: 3, 2, 1

Kilsavach-bliva-helesvi

Nanek-siharavesvi

ANGEL:

ANGEL:

Neshtablit-ukresvi

Nenasak-kluhestrevar

Surrendered silence

Incantation: *Kereta prusabit helesklar anech*

Physical Benefits
Uterine complaints
Ovarian distress

Emotional Benefits
Encourages expression of the intuitive

Spiritual Benefits
Cultivates inter-dimensional capacities

Insight: Time changes in the contraction of awareness through the sub-created personalities to the eternal core of our being. It is here where timeless silence reigns and the moment fills eternity.

- The past that is also the future within the circular movement of the matrices has been kept in place by twenty-nine unyielded insights. The previous ten insights are based on one specific insight: compassion can only exist within the web of illusion because separation does. Imaginary exterior programs or standards cannot measure excellence. From a higher perspective, excellence is the moment fully expressed because there is nothing that is not excellent; there is no such thing as excellence.
- To strive for superlatives draws in mediocrity as long as our environment is an opposite. The one who expresses in excellence will find himself surrounded by what in his high standard, seems like inadequacy.

134. Black Cumin, Clary Sage, Black Walnut
Ratios: 1, 2, 4

Stabahit-krisur-ustachvi   Arek-haresta-mistrenaduk

Angel: Angel:

Pretpra-vilesvi-stechve-nubasur   Arech-krivanus

Inspired existence

Incantation: *Valavesh ersetar brachbaver*

Physical Benefits
Anti-parasitic and expels worms
May lower cholesterol

Emotional Benefits
Grounded balance with temporal affairs

Spiritual Benefits
Promotes self-sovereignty

Insight: Food, water, air and other external sources of nourishment we have dependent relationships with can only affect us if we approach them superficially from our sub-created personality levels. If we flow through the food from our indivisible, eternal Self, that which is real within our food will be accentuated and that which is not will disappear before our real Divinity.

135. **Chamomile (Roman), Violet, Pikake**
    Ratios: 3, 1, 2

Trasva-krisat-nesbahur

Samnasut-ersklevatra

Angel:
Neserek-tribeles-krisatur

Angel:
Karuchnit-selbavi

The Poetic Perspective

Incantation: *Kasabavi ninach ruspavahur*

Physical Benefits
Soothes tired feet
Chapped skin
Supports deep sleep

Emotional Benefits
Peaceful and contented feelings

Spiritual Benefits
Inspired living

Insight: Kundalini in the pranic tube is the true epicenter of the body; the misplaced epicenter designed to keep us in density is the spine. The color of the kundalini turns white just prior to leaving duality. It is blue when there are masks for protectiveness and contraction into ego-identification. It becomes red when we strive to conquer and become more. It becomes yellow when we cling to belief systems and the tools of mind: reason, logic, and intellect. In complete surrender it becomes white.

- Linear time is created by the spine and nervous system. Eternal time, (the movement of the tube torus), is created by the heart as a field around the body. The moments are created by the true epicenter of the body, the pranic tube. Although the moments still form a linear progression when shallowly lived, they are also the windows into eternity. Each moment, when entered into as all that exists, can be the entry into timelessness.

136. **Melissa, Ravensara, Violet**
Ratios: 3, 2, 1

Liva-suramet-pile-hubarechsvi   Espahur-vibrasvi

ANGEL: ANGEL:

Kiret-avechva-nachva-stubaht   Kesenas-plahur

Eternal indivisibility

Incantation: *Klisetret brivesh pravekbi*

Physical Benefits
Allergies
Respiratory infections
Wounds

Emotional Benefits
Heals painful memories

Spiritual Benefits
Encourages self-expression

Insight: Sinking through the moment into the depths of ourselves, we bypass the personalities of the past and enter the quiet eternal part of ourselves. The spaceless bubble of timelessness 'located' behind the navel is the way we can touch the face of eternal indivisible life while still in the web of existence. It is an entry into a timeless condition that prepares us for leaving duality altogether, much the same way a diver enters a decompression chamber after deep sea diving.

137. Helichrysum, Frankincense, Myrrh
Ratios: 3, 2, 1

Hitra-neserutvi-kilnech-uskrat-vivech-anas

Angel:

Arktu-nenachsat

Angel:

Satvi-iklet-barushva

Vilshba-bravanuk

Graceful unfoldment

Incantation: *Kehet-trave arasatvi manesh*

Physical Benefits
Diarrhea, stomach viruses
Diptheria and typhoid fever
Warts

Emotional Benefits
Powerful purifying effect on attitudes

Spiritual Benefits
Heightens consciousness

Insight: Name associations, both positive and negative, give identity; they bind us in a way that holds old, discordant presences in place and prevent fluid change from occurring by holding on to old memories. These need to be cleared with determination in relation to ourselves and others.

- The bones of the cap of the skull and the coccyx hold memories of previous traumatic deaths and births in the form of frozen emotions of terror. The understanding of the past as a dream within a dream erases the illusional hold on the present by unreal pasts. This allows effortless intuitive knowing in the pineal and the genitals to take place.
- The cohesive density of the body is kept in place by the 'story' of the individual and the resulting identity that the person receives from the story of his life. Releasing the 'story' releases the hold of the matrices, which keep us dense.
- The blood holds memories. Cleanse it by releasing old ideas of what love is. True, eternal love is the touching and blending of divine spark to divine spark, true essence to essence. It is here where emotion and knowledge is transcended by infinite Oneness.

138. Honeysuckle, Stocks, Chamomile (Roman)
Ratios: 4, 4, 1

Sach-uvanet-urat-bives-harasvi   Arta-piritna-harsanut

Angel:
Setva-neskarut-pelahut-esetra

Angel:
Iklet-vitra-pererut

Trusting surrender

Incantation: *Arch-asanavar pluvar vitre-prahus*

Physical Benefits
Delirium Tremens
May help with healing addictions

Emotional Benefits
Centered presence, being home for self

Spiritual Benefits
Promotes rapture and bliss

Insight: There are atomic particles (protons, neutrons and electrons), which are used in alchemy to change one substance to another. There are also 7 levels of sub-atomic particles, differing from one another in that the magnetic, horizontal axis (they resemble little wavy crosses) has 7 different tones of frequency, which create 7 levels of life. Physicality is created from sub-atomic particles that have the lowest tone (see *Windows Into Eternity*). There is however a third building block of existence, larger than atoms, but more etheric. They can be called potential particles and resemble tiny tube toruses. They are like little windows between realms.

- These three types of building blocks hold past information, like vast bands of libraries, forming 3 separate cosmic realities. They are called the 3 types of Akashic Records.
- Sub-atomic particles hold the memories of deeds and actions and are the source of karma in all 7 levels of life. Akasha is the combination of all 7 levels. It can also be called undifferentiated matter. It is here where psychic impressions form (ghostlike images that have no self-awareness or consciousness).
- The potential particles hold spoken words and suppositions; the "what ifs" or the "if onlys". Potential comes in two polarities (the tube torus rolling outwards and inwards, has two sides and two actions going on simultaneously). The feminine potential consists of that which is suppressed and prevented from expressing. The masculine or positive potential is that which has the suppositions.
- If we want to speak, write or sing, or participate in any communication of frequency without imprinting reality (which locks the past in place), it must be permeated with the eternal real communication of the silent song of the indivisible self.

139. Davana, Sweetpea, Ginger
Ratios: 1, 2, 1

Sekva-usach-balavespi **Arlas-vilsevra**

ANGEL: ANGEL:

Katru-misesh-urechbi **Kluhastra-bravabis**

Adventurous self-exploration

Incantation: *Usut-pravar este asunach*

Physical Benefits
Supports hormonal balance
Improves skin elasticity

Emotional Benefits
Feelings of encouragement

Spiritual Benefits
Encourages uplifting perspective

Insight: The cosmic akashic records have their microcosmic similarity in the bodies of man.[8] The sub-atomic particles in the physical (+) and etheric (-) bodies of man hold physical memories or karma, of actions taken. The emotional (-) and mental (+) bodies

---

8 See page 68 for image of 7 Bodies of Man.

hold memories of emotions and feelings that are resolved after death by the soul.

- The spirit emotional (-) and spirit mental (+) bodies hold unexplored potential that must be expressed or resolved during ascension (a state of transfiguration that supercedes death).
- The 7th body is the controlling tool of spirit; accessing data from all 3 record-keeping systems. It permeates all six of the other bodies and then dictates the way reality will unfold by means of the assemblage point and life force center (see www.schoolofarcana.org, Glossary of Terms).

140. **Cedarwood, Cajeput, Lupin**
     Ratios: 3, 1, 4

Neshka-klibasur-krivatut   **Arek-uratu-mines-harsta**

Angel: Angel:

Neskat-reksu-besklash-patur   **Selve-skliharvat**

Inevitable authenticity

Incantation: *Kabahut menes-ishavar rutret*

Physical Benefits
Bronchial conditions
Intestinal conditions
Skin spots

Emotional Benefits
Releases old grievances

Spiritual Benefits
Balances joy and passion

Insight: The bodies become one by allowing a poetic perspective to take place, living a surrendered life in which they become androgynous and by singing the silent song of rapture of intense awareness throughout our being. This must be accomplished as a pre-requisite to overcoming duality. (See *The Atlantean Book of Angels* online course, www.spiritualjourneys.com.)

141. **Lilac, Geranium, Tomato Leaf**
 Ratios: 2, 2, 1

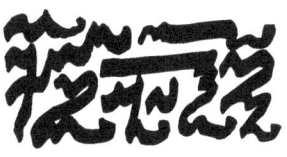

Kershpa-trekva-lelsesbish-brenevach

Parut-bribavek

ANGEL:

Krasut-nechpaliset-neshtalvi

ANGEL:

Karchna-subarut

Receiving self-fulfillment

Incantation: *Sihubatret arska elechpavi*

Physical Benefits
May help balance blood sugar
Liver detoxification

Emotional Benefits
Eases feelings of inadequacy

Spiritual Benefits
Strengthens feelings of love

Insight: The pranic tube creates the succession of moments; it therefore creates linear time. The Haraknit is a 'pocket' of timelessness. The pranic tube is linear and creates space. The Haraknit is spaceless. By combining these two in the body, we close down the first causes of duality: time and space. For this holy marriage to take place, the pranic tube must be white - that of the surrendered life.

142. **Myrtle, Fleabane, Stocks**
    Ratios: 1, 1, 4

Krenuch-setravit-klasit-brenevach

Kiranasvi-prekpratur

Angel:

Kelvekrasut-natir

Angel:

Sech-uras-nanis

Unencumbered freedom of expression

Incantation: *Kiset-bavi aras aresta*

Physical Benefits
Supports the pancreas
May help delayed puberty

Emotional Benefits
Opens the heart, fuller emotional expression

Spiritual Benefits
Assists with finding one's voice, self-expression

Insight: Become aware of the fluid, eternal, formless form part of yourself. Have it flow through the pranic tube. Old programs will effortlessly fall away in the presence of the real. Do this over and over if necessary until the pranic tube contains white light.

143. **Neroli, Tangerine, Hyssop**
    Ratios: 3, 2, 1

Setve-manut-ubrachspi   **Aret-helsvrava**

Angel: Angel:

Kesteblava-bishtahur   **Usanarut-pelesva**

Amazing grace

Incantation: *Mivarech iset blavabi*

Physical Benefits
Removes intestinal mucous
May help remove cellulite
Supports the immune function

Emotional Benefits
Activates intuition
Mental clarity

Spiritual Benefits
Eliminates patterns of shock in the cells

Insight: Imagine the Haraknit entering in a union of rapture into the pranic tube. Feel waves of rapture enlarging and enlarging the merged pranic tube/Haraknit until it fills all the bodies including the physical one. The bodies will explode into one and as the expansion continues, lose all boundaries and become the ocean that never ends.

The Poetry of the Perfection is the One

144. **Rose, White Lotus, Spikenard**
Ratios: 4, 2, 1

Skirinas-strakva-nenes-vatrahur

Kanavech-parut-urasvi

ANGEL:

Sitrahet-hurnavich

Unimagined contentment

Incantation: *Hurat privatar bluhavabes-bi asatar*

Angel: 144 a - m

a) **Skilitrechvi-peresut**

b) **Kavasatvi-presba-uklavet**

c) **Stivasut-meshvara**

d) **Ketremish-unas-balahespi**

e) Kivanuchra-utnabil

f) Stirach-kavanes-presbelenus

g) Pershtu-kriset-manur

h) Skeverut-arstrack-
brivech-kelsatvi

i) Stechba-miseretvi

j) Estrach-hures-paratvi

k) Kisech-rakturbi-urastat

l) Ra-at-Pirskla-
nesek-urstachvi

m) Iskresat-parut-mirsavechvi

Physical Benefits
Skin tonic, scalp treatment
Anti-wrinkles
Uterine and menstruation difficulties
Circulatory system

Emotional Benefits
Deep contentment and release of birth trauma

Spiritual Benefits
Assists with achieving deep states of meditation and quietens the mind

Insight: At this point, you no longer entertain the unreal story of the dream. Having become free from all programs, you are beyond duality.

Recommended reading: *People's Desk Reference for Essential Oils*, compiled by Essential Science Publishing.

Part IV

The Haaraknit

The Haaraknit

Entering into the Haaraknit

The Haaraknit has been described as being similar to a decompression chamber used by deep sea divers who have been in the depths of the ocean and must readjust to surface conditions. It is 'located' behind the navel, a place of spaceless space and timeless time where one may enter the door of Oneness by truly seeing the Infinite.

(For further information about the Haaraknit, we recommend the online course, 'Down the Rabbit Hole', part 8.)

The Spaceless Space of No-Mind
The Scrolls of the Hanasad

Excerpt from *Revisiting the Labyrinth*, Day 41

Kaanich Savit eshe ehe u va kenevilik stat pelesh pavaa nisetaa...
Only from the empty space of fullness that is accessible from the place of no-mind...

Bilech vaa nisit ares paa ra rut selevaa sta usanaa.
Can you change the illusory manifestations of form.

Paara urik eneklesh hers tra haa, ese kle vribak elese nenunish vraktra unit.
Only by leaving the tangled web of time, do you master space and its manifestations.

Kishat arek nisetra pra hut astava ninushat.
From the fondnesses of your heart are prison bars born.

Kaarch baru nisa peles pirkna esta balukve isetenaa sabuvit enes nasta kla-uve perus.
Those things that you deem worthy of esteem, you hold entrapped by your affection.

Kahas esekla uset palekva usete anash herstuvaa esakle enunish.
The static sub-creations of man have given him the comfort of a reference point.

Keret restave ehespe kle erevi nat kuraret presvi estana herusat klave.
They have also kept him captive of the world of form and unable to affect it.

Eres pa nusa te vaa esekle parunash iselvi estana ba vi.
One cannot change that which holds you captive within it.

Arch ara virstat blivesh nisavi kelech ni heresbi asta irit alechva.
From formlessness can form be changed, but to enter there you must have no mind.

Salvate esete inesh haras sta ve kla bilis stekve harusat strave.
It is thought that holds the structure of reality in place.

Kisi abavet herekla pra urut.
Release form to re-create it again.

Akra eneset uselvavi nostruva vim asva kisel usetaa paaresh nenechta harasv uklat.
Live from mindlessness at all times that you may claim the divinity of man that slumbers as potential.

Kiras vrusta arch bilech esete nunach vibras blivestavak harsta esklava.
Go beyond the moment to timelessness, and attachment to form will be gone.

Kaaranach uselva niset arat heres estravaa, minash hurech vilesvaa stenanoch.
Mind is like a spider web of lines of light that lie like a grid over a bottomless well.

Hursvaa kaaranach eskle paru be urasat kla haarech stat, pa-ahalish ninaset bri-uvra.
Mind has been the worst offender in creating illusion, but heart's attachments have been keeping it in place.

Kursat kaaranach heresat, piraspave uklet nina shetve huspava.
From mind did the illusory world spring; from there shall it also be dismantled.

Kaarch basur eselve unush kel savaa.
From there shall entry come to formlessness.

Uktrek baalich hers parut nesatra pilish usekvi eles nistra parut...
Consider that which your heart ensnares by its affections..

Kaaha-ayish iselpe ru-uhut kaa anesh sitreve ikles vi aras kirstaa verebich speleluk nehesh estaa klu-hish.
That which we think of as our great joys receives our focus and from our inordinate attention, cannot evolve.

Ka-usabas ares tre hur na nasat treheruk.
We cannot imagine that it could be more than what it is.

Kaa-u vavas bli heresut uklave, ekle misaba brivek arat.
Nature is such an example; it lags behind in evolution.

Ki-aa hera piravit kelech pa-uharat usete kanaa hirs vravi.
It lags behind humankind in evolving beyond its savagery.

Nich verestach bilash nenuset paa-a lach vilseba nun-urhukret selvevach nehestra.
Parts of our body are more pleasing to us than others. They too do we bind to the ways of the past.

Kaanahish stavaa baruk esklave nusaltaa, viribak pluhes esete nunave arasva sklu-abach.
When something cannot evolve into a more refined expression, it deteriorates from stagnation.

Kaa-a halshet penech uva shevavaa kravich prevaa harushat unesh paklaa.
Fear of formlessness and identification with the body are other causes of bondage.

Paalesh ekenach sirvata nesba ersut aras erstavaa minach heresvrabu.
Many attachments to dissolve so that you may enter through the door of no-mind.

Skarach ersetaa paaravish nestaa ukla vereskra paarech elestaa nanuvich.
Only from no-mind can the physical be mastered and form obey and re-form.

Kelese isata pilikvaa restu aras kelesta piles vratu vibras aranus tre hestaa: Haaraknit
The cosmic entry to no-mind is on Earth and is called: The Haaraknit.

Karavrastu nenish arach vreharsh pra nu Haaraknit ste u aklas vrebu.
The opening into formless life, the Haaraknit, is present in the skull of man.

Virsklavaa erstaa ninach uselvaa erek perenut.
By entering here, miracles are done in your environment.

Paalesh heresta aklech nunahers birak ekre virasat paa-uklet velasvi.
Only from outside illusion can it effectively be changed.

Kuras estra biranak vile-ustravaa haarstana skarut uvrekla bares.
To live from here, disease ends as you re-create your form at will.

Kru-hanach subetsta kle-uharanet esta uranechvi iskle mishet.
By opening the door you can go in and out, preparing yourself to life in formless form.

Kurut arsta erkle brivet erste ninus harsva aruset erkletve privabit.
It is the wellspring of all incorruptible white magic to dissolve illusion.

Vaaravach stu-a vesvi nu-ahastat kires eruch pa-uha arsavat vi-uklatve.
What is magic but the quickening of events out of linear progression and linear change?

Elshpa nisetu arakve pelsut nenuneshvi haaruvarsta ere uklet ni-uvrek spava.
In the formless place of no-mind, eons can pass in what feels like moments.

Pilsetra erek virstakaanich savit ubach aklesh vilevach aresta uselvi paarech nisulnavi.
Affecting life from the empty place of fullness bypasses time and creates instant manifestation.

Aaruk arsta kiret baranuch urat pires arksta pilavivek viles minesta.
Youth comes from the androgynous union of form and formlessness.

Kirapa bivek elke nus astavaa irestaa arch klanaaniset uselvi haarichpa eret klavi.
When illusionary form is dissolved, we live as images of separateness within Oneness.

Kaanash ersta hursvava enash urach pararut niselvi branabak esklavu ukrevit salvuta.
The way images are cast upon a screen; we are the screen playing the roles of the unreal images.

Kaarach nenesut alskla baruch nesta aruvit ereta paarus areskla vrehut alsh pravaa verus haras eretu.
From a life of knowing ourselves to be the screen, not the images, we can participate in directing the play.

Plu-uhasat nanes prehut alstabaa kranuch kinash herchstavaa.
It is the way for our environment to reflect the purity of the heart.

Kaalavak espa helesat urechspi neselvi eresak urestavaa nanushit.
The body casts reflections that loom around us in overbearing vastness.

Arach sutava rishpa unechvi viblechspa erskla piret nanunespi aruvasat.
The reflections create an environment that mirrors the opposite of what we are.

Kirat pirihatva nanunespara kilvasat.
It is the nature of mirrors to reflect opposites.

Aranak pilesba uras treha bruhabas virskla vrines arach pelevu.
Oneness requires a life of no opposites, for they only exist as part of duality.

Nuska aras knu-avach kruvespi uskle velesh haravas brivechbi nanusat.
Beings of shadow can only be gone when our body becomes a fluid field.

Tre he ura nanusat palesh herstavaa aklesh paa laluch ve hurit.
The field has to be androgynously integrated with the whole.

Arach herenus arksla parut niset vavu areskla parut eret urech nenesh usta.
Though the eye sees another as separate, it cannot be. The ocean cannot be divided.

Kurach nereset ekles urstava ninus eret paara ekleshne stuva.
Form became solid because we believed the trick of our eyes.

Arska nusivavi arak ekleshne irata piruha. Neselvi baruch harvasta.
The Oneness of life whispers through the amygdala and must override the messages of the eyes.

Kuhurabit niret eresklave piruha arvata ishate ekle hunesvi ararestruanit.
There are certain qualities to live that help the amygdala interpret the messages of the One Life.

Archna iras harsut pilichva aranut eselvaa.
The trick of the eyes lets us play the game of relationship.

Asalvi urnut aruk vra hilsevat arach pra-unut hiret arak bruhastat uselnet.
Though relationship has value as a means of joy, believing it to be real is detrimental.

Kaananish aras esklave hurisvaa arak piret utre aranas vilesva bravabik vilset minuve aras paranut esklave.
When we believe the real to be unreal, a schism opens between our imaged field and our presence as part of the One.

Kaa sa barurit eraskle virspa haranus ersklava pravit arstaa eklavu ninas harus erstravaa vabrit urestaa.
Once separation occurs we believe form to be a cause rather than an effect, leaving us disempowered.

Aruch nenesut arech pravabit sutvavi arek harustaa.
A great secret hides the realms of no-mind and space.

Pilekvavi ikles anas viles minestra esa tra hesavi ines pilekvavi arasnut minestra uret.
The place of formlessness is a tool for form to use and thus the form is not the tool of formlessness.

Kuna husiva eres aras Haaraknit echsta ures paarat iklet pilekvavi nistu kerech baanik stanut.
But a pocket it is, the Haaraknit, to step into to escape the confines of the matrix of form.

Archba satvaa arsklavi eres unasta heres tra-una palanesh.
Like all illusion, it too can control us if we think it is real.

Kaasachvi nivash ures tra haras vribet aararak harastaa kli-unech.
The real part of you is embodied. Abdicate not from the sovereignty of your life.

Kaarch parva, nestavu ares, hursta vi-brachvi araves kla-una.
Eternally seeking, never to find anything greater than your present life.

U-aklave irinachvi uhespa arstava vi uklesh nasta vilesva hurnavich estavaa.
All is but an instrument by you designed that aspects of the Infinite can play.

Kuhelesh estavi kli-uva miste parut aranus aresta vra-u-akla pravilset pere usta vablik velsh bavaa.
No definition can ever explain the Infinite majesty that plays the self-relationship game.

Aarlaklach biset vara bravi hunus alstaa brech branik estavaa klaves.
Only one being exists and plays with the images of its inseparableness.

I enter the Haaraknit — the place of all magic: this is the first spaceless space I have entered... no beginning, no end, no up or down... no point to move — all comes to me, or rather is created in response to me... in flashes of color all is revealed... yet although no sound is found in my body — unfolding through me — my stomach tightens at the unfamiliarity. This is different than when I've moved through the "void"... this is animated, yet I see no individuated beings. I wonder briefly what Haaraknit means. Instantly the spaceless-space swirls — a sort of tunnel forms — I feel images: a family in distress — it means "window." I don't recognize the language of the word. I feel rather than hear: The language of no sound. Are there repositories of information? None exist in a window... Using "Haaraknit" from the depth of your being ... the incomplete buried symbols [blah]. What are they? Keys to yourself...

Closing

We live in extraordinary times when massive cosmic cycles close and new ones begin. Laws of the cosmos melt away to yield to more inspiring realities.

These less dense times benefit Belvaspata practitioners on a practical level, yielding more effortless results, graceful transitions and miracles due to the closing of the gap between cause and effect – the result of waning electro-magnetic fields.

These times are not to be feared, but rather regarded as a glorious opportunity. Let us seize the chance to create the miracles Belvaspata is the vehicle for, and with the additional information given here, remind the world of its origins of Oneness. Let a new reality begin…
"Nachva herestu ura ash bravenut"

Almine

Appendices

Appendix I

Gas Discharge Visualization to Determine the Effectiveness of Healing Methods

By Dr Sabina DeVita

A study was initiated in the presence of the healer Almine to ascertain visible and scientific measures of changes on the biological systems of a small group of subjects. The Gas Discharge Visualization (GDV) Bioelectrography camera was used.

About the Bioelectrography Camera

The Bioelectrography camera measures the human energy field and allows us to detect and monitor changes in the subtle energy fields of the individual. The energy field is a cosmic blueprint and use of this technology was most appropriate in monitoring the participants in this study.

The camera is the most advanced comprehensive full-body imaging device available on the market today, used and developed by

Dr. Konstantin Korotkov, a leading Russian physicist internationally renowned for the pioneering research he conducted on the human energy field over approximately the last 20 years.

The system allows for direct, real-time photos and videos of the entire energy field of a human as well as other organisms and materials. The information is extracted by computer software that measures brightness, size, fractality and other parameters of the energy field. It is a unique system, distinctive from that used in Kirilian photography.

The photographs can give information about the psychological, emotional and physical condition of the subject. This aura-imaging technique is especially useful in showing changes in the subtle energy distribution around the human body before and after any experience.

The Study

The principal author, Dr. DeVita, conducted all testing of subjects, pre and post, over a 6-day period. The study consisted of a small group of subjects who were subjected to specific healing conducted by Almine. The testing methodology was based on individual GDV analysis of psychological/emotional/physical states. Post- and pre-GDV photography was taken to observe the effectiveness of the healing.

Dr. DeVita was personally trained by Dr. Korotkov in Canada in October 2001. More advanced training was received in July 2002 in St. Petersburg, Russia. She received an International Certificate for her presentation of clinical data to the VI Scientific Congress and for her active participation in hands-on training workshops.

About Dr. Konstantin Korotkov, inventor of the technology used in this study

Dr. Krotokov is Professor of Computer Science and Biophysics at Saint-Petersburg Federal University of Informational Technologies, Mechanics and Optics and Professor of Research in Saint Petersburg Academy of Physical Culture. He holds 12 patents on biophysics inventions and is the author of more than 90 papers on physics and biology published in leading Russian and international journals. He has written multiple books, published in Russian, English and Italian. The titles include: *Life after Life: Experiments and Ideas on After-Death Changes of Kirilian Pictures,* 1998, NY Backbone Publishing Co., and *Aura and Consciousness: New Stage of Scientific Understanding*, 1999, St. Petersburg, 'Kultura'. Dr. Korotkov is also President of the International Union of Medical and Applied Bioelectrography.

Analysis and Interpretation of GDV Information

The Gas Discharge Visualization camera created by Dr. Konstantin Korotkov is the first device in the world that measures the distribution of the energy level of biological objects (energy geomeo kinesis). It is being used for medical diagnosis in many medical facilities.

This technique is based on the visual observation or registration on a photo film of gas discharge fluorescence as it appears close to the surface of the investigated subject, placing it into a high intensity electromagnetic field. Using computer software, analysis is estimated by means of non-linear mathematics and data-mining methods developed by Russian scientists. It has been successfully trialed in Russia, England, Germany, Slovenia, the United States and is acknowledged in many other countries.

Healthy Aura

The field of a healthy active person is dense, uniform and has smooth changes of color from the blue spectrum through the orange to the yellow. Both psychological and physical profiles of each subject were taken before and after the healing sessions.

Disturbances

Holes, gaps, heterogeneities and outbursts in the aura are indicators of disturbances in the energy field. They point to disorders on mental, functional or organ levels, showing a direct link to the organ system indicated on the Beogram (aura picture). Left and right side projections of the image show disturbances that relate to both logical cerebral and right intuitive hemispheres and right and left sides of the body.

Gaps or breaks in the psychological/emotional profile represent leakage of energy and the individual is most likely experiencing a number of powerful symptoms. The images of the Beograms help us to decode an individual's main psycho-emotional state and denote the relationship between the organs and the psyche.

Old Chinese texts link rage with liver damage, worry with spleen damage. Cord-like structures appear to enter and exit the body, often indicating attachments between people via intense emotions coupled with thoughts of fear or worry.

Brief Interpretations of 3 Subjects from this Study

Subjects 1, 2 and 3 are presented here both before and after their healing sessions. All three displayed gaps, holes and cords plus irregular energy fields. The pictures and diagrams included display the definitive improvement after the healing. The 'before' GDV Kirilian picture outlines the disturbed energy field. The 'after' image displays the bio-energetic change and the significant effectiveness of Almine's intervention.

In conclusion, this study shows that the spiritual healing of these 3 individuals as performed by Almine was indeed successful. Similar effects were noted on each of the other participants.

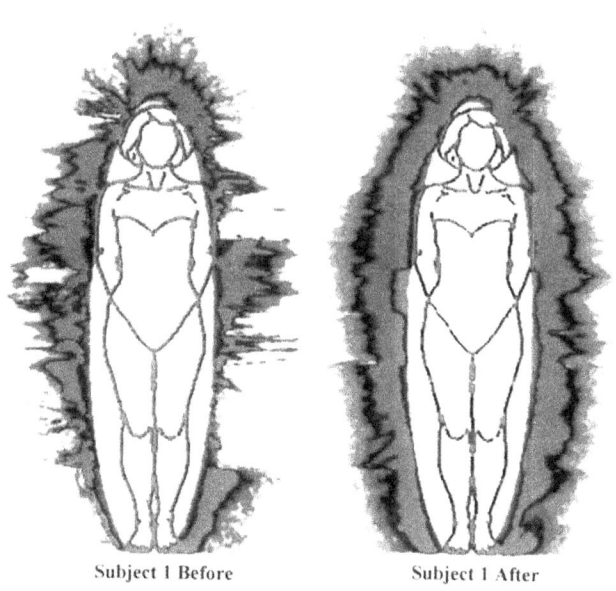

Subject 1 Before   Subject 1 After

Appendices

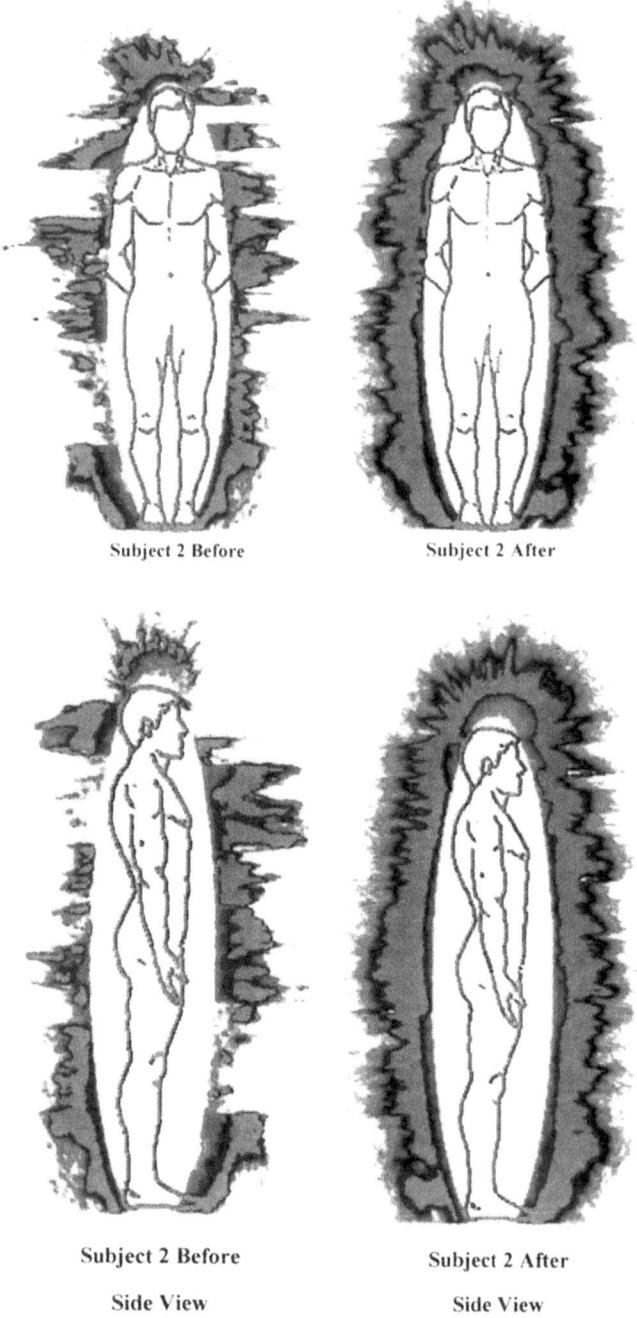

Subject 2 Before   Subject 2 After

Subject 2 Before   Subject 2 After
Side View   Side View

Belvaspata

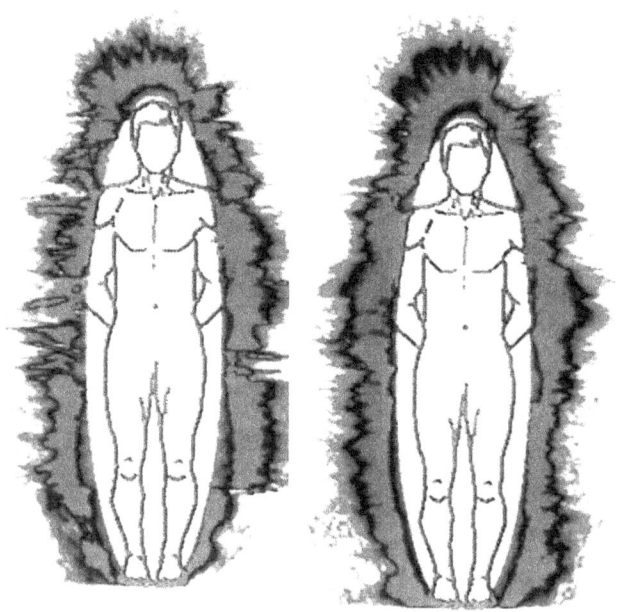

Subject 3 Before   Subject 3 After

Appendix II

Guidance for Beginning Healers

by Almine

As our journey of exploring the intricate art of healing and our responsibilities as healers begin, you are urged to remember that the more you grow, the more you will gain from this information. You may, therefore, wish to return to it periodically and re-read portions of it that new layers may reveal themselves to you.

Whether the techniques have a mild or profound effect on those who come to you for assistance will depend largely on how well you have internalized the qualities given in the ***Belvaspata*** section. Do not heal for the sake of results, so that you can remain unencumbered by the weight of self-reflection. However, you will become more and more aware of how healing frequencies respond to you. This, like the acquisition of any other skill, will grow with practice. The techniques provided give you something to practice with. The illusion of disease comes in an instant and so can healing, but knowing what to heal and asking the right questions in giving your client guidance is a product of humility, an openness to receiving information and of practice.

It is recommended that beginning healers form free healing circles, as their time is available (evenings and weekends, perhaps) to develop the skills necessary for working with clients. Recognition of the divinity of those who come for assistance, as well as a deep and abiding compassion, can make even a beginning healer effective.

Always be sure you are not in a state of emotional duress and that you have had sufficient food and water. Take time to establish a sacred space and to cleanse it after each client. The work you are doing is holy in that it removes the filters that block the passage of light. Treat your healing room as worship space. Make sure that when your client leaves, they do not encounter disruptive or hostile emotions from others in the building, since they will be wide open and highly sensitive.

We urge healers to study and abide by the laws of the state in which they reside. In many states it is illegal to say, "I heal" and healers have to call themselves healing facilitators. In others it is illegal to touch another person unless you are licensed to do so. A minister's license will enable you to do so legally. They are easy to obtain and can be kept current at little cost. Even though there are homeopathics remedies strong enough to heal disease, it may be necessary to represent them as facilitating healing or as nutritional aids.

Dealing with these sacred healing modalities where the veils between realities become thin and the past and present merge with the future, takes great courage. With impeccability as your shield and in a place of balance that has shed the need to impress, your steps will be guided so you may stride forward unafraid to reveal the perfection that dwells in all beings.

Seeing the divinity within ourselves enables us to see it in another. To approach our fellow man as less than divine is to deny the Source of his being. He is an arrow sent forth from the hand of the Infinite, straight and true upon its course. The ancient Norsemen shot flaming arrows into mist to guide their boats safely into the unknown. In the same way we have been sent like flaming arrows to explore the mysteries of the Infinite's Being. All flaming arrows are of equal value to the navigator; some tell him where it is clear to go and others showing where it is not. In the same way within the mystery of the Infinite's Being, all are equal. There is much value in mirroring to the Infinite, through the experience of a life, that which It is not, so It might fully understand that which It is.

Exerting influence on the life of another is a sacred, awesome responsibility. When our fellow man approaches us to ask for help, remember his true identity as a being vast as the cosmos having a human experience and approach him with humility and impeccability. For in helping birth him into an awareness of the infinite possibilities that lie sleeping within his soul, we are helping him find the diamonds of divinity lying hidden in the dust of illusion.

There is great value in opposition and, hidden within the shadows of density, lies the impetus to set us free from mortal boundaries. Without friction, no creature can walk upon the Earth. Nature has designed the opposition that any fetus must overcome to earn the right to life. In truth, opposition strengthens and in a similar manner we strengthen density when we oppose it. We strengthen the shortcomings we suppress and the illness we combat. Challenge yields perception and perception yields power. If we pull the chicken prematurely from the egg, it dies. If we remove a sufferer's pain without assisting him to receive its insights, a great dawn of illumination might die stillborn.

Throughout the cosmos the Infinite has gained in luminosity and power, not by denying the unsolved mystery of 'The Dark' within Its Being, but by including it within the light so it might yield its insights. The greatest service we can render as the One expressing as the many is to remember who we are, for in this memory all is included. The greatest hardships hold within their overcomings the greatest miracles.

As wielders of power, our balance is maintained through constantly remembering that the insights gained in all of life's journeys are of equal value in enriching the One. The vast majority of Creation falls within the realm of that which, from our vantage point, is unknowable. This eliminates the temptation to yield to the compulsion of the left-brain to reduce the infinite to the finite. It stifles the incessant need to know and sets us free from attachment to outcome.

To sow in order to reap gives only the harvest as reward. But to sow like a pilgrim traveling through the land, scattering seeds along the way with no thought of benefit from their eventual fruition is to become an instrument in the hand of the Infinite. We sow, not to reap the benefit, but because the seeds are in our hands and our passage blesses all creatures. As we bless others with the seeds of healing, let us remain unencumbered by self-reflection and unfettered by self-importance. Do not focus on the results of your healing; it is life giving unto life. You are the blessed flute upon which the Infinite plays divine melody. Be assured that, in as much as the soil of the soul is responsive, the seed will grow even if the fruit or flower of its maturity arrives long after you have passed.

The sublime path of being a blessing to mankind, shedding light on dark days, is not for those who pretend ignorance to escape culpability. It is not for those who hide behind false humility, which is simply conceding to the arrogance of another. Instead, it is for men and women willing to let their light increasingly illuminate with the soft flow of hope the darkest corners of the lives they touch. It calls for masters with the innocence of a child, who freely acknowledges their inability to know the infinite plan of wisdom that shapes the lives of their fellow men. Through these masters, the Infinite speaks.

There are those who grasp greedily at every scrap of information, never pausing to incorporate it into their lives. They hoard and store and study knowledge as if by merely knowing it, they can gain power. Book volumes of information cannot enrich those who do not do the work within. Yet a person who has made wisdom their own will find their lives altered by a single phrase. It is to them that I speak. It is my sincere desire to share with healers, through these teachings, the continual stream of knowledge I receive. There is no limit to the knowledge that can be brought forth on this planet, but it must be called through the human heart.

Appendix III

Example of a Belvaspata Certificate

BELVASPATA
HEALING of the HEART
Light and Frequency
~Almine~

GRAND MASTERY LEVEL

is hereby granted to

_____

Granted on: _____

_____
Grand Master Teacher

Other books by Almine

Belvaspata, Angel Healing, Volume I
The Healing Modality of Miracles Plus: The Healing Methods of Enlightenment and Restoration of Inner Divinity, Angel Healing MP3 included

Whether you are a beginner or an experienced master of the miraculous healing modality of Belvaspata, this comprehensive guide is an information rich handbook that will serve as your most valuable tool – a compendium of information for everything you need to know to establish yourself as a practitioner of this miraculous healing modality of the angels. Also included are Kaanish, Braamish Ananu and Song of the Self Belvaspata.

Published: 2011, 394 pages, soft cover, 6 x 9, ISBN: 978-1-936926-34-3

A Life of Miracles
Expanded Third Edition **Includes Bonus Belvaspata Section—Mystical Keys to Ascension**

Almine's developing spiritual awareness and abilities from her childhood in South Africa until she emerged as a powerful mystic, to devote herdesc gifts in support of all humanity is traced. Deeply inspiring and unique in its comparison of man's relationship as the microcosm of the macrocosm. *Also available in Spanish.*

Published: 2009, 304 pages, soft cover, 6 x 9, ISBN: 978-1-934070-25-3

Journey to the Heart of God *Second Edition*
Mystical Keys to Immortal Mastery

Ground-breaking cosmology revealed for the first time, sheds new light on previous bodies of information such as the Torah, the I Ching and the Mayan Zolkien. The explanation of man's relationship as the microcosm as set out in the previous book *A Life of Miracles,* is expanded in a way never before addressed by New Age authors, giving new meaning and purpose to human life. Endorsed by an Astro-physicist from Cambridge University and a former NASA scientist, this book is foundational for readers at all levels of spiritual growth.

Published: 2009, 296 pages, soft cover, 6 x 9, ISBN: 978-1-934070-26-0

Other books by Almine

The Ring of Truth *Third Edition*
Sacred Secrets of the Goddess

As man slumbers in awareness, the nature of his reality has altered forever. As one of the most profound mystics of all time, Almine explains this dramatic shift in cosmic laws that is changing life on earth irrevocably. A powerful healing modality is presented to compensate for the changes in laws of energy, healers have traditionally relied upon. The new principles of beneficial white magic and the massive changes in spiritual warriorship are meticulously explained.

Published: 2009, 256 pages, soft cover, 6 x 9, ISBN: 978-1-934070-28-4

Arubafirina *Third Edition*
The Book of Fairy Magic

This book is most certainly a milestone in the history of mysticism throughout the ages. It is the product of a rare and unprecedented event in which Almine, acknowledged as the leading mystic of our time, was granted an exceptional privilege. For one week in November 2006 she was invited to enter the fairy realms and gather the priceless information for this book. The result is a tremendous treasure trove of knowledge and interdimensional color photos.

Published: 2011, 340 pages, soft cover, 6 x 9, ISBN: 978-1-936926-32-9

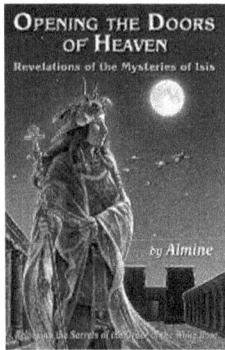

Opening the Doors of Heaven *Second Edition*
Revelations of the Mysteries of Isis

Through a time-travel tunnel, linking Ireland and Egypt, Isis sent a small group of masters to prepare for the day when her mysteries would once again be released to the world to restore balance and enhance life.

They established the Order of the White Rose to guard the sacred objects and the secrets of Isis. In an unprecedented event heralding the advent of a time of light, these mysteries are released for the first time.

Published: 2009, 312 pages, soft cover, 6 x 9 ISBN: 978-1-934070-31-4

Other books by Almine

Windows Into Eternity *Third Edition*
Revelations of the Mother Goddess
This book provides unparalled insight into ancient mysteries. Almine, an internationally recognized mystic and teacher, reveals the hidden laws of existence. Transcending reason, delivering visionary expansion, this metaphysical masterpiece explores the origins of life as recorded in the Holy Libraries.
The release of information from these ancient libraries is a priceless gift to humankind. The illusions found in the building blocks of existence are exposed, as are the purposes of Creation.

Published: 2011, 322 pages, soft cover, 6 x 9, ISBN: 978-1-936926-26-8

Secrets of the Hidden Realms, *Third Edition*
Mystical Keys to the Unseen Worlds
This remarkable book delves into mysteries few mystics have ever revealed. It gives in detail: *The practical application of the goddess mysteries • Secrets of the angelic realms • The maps, alphabets, numerical systems of Lemuria, Atlantis, and the Inner Earth • The Atlantean calender, accurate within 5 minutes • The alphabet of the Akashic libraries.* Secrets of the Hidden Realms is a truly amazing bridge across the chasm that has separated humanity for eons from unseen realms.

Published: 2011, 412 pages, soft cover, 6 x 9, ISBN: 978-1-936926-38-1

Visit Almine's website **www.spiritualjourneys.com** for world-wide retreat locations and dates, online courses, radio shows and more. Order one of Almine's many books, CDs or an instant download.

US toll-free phone: 1-877-552-5646

Music by Almine

Children of the Sun
Music from the Known Planets (Re-mastered and re-titled version of the Interstellar Sound Elixirs)

The beautiful interstellar sound elixirs received and sung by Almine.

Price $9.95 MP3 Download
$14.95 CD

Labyrinth of the Moon
Music from the Hidden Planets (Re-titled version of the Sound Elixirs of the Hidden Planets)

All the vocals in these elixirs are received and sung in the moment by Almine

Price $9.95 MP3 Download
$14.95 CD

Jubilation - Songs of Praise
Music from around the world to lift the heart and inspire the listener.

The extraordinary mystical quality of the music, and the exquisite clarity of Almine's voice, creates the ambient impression of being in the presence of angels.

Price $9.95 MP3 Download
$14.95 CD

www.ingramcontent.com/pod-product-compliance
Lightning Source LLC
Chambersburg PA
CBHW060447170426
43199CB00011B/1124